Archaeology: The Basics

'Strongly recommended for novice undergraduates . . . makes an absolutely excellent case for archaeology as a discipline.'

Antiquity

From archaeological jargon to interpretation, this volume probes the depths of this increasingly popular discipline, presenting critical approaches to the understanding of our past. A piece of broken pottery will never seem the same again.

This ultimate guide for all new and would-be archaeologists, whether they are new students or interested amateurs, introduces its readers to archaeological thought, history and practice.

Lively and engaging, *Archaeology: The Basics* fires the archaeological imagination whilst tackling such questions as:

- What are the basic concepts of archaeology?
- How and what do we know about people and objects from the past?
- What makes a good explanation in archaeology?
- Why dig here?

Archaeology: The Basics provides an invaluable overview of a fascinating subject.

Clive Gamble is Professor of Archaeology and Director of the Centre for the Archaeology of Human Origins (CAHO) at the University of Southampton.

Archaeology:
The Basics

■ Clive Gamble

This reissue first published 2004
by Routledge
2 Park Square, Milton Park,
Abingdon, Oxon, OX14 4RN

Simultaneously published in the USA and Canada by Routledge
270 Madison Ave, New York, NY 10016

Reprinted 2005 (twice), 2006

Routledge is an imprint of the Taylor & Francis Group, an informa business

Typeset in Times by
Florence Production, Stoodleigh, Devon
Printed and bound in Great Britain by
TJ International Ltd, Padstow, Cornwall

British Library Cataloguing in Publication Data
A catalogue record for this book is available from the British Library

Library of Congress Cataloging in Publication Data
Gamble, Clive.
Archaeology, the basics / by Clive Gamble.
p. cm
Includes bibliographical references and index
1. Archaelogy. 2. Archaeology–Philosophy. 3. Archaeology–History. I. Title
CC165.G23 2000
930.1-dc21 00-059183

ISBN10: 0-415-34659-2
ISBN13: 978-0-415-34659-7

Contents

Illustrations

Illustrations

Boxes

To the reader

The book in your hand is not a textbook: it makes no attempt at comprehensive coverage, and it contains no exercises. Instead, it aims only to get you thinking about one of the most important and fascinating topics you could ever hope to encounter: archaeology, the investigation of the human past. Our created past surrounds us and it matters. Indeed, it is probably our most important legacy. I hope this short book will quickly persuade you of this and show you that nothing is more interesting, more stimulating or more rewarding than the study of archaeology.

My book is designed as a basic introduction to the subject. I have chosen eight aspects of archaeology and covered one in each chapter. Archaeologists do not always agree and I have set out some of the current debates as well as several of the major questions that archaeologists are tackling, whether as researchers, managers, curators, specialists or a combination of all of these aspects of the profession.

The reader I have in mind for this book is someone who has not yet entirely made up their mind about archaeology. This means they are not sure if they want to find out more; whether ley lines and the Bermuda Triangle are more interesting (believe me they're not!) than the everyday life of a medieval peasant or the evolutionary origins of humans. I have also written the book for those who are a few steps further on. You have been bitten by the archaeology 'bug' and want to know more. You may be reading archaeology for pleasure, studying it at university, taking it in conjunction with another subject or just intrigued by a Web site you have browsed or a museum or monument you have visited.

What this book is not about are the techniques of field archaeology. Many excellent books already exist on that subject and I would recommend Philip Barker (1982) and Jane McIntosh (1999). What I hope my book will do is kick-start your archaeological imagination so that the experience of handling and studying objects, fieldwalking and surveying landscapes and buildings, arranging exhibits and presenting the past to the wider world will become even more immediate and rewarding.

Acknowledgements

Of the very many people who over the past 30 years have shaped my interest in archaeology I would like to single out the following, who not only made this project possible but also made it fun: Vicky Peters of Routledge for suggesting the idea and Polly Osborn and Julene Barnes for seeing it through to completion; Chris Gosden, Randy McGuire and Tim Darvill, who provided invaluable and insightful comments on the manuscript; Penny Copeland, who illustrated it so well; all my students, too numerous to mention, who can now really say they have heard it all before; and my friends and colleagues at the University of Southampton (http://www.arch.soton.ac.uk), particularly Justin Dix, Yvonne Marshall, David Peacock, Simon Keay, Thomas Dowson, Martin Millett, David Hinton, John Robb, Dave Wheatley, Elaine Morris, Stephanie Moser, Jon Adams, Tim Champion, John McNabb and James Steele, as well as those who have moved on elsewhere, Colin Renfrew, Arthur ApSimon, Brian Sparkes, Stephen Shennan, Peter Ucko, J. D. Hill and Julian Thomas. For financial support and research leave I should like to thank the University of Southampton. And finally an apology to Melissa Gamble and Tom Gamble, who finished their archaeological degrees before I finished this book, the past is always in front of you.

Chapter 1

What is archaeology?

The archaeological imagination

Archaeology is about excitement. It is about intellectual curiosity and finding ways to turn that curiosity into knowledge about people in the past. It is an excitement that comes when we use what Julian Thomas (1996: 63) calls, in a borrowed phrase, 'our archaeological imagination'. This allows us to go where we can never travel, to the past, and to think about time and objects in very different ways to our everyday experience.

An archaeological imagination must be as old as the human species. At one level it is that taken-for-granted ability to reconstruct in our daily lives what went on from the evidence left behind; footprints in the sand point to visitors, a room littered with glasses and bottles adds up to a party. At another level this imagination has been sharpened and refined in the past 200 years into a professional discipline. This is the sense in which I will use the phrase throughout this book. We now routinely excavate, catalogue, measure,

describe and analyse the objects and monuments of the past. Most importantly we have also developed a way of thinking, which these methods assist, that represents a scheme of things long gone. This is the excitement of archaeology. Discovering unplundered tombs is one thing, but to explore our capacity to think well beyond everyday experience and to incorporate into our lives the activities and artefacts of former people are riches indeed.

Three political contexts

Archaeology emerged gradually during the past two centuries as a systematic study of the past. The timing is all important. It is a pointer to the forces that created the discipline and continue to sustain it as an activity.

The driving force was the new political, social and economic order stemming from the industrial revolution, first in Europe and later in North America. Bruce Trigger (1989) has identified three political contexts (Box 1) within this revolution that directly affected the archaeological imagination.

A reaction in some quarters to Triggers' third context, with its universal approaches, has emerged through organisations such as the World Archaeological Congress and its prolific *One World Archaeology* series. In this 'United Nations' of Archaeology alternative viewpoints are welcomed rather than excluded. A forum is provided for the many, and often contradictory, readings and uses of the past. Membership is drawn from all three of Triggers' political contexts and a new orthodoxy created.

How did archaeology get started?

The study of the history of archaeology has recently emerged from a chronicle of discovery, and a gallery of eccentrics, to reflect on the wider movements that created and still feed the discipline (Trigger 1989). I will return to these forces in the chapters that follow, especially Chapter 8 when I discuss nationalism and ethnicity.

But a good place to start is to see how the stuff of the past, monuments and ancient cities as well as objects dug up for the

Box 1: The political context of archaeology

Nationalist: Monuments and artefacts were frequently used to forge the identity of the new nation states of Europe. These emerged during the process of industrialisation and particularly in the nineteenth century (see Chapter 8). To understand the history of archaeology and the aspirations of archaeologists you definitely need to appreciate the force of nationalism (Díaz-Andreu and Champion 1996). The trend continues. The state of Israel, for example, places great emphasis on monuments, such as the fortress of Masada, sacked by the Romans in AD 73, as symbols of resistance and sacrifice en route to nationhood in 1948. The significance and interpretation of such monuments are often contested, as indeed are the boundaries and existence of many modern countries.

Colonialist: The European colonial powers, particularly Great Britain, investigated the archaeology of their dependent territories in Africa, India and Australia. Interpretations were often highly coloured by a colonial viewpoint that liked to see all change and benefits as coming from outside. The explanations for the ruins of Great Zimbabwe in what was Rhodesia are a good example. Until recently African origins were usually discounted. The spectacular city was put down to the influence of either European or Arab traders even though no evidence existed for such claims. On independence colonial archaeology becomes nationalist, as again, in the case of Rhodesia; Zimbabwe became the symbol and the name of the country in 1980.

Imperialist: The three great empires of the modern world, those of Great Britain, the United States and the former Soviet Union, all developed a form of world archaeology. A world archaeology is a universal way of looking at the past, usually from a single viewpoint. Soviet archaeologists followed a Marxist stance on the construction of history (McGuire 1992: 56–62). The British model was comparative, seeking to establish a league table of achievement by period, region and continent. Hence Grahame Clark's description of technology in prehistoric Australia as 'crude and rather colourless' (1968: 21). Unsurprisingly, given its super-power status after World War II, the United States model has been the most widely followed. Trigger regards the 'new' archaeology of the 1960s (see Chapter 2) as an example of this imperialist approach. More widely known now as processual archaeology, it champions a scientific approach, in both methods and explanation, to the study of the past.

antiquities trade and other purposes, was turned into information about the past. This was done through the application of distinctly archaeological methods (for a full description see D. H. Thomas (1998: 332)). Two important methods are the analysis of *style* (see Chapters 3 and 5) and *seriation*, which I discuss briefly below. These methods are in turn based on and integral to the principles of *popularity* and *stratigraphy* (Chapter 3). These methods and principles (Box 2) were the building blocks in educating the infant archaeological imagination.

Uncovering riches

Briefly, these are the discoveries. The base from which archaeology was fashioned reaches back to the British antiquarians Camden and Aubrey, of the sixteenth and seventeenth centuries, just prior to industrialisation. There then followed, in the eighteenth century, a growing fascination with the classical monuments of Greece and Italy which fuelled treasure hunting in buried cities such as Pompeii and Herculaneum. Classical architecture, artefacts and literature provided an ancient authority to establish the new world order. But the process went further. The sand was first removed from monuments in Egypt in 1798, so that they could be recorded, while the hard task of hacking the jungle from the ruins of Borobudur in Java began in the 1810s and from the Mayan ruins in Central America in the 1840s. At the same time investigations began in the Mesopotamian cities of Nineveh and Nimrud.

The languages of these ancient civilisations needed deciphering. This was achieved for Egyptian cuneiform in 1802 and for Babylonian and Assyrian by 1857. Once deciphered, the lists of kings and pharaohs supplied a chronology for the wealth of discoveries that fleshed out civic and artistic achievements.

Christian Thomsen and the Three Age system

Much of this early work was text based rather than object based, its focus historic rather than prehistoric (for a review see Andrén 1998). The widely recognised turning point came in 1819 when C. J. Thomsen classified the collections of the Museum of National Antiquities in

Box 2: Four basic archaeological concepts

Style: Many definitions have been put forward. However, the bottom line in a stylistic analysis is assessing the degree of visual resemblance between objects. That sharing leads to the classification of types because they are stylistically similar (see Chapter 5).

Seriation: A technique to order stylistic units, such as types, into a relative chronological sequence. As described by David Hurst Thomas, seriation is based on the assumption that cultural styles, what he calls 'fads', change, and that the popularity of a particular style or decoration can be associated with a certain time period (Thomas 1998: 246; see Chapter 3).

Popularity: Does nothing more complicated than summarise the frequency with which objects and types are found in archaeological units such as assemblages and cultures. Popularity assumes that over time change will happen and that archaeologists can show this because styles wax and wane. Changes in popularity are interpreted in many ways; for example, the movement of a people with their culture, the in-situ evolution of society, and the spread of technological ideas (see Chapter 3).

Stratigraphy: The law of superposition states that the book at the bottom of the stack was put there before, and is therefore older, than the one placed at the top. Sediments generally obey this principle as well as the archaeological materials they contain. Stratigraphy is an interpretation of the many structures revealed during archaeological excavations that this simple law produces (see Chapter 3).

Copenhagen in terms of a three-age, chronological model. Since he was dealing with prehistoric objects, his scheme stretched the archaeological imagination well beyond texts. Thomsen, of course, had no dates either from calendars or king-lists to guide him and the chronological aspect was expressed in two ways. Technology provided the first with his division of materials into successive Stone, Bronze and Iron ages. Seriation, though he would not have called it that, provided the second. He took the finds that the museum had acquired and looked at the changing proportions of items in each collection. This allowed him to establish what repeatedly went with what as well as to spot changes. These patterns among the artefact types confirmed the basic technological divisions. It is for this reason, rather than a lucky guess that stone came before bronze and bronze before iron in the history of technology, that his scheme has stood the test of time.

Thomsen's three-age model represents a fine example of empirical, inductive research, where a classification is built by observing patterns in the data. It is clear from his famous guidebook to the collections, published in 1836 and translated into English in 1848, that Thomsen attached great importance to contexts and associations of finds in devising his scheme. In this respect an interest in coins may have given him the inspiration to see stylistic change in prehistoric artefacts. However, as Trigger (1989: 84) points out, Thomsen did not borrow a dating device from a subject such as geology but instead developed a new technique, seriation of types, that was appropriate for archaeological evidence. Furthermore, he never gave the impression of having been influenced by Adam Smith writing in 1763 or Thomas Malthus in 1798, who conjectured that society had progressed through stages en route to the present – an age of hunters, then shepherds, then agriculture, and finally their own age of commerce. If he had, then his scheme might be described as deductive, testing a hypothesis – the progressive nature of social change – with archaeological observations. Others did just that, notably Sir John Lubbock (1865), while E. B. Tylor (1865) and Lewis Henry Morgan (1877) built similar schemes by ranking the contemporary cultures of the world in ascending, and by inference ancestral, order.

How has archaeology changed?

The principles of popularity and stratigraphy and the methods of seriation and the stylistic analysis of artefact types (see Box 2) were the basic breakthroughs. Today we also have scientific techniques to find out how old a building or a bone might be (Chapter 3). But basically the methods, using time and space as a framework, to carve the continuum of the past into categories were worked out over 150 years ago.

In the meantime archaeologists have not simply got better at doing stylistic analysis or logging their stratigraphic sections more precisely. Instead the discipline has been swept along by the changing political, social and economic climate. Many of its present aspirations would be unrecognisable to archaeology's founding fathers such as Thomsen or Lubbock.

Anthropological archaeology

The big change has been the development in the past 40 years of an anthropological archaeology. This is a broad umbrella which shelters most of the approaches discussed in Chapter 2. Some of the keywords are science, theory, relevance, quantification and interpretation. Prior to its appearance the practice of archaeology was dominated by culture history. Colin Renfrew (1982: 6) has rightly referred to a period of some 80 years from 1880 to 1960 before anthropological archaeology as the 'long sleep of archaeological theory'. Culture history, started by Thomsen and fuelled by evolutionary thinking in the nineteenth century, continues to emphasise progress, description, dating and ethnicity.

Forty years later and Charles Orser (1999: 280–1) sums up the changes not only for his period, modern-world archaeology, but for the entire subject (Box 3).

This is where the archaeological imagination has got to today. Of course not everyone agrees. Many archaeologists regard self-reflection as a sign of weakness. Still more find the 'basic stuff' of social relationships too vague. They prefer to deal in 'hard facts', while at the same time networking madly to raise funds, get their work noticed and be part of the professional archaeological community, as well as enjoying a life outside the subject. Precisely the 'basic stuff' that structured the past.

Two basic concepts

Accepting the changes Orser describes leads to some important conclusions. Archaeology is what we make it, not what was made for us. The past needs our concepts. Without them it has no significance. With

Box 3: The four characteristics of archaeology today (Orser 1999)

- It is globally focused. Although you can dig only one site at a time, the aim must be to place it within a wider world. You need to look beyond the physical boundaries of your bit of data and see its wider significance (Chapter 6).
- It is mutualistic, which Orser explains as the basic stuff of human life in all times and places. The 'basic stuff' are the social relationships that people create and maintain. The best way to conceive of these is as networks (Chapter 6) that for all sorts of reasons overlap, shift and change. Hence they are mutually inter-related rather than independently associated.
- It is multiscalar. How can we go from the single potsherd to the civilisation of which it was a part (Chapter 4)? How do we match up the micro-scale, everyday activity of someone making a pot with the long-term macro-scale experience of the formation and collapse of the Mayan empire (Chapter 7)?
- It is reflexive. We have come to realise that archaeological data are not just curiosities but powerful knowledge for people alive today. By reflecting on what they do, and why, archaeologists think about their research and the impact it can have on other people. The most striking examples lie in the impact on indigenous, First Nation peoples, for example Native North Americans and Australian Aborigines, who until recently had no voice in the investigation and interpretation of their past. The return of cultural property and the claims of ethnic identity on archaeological evidence provide further examples (Chapter 8).

them it takes on many different meanings and so contributes to modern life. This may at first seem rather confusing. Surely, you might say, the past is about finding and describing objects. Why then do archaeologists disagree and why are there so many different theories (Chapter 2)? I will come back to these questions in the following chapters. Here, however, I feel we need to be very clear about two further concepts. These are:

- facts, and
- essence.

Facts and stories

Facts, or rather observations of data, are never simple. Neither are they neutral or value free. Facts are theory laden. They cannot be read objectively but come ready interpreted, owing to such factors as the history of the subject and how they have been interpreted within the narratives we use. The archaeologist does not so much breathe life into them by, say, placing pots in a battleship curve (Figure 3.5) or analysing animal bones as evidence of how a prehistoric butcher made decisions, but rather his or her interpretation is already driven by theory, however implicit and unrecognised.

Facts become meaningful when they are contained within stories. Rather than striving for a single narrative, which some archaeologists still favour, the current trend is towards variety. Now you may feel unhappy with the idea of many pasts. You may feel that certainty rather than a myriad alternatives is what your archaeological imagination needs. Wouldn't life be easier with just one version of the Neolithic or the Roman Empire?

The philosopher Daniel Dennett (1991), using a Darwinian approach to the question of explaining human consciousness, came up with a computer-based metaphor that may help your bemused archaeological imagination. Consciousness, he proposed, is like the multiple drafts that are now produced on a word processor to write a book like this one. Constant revision and updating takes place – nobody expects to get it right first time. The successive versions do, however, bear similarities to each other; change and stability can be traced. Dennett's idea is that the process leading to those changes is a form of natural selection: only certain sections, sentences, words will get through to the next 'generation' of drafts. On a much wider scale this is what is happening to all the writings, projects and activities associated with the past. It is not just a case of ideas standing the test of time or waiting for new data to overturn them. We are now attentive to the process by which our knowledge of the past is created.

Essence and essentialism

How can you spot a theory-laden fact? Easily. Just ask yourself what essences or properties you believe it has. For example, a Roman burial in a lead rather than a wooden coffin already suggests, before we open it, that we are dealing with someone rich, important and therefore 'naturally' concerned about preservation. Alternatively, consider the biological essentialism found in so many representations of the past in books, magazines and museum dioramas that men hunted and made spears, while women gathered and scraped hides (Gifford-Gonzalez 1993; Moser 1998). Such essentialism is a very common approach to classification. It is particularly strong in archaeology. What happens is that things are defined by the properties, or essences, they are expected to have in the first place.

It was Charles Darwin's great insight to challenge the inherent notion of essentialism in biology. His mechanism of natural selection (Chapter 2) overturned the much older idea that a species was fixed and unchanging because it was made up of a set of essences. For example, this approach would define the essential features of a house mouse as a set of whiskers, a long tail and a fondness for cheese. Now Darwin showed that such essences, which produce an *ideal type* of house mouse, were not fixed for all time but capable, under selection, of change. An example of the process had been going on for millennia as farmers selectively bred bigger cows to make larger cheeses, and possibly cleverer cats, all of which changed the selective pressures on mice.

Archaeologists have also based their classifications on the uncovering of ideal types. We will see in the following pages how at Sutton Hoo combinations of objects are believed, rather like perfume sprays, to exude 'essence of kingship'. I will examine in Chapter 5 how our key concept of style is also based on expecting essences to be *in* the object rather than dependent upon the item being part of a network of social relationships.

Changing Anglo-Saxons: a case study

The developments in archaeology over the past 50 years, from culture history to anthropological archaeology are very well illustrated by the three major investigations of the Anglo-Saxon ship-burial site of Sutton Hoo in the county of Suffolk, eastern England (Carver 1998).

The spirit of place

The cemetery with its mounds and earlier prehistoric settlements had been hacked into by grave robbers in the seventeenth century and by antiquarians in the nineteenth century. All we know about them are the holes they left. Our knowledge of what they missed begins when Mrs Edith Pretty, a practising spiritualist, decided in 1938 to hire a local, self-taught archaeologist, Basil Brown, to find out what were in the mounds on her land at Sutton Hoo. Brown trenched several of the mounds and in 1939 returned to the largest. Here he uncovered with great skill the trace of an Anglo-Saxon long-ship which had been dragged up on to dry land to act as a giant coffin 1300 years ago.

Long before the invention of CNN, news of such a spectacular find quickly spread along the very small archaeological grapevine. The powers-that-be intervened. In the interests of national importance the authorities, represented by the British Museum and the Government's Office of Works, replaced Brown and his advisors at the local museum. They gave the plum job of digging the burial chamber within the ship to a Cambridge archaeologist, Charles Phillips. He in turn brought in Stuart Piggott and W. F. Grimes, who later became professors at, respectively, Edinburgh and London universities.

The spectacular array of 263 objects, including silver bowls from Constantinople, exquisitely crafted gold buckles, royal insignia, a lyre and the occupant's sword and helmet, were uncovered in only 17 days during the summer when England declared war on Germany. As Martin Carver describes it:

> It had been one of those magical excavations that few are given to experience: when every day brings a new discovery, and each find discovered reveals the glimmer of the next. Moments of

> disciplined restraint and stiff upper lip, while photography and drawing are undertaken, are followed by gasps of excitement and jubilant chatter, taking stock and racking the imagination for every eventuality before the tense commitment of raising the object from the ground.
>
> Carver (1998: 16)

Then, in what is still the greatest act of individual generosity in respect of excavated treasure, Mrs Pretty gave the entire collection, worth millions, to the British nation for nothing, not even an honorary title.

Sutton Hoo science and scholarship

The second campaign was slower. Led by Dr Rupert Bruce-Mitford from the British Museum, it was meticulous, scientific and very scholarly. The two watchwords in 1939 had been recovery and recording. In Bruce-Mitford's reinvestigations between 1965 and 1971 they became authenticity and accuracy. His was not an anthropological approach. The ship was redug and the corroded artefacts reassessed and reassembled. Brown's spoil tips were sieved for anything that might have been missed. Parallels to the artefacts were hunted down and everything recorded in three massive volumes completed in 1983. Here was the State reporting on one of its assets.

Science-based archaeology played a key role in the second phase and made it possible to realise the goals of accuracy and authenticity. For example, a little bronze stag had originally been thought to come from the top of the helmet. But when the composition of the alloys in the stag, the helmet and the metal surrounding a great whetstone were analysed the match showed that it should be reunited with this last object. That is how you can now see it on display in the British Museum, where it is known as the King's 'sceptre'.

Sutton Hoo in a managerial age

How much more remained to be discovered? The third and latest investigations employed new scientific advances in prospection and excavation techniques, but most importantly the archaeologists now changed the questions. The Sutton Hoo landscape, with its evidence for multi-period occupation, rather than the mounds alone became the prime focus.

The campaigns between 1983 and 1992 were led by Martin Carver. His research proposal was selected in open competition by the national management committee responsible for the site. It was the first British archaeological project to have a published, and publicly scrutinised project design. The questions it framed drew on information from an 'evaluation' and 'strategy' phase that was carried out before any digging began (Carver 1998: 176). How different to 1938 when it had been curiosity, perhaps tinged by spiritualism, that motivated research, and even 1965 when plans were very much kept in-house and played close to the chest. Carver's investigations were part of wider changes as British archaeologists accepted that if their discipline was to grow, then it had to adopt professional standards. The watchwords in this third phase were management and accountability.

The project design set out to place Sutton Hoo in its archaeological context. Carver's investigations tackled the question at a variety of analytical scales and with an armoury of techniques. Non-destructive methods such as ground-penetrating radar and geophysical survey were used to find out about the site. Greater time depth was achieved by sampling the prehistoric settlement. More of the cemetery was excavated to better judge the status and position of the original finds within the wider Sutton Hoo society. Graves, with much less in them, now took months rather than a fortnight to dig and record. As a result, bodies were found as traces in the sand. The surrounding region was systematically studied through The Kingdom of East Anglia survey. The pattern of land use and settlement was reconstructed to answer the question why such wealth should have been found in what today is regarded as a rural backwater? And in order to meet the accountability criteria, Carver set out to explain and interest the public in the work. After all, the public had benefited from Mrs Pretty's generosity and it was in their name that the site had been placed under State protection through existing Ancient Monument legislation. Television coverage, impractical in 1939, meant that 13 million people watched the excavations in the 1980s, as compared with perhaps a hundred who visited the original dig.

Sutton Hoo as a heritage issue

The latest investigations at Sutton Hoo were partly prompted by the threat of treasure hunting using metal detectors. It is ironic that science should provide the means both to aid and to destroy archaeology. It is also ironic that Mrs Pretty's selflessness should be matched by others' greed for treasure. Such venality has extended in many directions. At the close of the project, the Nation, in the shape of the appropriate government agency, was invited to buy the site but valued it at only £3000. A plea for private sponsorship failed. Eventually the National Trust stepped in and with £3.6 million from the Heritage Lottery Fund the site was secured.

We should not be surprised. At the same time archaeologists had discovered in London the remains of the Rose theatre, where all of Christopher Marlowe's plays opened and where Shakespeare's *Titus Andronicus* was first performed in 1592. A site of unquestionable national significance, the Rose now lies wrapped in clingfilm and covered by sand in the basement of the office block that stands there (Wainwright 1989). Preserved for the future, yes, but hardly accessible to the present. The State likes its heirlooms but will not fork out the financial compensation that is entailed by stopping a city office block from being built.

Sutton Hoo provides in microcosm the change from an amateur to a professional discipline. At the same time the conceptual framework has shifted from exclusively culture history to consider the wider issues raised under the umbrella of anthropological archaeology (Chapter 2). The process could be repeated in every country over the past 60 years. The move also involved the increasing use of science to validate claims and an awareness of contemporary issues. 'Who owns the past?' is a big question that all archaeologists now face. Flashpoints such as the Rose theatre are extreme examples which polarise the various views and raise critical questions of professional ethics. Do you, as an archaeologist, side with the heritage lobby and the famous actors who claimed the site must be saved and displayed, or with the developer who was guided by planning legislation and arrived at a solution, preservation in situ, with the proper authorities? Should the past halt progress, even if it is just another office-block?

Would the arguments have been different if a hospital had been planned for that location?

At Sutton Hoo the move from individual ownership to protection by a national heritage organisation also involved controversy. Some archaeologists questioned whether the 1980s excavations were appropriate. Now they are divided over how to develop the site as a tourist and educational attraction, as proposed by the saviours of the site, The National Trust, ('Tourist centre "would destroy Saxon site"', *The Guardian*, 11 October 1999).

The lesson to take away is that archaeologists do not just dig things up. Our campaigns also create the symbols that people use to contest fundamental issues of concern in the modern world (Chapter 8).

The archaeological cafeteria: is that really archaeology?

By now you are probably thinking that the answer to 'What is archaeology?' is much more complicated than you first thought. What was it that fired your archaeological imagination to find out what makes the subject tick beyond the everyday, the common-sense and the familiar? Was it Lara Croft, or Gladiator? Dusk in the Valley of the Kings, in Egypt, or dawn at Petra, in Jordan? A beep from your metal detector? The stones of Stonehenge, the mounds of Moundville or the Roman baths at Bath? Will you own up to an autographed poster of the *Time Team* on your bedroom wall? Was it a museum display or, what did it for me, an artists reconstruction in a book of life as it once was. Remembering the spark that kindled your archaeological imagination now seems the easy bit, where next?

Let me try and help by providing first a definition and then a menu of how archaeology is encountered.

- Archaeology is basically about three things: objects, landscapes and what we make of them. It is quite simply the study of the past through material remains.

In the rest of this book I will expand on this definition by examining major themes: objects (which range in size from a spearhead to a city), time and space, people, change and stasis, and identity.

Box 4: Subject list for UK university and college archaeology (prepared in 1999)

Theory and techniques

Archaeological theory

- History of archaeological thought
- Social archaeology
- Anthropological archaeology
- Identity (including gender, ethnicity and nationalism)
- Philosophy of archaeology (including interpretive archaeology, post-processualism, social theory)
- Art and representation
- Material culture

Archaeological field practice

- Archaeology of buildings
- Excavation
- Landscape archaeology
- Underwater archaeology

Environmental archaeology

- Faunal
- Botanical
- Landscape, soils, geomorphology

Technology and materials science

- Lithics
- Ceramics and glass
- Metallurgy

Scientific dating

Biological anthropology

- Osteology and palaeopathology
- Forensic archaeology

Archaeological computing and statistics

Archaeological prospection

Archaeological conservation

Heritage management and interpretation

Box 4 *continued*

Periods and regions

Human origins

British archaeology

- Early prehistory (Palaeolithic–Neolithic)
- Later prehistory (Bronze Age–Iron Age)
- Roman
- Migration and Medieval
- Post-medieval (modern world) and Industrial

European and Mediterranean archaeology

- Early prehistory (Palaeolithic–Neolithic)
- Later prehistory (Bronze Age–Iron Age)
- Graeco-Roman
- Medieval
- Post-medieval (modern world) and Industrial

Archaeology and history of ancient civilisations

- Anatolia
- Near East
- Egypt
- New World
- South Asia, India

World prehistory and pre-colonial archaeology

- Africa
- The Americas
- East and Southeast Asia
- South Asia, India
- Pacific and Australasia

Historical (modern world) and ethnohistorical archaeology

- Africa
- The Americas
- East and Southeast Asia
- South Asia, India
- Pacific and Australasia

What archaeologists actually do is another matter and again very varied. To define an archaeologist just as someone who studies the past is now far too narrow. The profession, though small in numbers, has many constituencies and interests. The past is not remote but a part of daily life. The issues archaeologists raise about investigative procedures, identity and ownership can be bitterly contested. This can be both among fellow professionals and with the varied constituencies that may either be friendly or hostile to the systematic, often legislated investigation of the past.

But how do I give you an initial taste of the types and varieties of archaeology that are on the menu? The Internet is one obvious way. Pick a search engine, type in 'archaeology' (and don't forget to try the alternative spelling 'arch*e*ology') and just see how many sites come up. Using Yahoo in December 1999 I found almost one thousand sites and over a hundred categories. Then try other search words – heritage, prehistory (66 sites in 1999), shipwreck, human origins, evolution, excavation, museum, new age (991 sites in 1999), megaliths – and the sheer diversity of the past will flood your screen.

If you don't have access to the Internet, pay a visit to any large library and search the catalogue. Browse your local bookstore and discover how erudite texts on the classification of stone tools are often shelved next to wacky solutions to the 'mystery' of Atlantis.

Another menu is provided by what is taught. Archaeology is not a common subject either in European schools or US high schools but it is on offer in many combinations at universities and colleges. Since I teach at a British university I am most familiar with what goes on there. However, my feeling is that almost anywhere that archaeology is taught a broadly similar range of themes will be covered, though the emphasis will vary. The major differences will be in the periods covered, which will in turn reflect the archaeology of the country concerned. A list of topics (Box 4), basically on the core of the subject, was recently drawn up to encapsulate the teaching of archaeology in Britain. Of course it does not list everything, but as an example of a structured *à la carte* menu from one country it gives you an idea of the choices on offer.

The list makes divisions between theory, techniques and professional practice, and periods and regions. Within each category will be many questions, such as the origins of agriculture or the Romanisation of Britain. The divisions and questions will be cross-cut by themes such as trade, religion, subsistence and the archaeology of death. These are too numerous to list.

It matters little how you participate in archaeology. What you will find by reading, surfing, excavating or learning about the subject is that there are major differences in approach. For example, these may be between those periods and regions that are aided by texts and those that are truly prehistoric. The rich historical traditions have been covered in detail by Anders Andrén (1998). His survey shows how texts and material culture can be integrated, although traditionally more importance, wrongly in my view (but then I am a prehistorian), has been placed on the texts. This is just one instance of the diversity of opinion and approach that you will encounter once you start following your archaeological imagination. One formal answer to the question 'What is archaeology?'

Luckily many excellent textbooks now exist to guide your footsteps. These include: Matthew Johnson (1999a) and Christopher Gosden (1999) on archaeological and anthropological theory; Robert Wenke (1990), David Hurst Thomas (1998) and Kevin Greene (1995) on aims, methods, theories and techniques; Colin Renfrew and P. Bahn (1991) on just about every topic; and finally the doyen of archaeological writers Brian Fagan (1991, 1992). Suitably shod we can now turn our attention away from the question 'What is archaeology?' to consider 'How many archaeologies are there?'

Chapter 2

How many archaeologies are there?

The past would be very boring if we all agreed about it. And archaeology would not last very long if we also thought we could work out a final answer to questions such as how we became human. As a result, no archaeologist I know believes there is one true past. The opportunity for fresh discovery keeps even the most anti-theoretical archaeologist quiet on that subject. Instead the trenches are dug between opponents according to their conviction of the right conceptual methods we should all use.

There are many types of archaeology but, as mentioned in Chapter 1, I like to boil them down to two: culture history and anthropological archaeology. These represent two alternative paradigms or ways of doing archaeology. A paradigm is a set of beliefs and assumptions about how the world, in this case archaeological enquiry, works and should be investigated in order to gain knowledge. There are disagreements, some of them serious, within each camp that can also be regarded as paradigmatic (Johnson 1999a). The arguments, like all messy divorces, is about custody of

the offspring. In this case the tug of war is over the future of our archaeological imagination.

Culture history

Culture history is the default setting for most archaeological inquiry. It has received a rough ride over the past 30 years, but even so Thomas (1995) estimates that in Britain over half of university archaeologists still come under this approach, though they might not realise it. On a world scale culture history also accounts for what the majority of archaeologists think they are doing. For example, Paddayya (1995: 138), writing of Indian archaeologists, concludes that most of them are at best disinterested in theory and regard the discipline primarily as a fact-gathering enterprise. The French archaeologist Paul Courbin is vehemently anti-theoretical, stating that the goal is the establishment of facts and nothing more (1988: 112).

Such statements should not imply that culture history is entirely without any concepts or theories (see Taylor 1948) but rather that its practitioners emphasise the primacy of data, facts and classification. They are truly Thomsen's children. Allied with this focus on facts is the notion that an inductive approach is best suited to archaeological enquiry. Putting things in the right order, chronologically and geographically, is the most important goal for the culture historian. Hence a synthesis such as Gordon Childe's *The Dawn of European Civilisation* went through six editions between 1925 and 1957. This reflects the culture history view that new data, rather than new frameworks, are the most important aspect in the development of archaeology. The framework allows the data to 'speak for themselves' and what they tell the 'listening' archaeologist is when change took place and from what direction it came. Very often any further interpretation is regarded as speculation and if it occurs it will only be found hidden away in the closing remarks rather than the body of the report.

Culture history: points for and against

Culture history has had many notable successes. Through the methods of stylistic analysis (Chapter 5), seriation and the principle of stratigraphy (Chapter 3) it has built up regional sequences in all parts of the world. These have been refined with the advent of absolute dating techniques such as radiocarbon dating (Chapter 3), so that the phases, horizons, periods and cultures now usually have a temporal as well as a geographical measure. For example, using the technique of 'ceramic stratigraphy', Alfred Kidder (1924) was able to produce, one year before Gordon Childe's ground-breaking survey of European prehistory (1925), a detailed synthesis of Southwestern prehistory in the United States. The explanation of change was either in-situ cultural development, where continuity could be traced among the potsherds, or a form of group diffusion from elsewhere if new pottery types with no antecedents appeared in the region.

Once available, culture history married up prehistory with the coin- or text-dated classical and historic periods. Conceptually, the majority of archaeologists in all three periods have always agreed over issues of method and explanation.

Culture history has also revealed broad patterns which have stood the test of time. We still use terms such as 'Neolithic' and 'Basketmaker' as shorthands to denote periods and phases, and broad agreement exists on their contents. It is also an adaptable approach that in some areas has continued to develop. The economic prehistory of Grahame Clark (1952) built on the earlier work of Worsaae and Kidder and proposed new investigations and frameworks for investigation. Major works appeared, including Henry de Lumley (1976) for France, Stuart Piggott (1965) for Europe, Gordon Willey (1966) for North and Central America, Peter Bellwood (1978) for the Pacific and Sigfried de Laet (1994) for the world. Finally, the hundred-plus books in the *Ancient Peoples and Places* series point to the synthetic achievements of culture history on a global scale.

But, as Lyman, O'Brien and Dunnell (1997) point out, what culture history has never developed is a convincing theory for either change or stability. Change is seen as an inherent property, an essence, of the system being studied. It depends upon common sense, expressed in simple language, to make this point. Change is attributed to migration, diffusion and innovation, since this is how modern societies apparently define what they are and how they became what they are. It is a transfer of their colonial experience (Chapter 1) to the societies of the past. Stability is a similar homespun tale of 'if it ain't broke, don't fix it'.

Anthropological archaeology

A new archaeology was required that reversed the stereotype of archaeologists as the stamp collectors of the past. This duly arrived in the 1960s but the newness of that first truly anthropological archaeology has to be put into context (Figure 2.1).

In the twentieth century there were at least three 'new' archaeologies (Box 5), all of them North American and all recognised as such at the time (Wylie 1993: 20).

Why the North American continent should be in a constant state of archaeological revolution can probably be explained by the four-field approach to anthropology that the ethnographer Franz Boas set

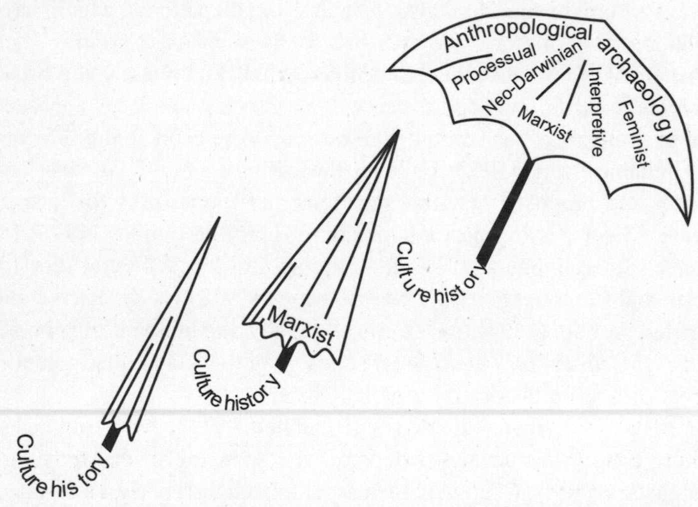

FIGURE 2.1 The unfurling umbrella of archaeological theory. When fully opened there are many theoretical approaches to be found under Anthropological archaeology, only some of which are shown here. However, you are still left holding the handle of the umbrella, the familiar Culture history

Box 5: North America's three 'new' archaeologies of the twentieth century. Are we due another one soon?

- 1910s – The stratigraphic revolution inspired by work in the pueblos of the Southwestern United States
- 1940s – Cultural ecology, which looked at the variety of human cultures and their adaptation to the environment. The importance of Native American ethnography was critical as a means of explanation
- 1960s – Processual archaeology, which proposed a scientific methodology including hypothesis testing and a call for archaeology as anthropology

in place at the beginning of the last century. The four fields, still available in many US teaching departments, are: linguistics and physical, social and archaeological anthropology. The pulls and pushes between these fields have always had repercussions. These have largely been unfelt in Europe, where archaeology tends to be taught either separately or as an adjunct of history with an emphasis on written sources as the way to understand the past (see Chapter 4, analogy).

Processual archaeology 1962–69

The third new archaeology (Box 5) is regarded as the big one. In print it began with a paper by Lewis Binford (1962) 'Archaeology as anthropology'. This short paper was concerned with process, how the various cultural systems that made up a society fitted together and worked. It dealt with the issues of adaptation and change in such systems by identifying three realms of behaviour – environmental, social and ideological – which could be inferred from artefacts and the contexts in which they were found. It stressed the importance of quantification and prediction to qualify archaeology as a scientific approach. Most importantly it drove explanation out from behind its hiding place of common sense and tradition. Explication, putting assumptions down and challenging them, was a key objective. Ten years later, and on the radio, Binford summed up as follows:

> The New Archaeology gives explicit recognition to the relationship between procedure or method and the kinds of questions we seek to get answers to. It also says that we must give priority to the testing of these general propositions in order to be able to make accurate statements about the past.
>
> Binford (1972b: 175)

Back in 1962 he supported his revolutionary programme with a regional example. In the process he sought to expose such fuzzy explanations for change as 'influence', 'stimuli' and the 'migration of culture' that culture historians applied.

Culture process

The accent on process and the system was crucial. Unlike culture history, where similarities and differences were explained by people sharing norms about culture, processual archaeology, as the new archaeology came to be known, explained variation in terms of differential participation in culture. Culture was our principal means of adaptation. Moreover, it varied as the situation demanded. It was not applied by a society, a cultural system, as a by-rote solution to its survival and existence at all times and places. Culture was instead presented as organisationally flexible. All aspects of it from the design on pots to coping with environmental hazards were under selection to adapt.

Processual archaeology then searched for the reasons why adaptive variation occurred. New archaeologists like Binford and Kent Flannery set great store by the philosophers of the scientific method who championed framing hypotheses and then testing them. What they were after were explanations that did not just rely on invoking the concept of culture to explain culture. This was a common criticism of culture history. Rather they were looking for cause, or as Flannery (1967) put it, looking for the system of organisation behind the Indian behind the artefact.

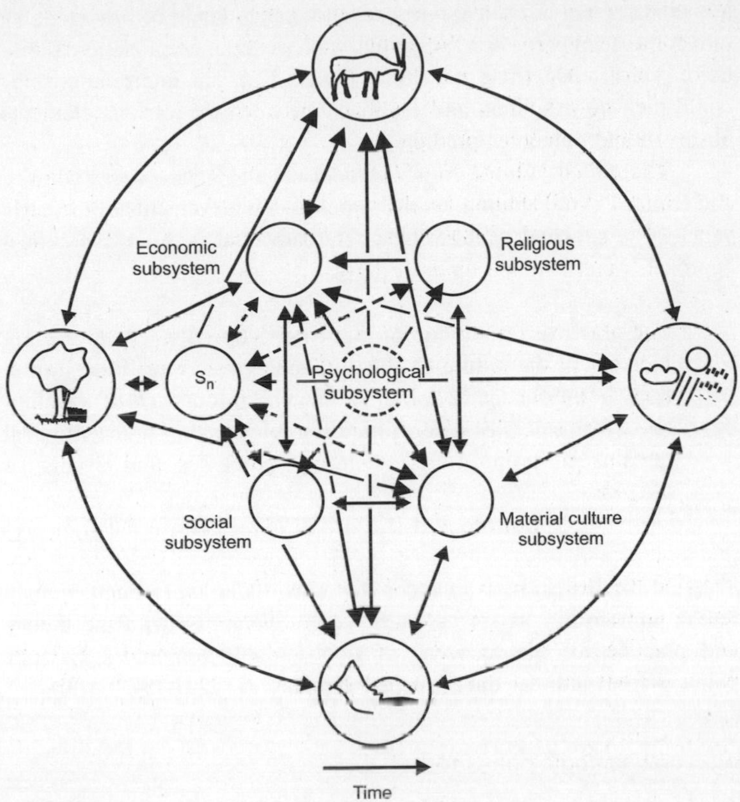

FIGURE 2.2 Analysing an archaeological culture as a set of interrelated subsystems (after Clarke 1968: figure 17). The five components of the internal system under study interact with each other and with the four components of the external environment: fauna, climate, geology and flora. The latter include another social system shown here by Sn

This search for cause also led them to consider why cultural systems did *not* change. Stability was approached from the perspective of ecosystem analysis, with inputs, outputs and self-regulatory mechanisms that balanced the whole system in what was known as homeostasis. For analytical purposes the system could be broken down into component parts, or subsystems, such as craft specialisation, population, subsistence, trade and ritual (Figure 2.2). The interrelationships could then be examined and feedback between the various elements observed and outcomes predicted.

The edited volume *New Perspectives in Archaeology* (Binford and Binford 1968) summaries the hopes and achievements of the early years of processual archaeology. The advantages of a theoretical approach were summed up as follows:

> The practical limitations on our knowledge of the past are not inherent in the nature of the archaeological record; the limitations lie in our methodological naiveté, in our lack of development for principles determining the relevance of archaeological remains to propositions regarding processes and events of the past.
>
> Binford and Binford (1968, in Binford 1972a: 96)

This led the British new archaeologist David Clarke, to pugnaciously define archaeology as 'in essence . . . the discipline with the theory and practice for the recovery of unobservable hominid behaviour patterns from indirect traces in bad samples' ([1973] 1979: 100).

Processual archaeology: points for

Trigger (1989: 2) made the important observation that Binford's lead suggested a more lucrative approach than culture history because he recognised two dialogues: an internal dialogue that archaeologists had had as they developed methods for inferring past human behaviour from archaeological evidence and an external one addressing general issues concerning change and the evolution of that behaviour. Without processual archaeology there would not be such a dialogue and the beginnings of a critical self-awareness of what archaeology is.

In order to get those two dialogues going common sense and in some cases plain language had to be jettisoned as new ways to express things were sought. I feel these were minor sacrifices to get the archaeological imagination working in productive, new ways. But the gripes about jargon rumble on rather like complaints about contemporary art. This just confirms David Clarke's view that 'each archaeology is of its time but since many deplore the time they will certainly be unhappy with its archaeology' (1979: 85).

Processual archaeology: points against

The major problem with processual archaeology lies in its avowal of a scientific approach that treats archaeology as akin to a repeatable experiment. In its early days it was strong on the discovery of laws of human behaviour.

It soon became apparent that the laws that were emerging were, in Flannery's phrase 'Mickey Mouse' laws (1973: 51). They dealt with small segments of behaviour in a rather obvious way; for example, 'as numbers of people increase on a site so too do the number of storage pits'. The general laws dealing with change have remained elusive.

The reaction starting in the 1970s has been to investigate middle-range rather than general theory (Box 6). As we shall see in Chapter 3, middle-range theory seeks to bridge the interpretive gulf between

Box 6: Middle-range theory: a set of bridging arguments from the present to the past

Middle-range theory is more a set of methods than a theory. They are middle range because the issues addressed are not grappling with the big theoretical issues needed to explain why culture changes or how humans evolved. Neither are they low level, such as the law of superposition (see Box 1).

Instead, middle-range theory reminds us that we still do not know that much about the archaeological record. We need to know how it was formed, what survives, and why, and how we can go from these inert observations in the present to the investigation of the once live action that produced the record in the past (see Chapter 3). Only with a better understanding of the archaeological record, and how we go about reanimating it, can we then return to the big questions with a better chance of getting an acceptable answer.

the static, dead facts we dig up and the invisible but once dynamic behaviour that created the patterns in the data that we study. By concentrating on middle-range theory as a methodological issue we have learnt a great deal about butchering animals, making pots and chipping stone. This is thanks to experimental and ethnoarchaeological studies. We know more than we ever dreamt possible about what hyenas can do to a bone (Brain 1981). What is not clear is how these observations on why decisions are made, which result in discrete patterns in the archaeological record, can then be built into a larger scheme of understanding. Some stay at the level of materials analysis (Skibo, Walker and Nielsen 1995), while others such as Binford foray into bigger questions such as Neanderthal behaviour and the transition to agriculture. But the overall picture is one of bits and pieces rather than overall structure. A harsh critic might say 'You have told me that people ate and made pots in the past. Now tell me something I didn't already know'.

The processualists would counter by arguing that we must understand the range of potentially relevant causal processes or we can say nothing about variability. They would regard the scientific approach as safeguarding the creation of a false past in the image of the present – a belief in a degree of objectivity and reliability that science confers but which in fact, we shall now see, is problematic.

Feminist archaeology

The development of a feminist archaeology provides a good example of the limitations of the scientific method. Contrary to many other disciplines where feminist approaches grew quickly, in archaeology the start has been slower (Nelson 1997). What began (Conkey and Spector 1984) as a long-overdue critique of androcentric notions and bias when interpreting the archaeological evidence soon developed into an exploration of gender. However, as Gilchrist (1993: 3–4) has argued, the continuing criticism from processualists that such studies need a methodology in order to identify gender from the evidence is misplaced. She asks why there is a need to find females among the archaeological evidence when there seems to be little need, because of existing assumptions, to find males.

The late arrival to archaeology of feminist critiques in general and gender studies in particular seems strange to many commentators given that gender is about male and female categories that are socially constructed rather than biologically given. Archaeology with its timespans and comparative samples would seem to have much to offer on this issue. As Alison Wylie has pointed out (1991), the long gestation cannot be explained by the old methodological chestnut that gender doesn't survive in the archaeological record. Instead, it is best explained as a conflict between the ideologies of powerful archaeologies. A processual approach, with its systems, categories and universal values founded on the authority of the scientific method, literally could not see a gendered archaeology. Vision was not restored until a feminist critique took place of such assumptions as 'all men hunt, all women gather', or that everything being equal (which it never is) women make pots and men make ploughshares. These are very obvious essentialist assumptions about the correlation of biological sex with status and activity. They have very little to tell us about the social construction of gender categories. Instead, they tell us a good deal about a powerful academic ideology such as processual archaeology. Since this approach was not looking at how categories were constructed, it could claim, with great methodological rigour, that no information existed. A case of: what you don't believe in, you won't find. So American archaeology in particular was a late addition to the feminist debate.

Elsewhere, the advent of gender archaeology was aided by critiques of authority mounted by interpretive archaeologists (see below), particularly in Europe, Australia and South Africa. When combined the advances are already considerable (Gero and Conkey 1991; Wadley 1997). By questioning the scientific method, and with it the processual interpretation of the past, archaeology has become a less secure discipline – in terms of understanding itself and protecting its interests. But it has also become a much more exciting one, intellectually. The great gain has been returning to the study of people rather than systems. Furthermore, these are often different people to the ones whose voices we normally hear in accounts of the past. This gain is well shown by Janet Spector (1993) as she weaves together her experience as an archaeologist with the Native American voice and foregrounds the experience of women in the past. Her focus is provided by excavated objects. Her narrative emerges from a sensitive reading of relationships and experience rather than the hard edge of science and systems.

The value of gender approaches will become apparent in the later thematic chapters (see especially Chapters 4, 5 and 8). Their ability to cross-cut approaches is one of their enduring strengths and a source of inspiration for the archaeological imagination.

Marxist approaches

Histories of processual archaeology can sometimes give the impression that they invented archaeological theory and opened single-handedly that umbrella of anthropological archaeology. This was not the case. One figure, the Australian born Gordon Childe (1893–1957), who was professor of archaeology at Edinburgh and London universities, stands out as an innovative, Marxist thinker working within the tradition of culture history.

Childe wrote many books on the evolution of prehistoric and state societies in the Near East and Europe. He adopted a Marxist approach to the study of change and emphasised the relations of production. Not surprisingly given his huge output and long career his views changed (McNairn 1980; Trigger 1989; McGuire 1992). His own intellectual evolution is a good example of how Marxism offers an interpretation of a changing world.

Childe remains the most widely cited archaeologist outside the discipline because he tackled the big issues of social and economic change. He is the classic exponent of the grand narrative that archaeology can provide. In *Man Makes Himself* (1936) he began to redefine the three-age model using two socio-economic revolutions that occurred in prehistory but which set in motion the modern world. These were the Neolithic revolution, when agriculture and villages appeared, and the Urban revolution that led to the earliest civilisations with writing, monumental buildings, bureaucracies, cities, trade and an agricultural surplus that was then unequally distributed to create a ruling class. These issues were explored, revised and repeated in his many books, including *What Happened in History* (1942) and *Social*

Evolution (1951). He also asserted archaeology's broader intellectual aspirations, as in *Archaeology as a Social Science* (1947) and *Society and Knowledge* (1956).

Childe died in 1957 at the age of 65. Through the scope and scale of his writings he moved archaeology away from the simple progressive evolution of Lubbock and the people-free typologies of Thomsen and Montelius, and provided an antidote to the racist agenda of the German archaeologist Kossina. Nearly all his work was written before the advent of radiocarbon dating, which provided the first truly independent check on the Montelian scheme. Such absolute dating saw the demise of the strong diffusion model of people mainly moving from the Near East that Childe favoured to explain changes in European prehistory, and allowed a fuller investigation of his socio-economic narrative (Renfrew 1973a).

Box 7: A seven-point plan for Anglo-American Marxist approaches in archaeology (adapted from McGuire in Thomas 1998: 388–9)

- Marx's writings are a starting point rather than an end point.
- Social relations are at the core of research in Marxist archaeology.
- Society is treated as a whole not as parts.
- Contradiction and conflict are regarded as crucial features of human society and these act as internal sources of change. This emphasis on the *dialectic* rejects the idea that society is simply a set of functional adaptations to external factors.
- Human action, or *praxis*, is given a significant role in the process of history. Notions of environmental, material or technological determinism in human society are therefore rejected.
- People make knowledge, and knowledge of the past depends on the social and political context of the time.
- The power relations of the modern, capitalist world are questioned and alternatives proposed.

Marxism is not, strictly speaking, a theory about the ancient past. However, because it provides a powerful analysis of human society it has proved very influential in the study of that central archaeological question: change (Box 7).

The wide impact on world archaeology of Marxist approaches can be found in many edited volumes (Spriggs 1984; Champion 1989; Miller, Rowlands and Tilley 1989) which cover all periods, as well as in regional studies which continue to explore many of Childe's interests in society and systems of production (for example, Kristiansen 1998). A recent, comprehensive review of Marxist archaeology is provided by McGuire (1992).

Interpretive archaeology

So far the four types of archaeology I have discussed – culture history, processual, feminist and Marxist – all have major followings on either side of the Atlantic and indeed worldwide. My last two approaches under the umbrella of anthropological archaeology – interpretive and neo-Darwinian – do not command such widespread support. Rather they reflect different interests between North America and in particular Europe. Interpretive archaeology, often known as post-processualism because of the approach it challenged, is more often than not dismissed as irrelevant in North America, while neo-Darwinian approaches mean very different things on different sides of the Atlantic.

Under the heading of interpretive archaeology we find a wide variety of theoretical positions and an unwillingness to set out any single goal for the discipline. Robert Preucell and Ian Hodder (1996: 7) present the variety as a fulfilment of the trend started by processual archaeology. This interpretive diversity began to appear in the 1980s and shows no sign of abating. However, this does not impress those who still hanker after a unified field and a scientific agenda with the goal that archaeology should aspire to be science with a capital S (Flannery 1973: 53). For them interpretive approaches are nothing more than 'anything goes'.

What this tells me is that the wheel has come full circle and that authority and status are at stake. This has happened before with the reaction of the culture historians to the new archaeologists in the 1960s. Then, in 1973, Flannery, a leading processualist, made fun in a poacher-turned-gamekeeper kind of way of the 'law-n-order' new archaeologists and their belief in self-regulatory systems. Processual archaeologists, like all good scientists, basically are interested in control, order and respect.

The particular tension in this familiar struggle is between the vast majority of North American archaeologists, now reared on either straight processualism or modified culture history, and a smaller band of mainly, but not exclusively, European archaeologists.

Interpretive archaeology is particularly concerned with two of Charles Orser's components of contemporary archaeology (Box 3). These are: the mutual character of social life and the reflexive attitude of archaeologists to their data and profession (Box 8).

Post-processualism

I will illustrate interpretive approaches by briefly looking at one self-proclaimed catch-all grouping. Post-processualism, it must be said, lacks the consistency of a strict creed and an appointed intellectual messiah, which was provided for processualists by the trinity of laws, science and explication, and by Lewis Binford. It does, however, have four British apostles: Ian Hodder, Christopher Tilley, Michael Shanks and Julian Thomas.

Post-processualism began as a thorn in the side of processual archaeology. It provided a critique of what archaeologists did and why. It sought in the books of Shanks and Tilley (1987a, 1987b) and through the movement known as the World Archaeology Congress to contextualise the knowledge of the past. On the one hand this involved asking what purposes were served by the production of archaeological knowledge? Who was it for and how had it been used? On the other hand it raised the possibility of alternative views of the past based on the opinions of indigenous peoples on whose lands archaeologists were often digging. The authority of the archaeologist to be the sole representative to talk about the past was therefore challenged.

This did not go down well. It was seen as nothing more than opening the floodgates to a subjective view of the past. How could

Box 8: Five elements of an interpretive archaeology

Symbolism: The key early work is *Symbols in Action*, in which Ian Hodder (1982) presents an ethnoarchaeological study of material culture in East Africa. He examines issues of ethnicity (as bound up in the culture concept (see Chapter 3), boundary maintenance and the power of individuals. In his book those elements dear to the processual agenda, such as diet and subsistence, are hardly touched upon.

Material culture: This is seen not just as things we create – extensions of ourselves – but as integral components of our personalities, inextricably linked to our social lives. Material culture is an active part of how we build our social relationships rather than a mirror reflecting the positions of authority and class in society. Pots, bronzes, even something as complicated as a city with its structures and public monuments, have biographies. Their multiple 'lives' are mutually involved in our activities. They are not just instruments for use but part of that surrounding environment from which individuals are indivisible (Chapter 4). Pots as people sums it up nicely (Chapter 5).

Hermeneutics: This is literally the study of interpretation and meanings in texts but applied by some to material culture (Shanks and Tilley 1987). More importantly, this approach questions the one-way interpretation of the scientist by contrasting it with a double hermeneutic – an exercise in translation between 'us' and 'them', subject and object. We move from our frame of meaning, which could be scientific, to that of the people being studied. Rather than imposing our view of how their world worked, we have instead a dialogue of difference. But what exactly the frame of reference of someone in the Bronze Age might be remains a problem (see Gosden 1994).

Narrative: The way we communicate is by telling stories. Facts get their meaning by being used in these narratives. The hypothetico-deductive programme of the processualists is just one form of narrative structure: the ethnic explanations of culture historians another (Alexandri 1995). Any narrative is structured in time and both simplifies and imposes its own order on reality (Gosden 1994: 54). The study of writing about the past therefore looks to the sources of authority that are being marshalled to make an argument about change and patterning.

Box 8 *continued*

Social theory: Archaeology is not alone in the move to critical self-awareness. Most academic disciplines since 1945 have gone through a similar loss of innocence. Four social theorists have proved highly influential in framing our debates about the mutualistic character of social life and the need for reflexivity. These are Martin Heidegger, Michel Foucault, Pierre Bourdieu and Anthony Giddens (for recent reviews see Gosden 1994; Thomas 1996; Jones 1997; Dietler and Herbich 1998; Meskell 1999; Dobres 2000; Dobres and Robb 2000). A common thread is the notion that much of what we do is practical, unthinking, habitual action. This is a form of practical consciousness, as opposed to a discursive consciousness when we are fully engaged, thinking about a problem. The French archaeologist André Leroi-Gourhan, who is best known for precise excavations and a structural theory of cave art, anticipated these concepts in 1964. But his book *Gesture and Speech* was only translated into English in 1993 and was much too far ahead of its archaeological time.

knowledge be verified? How could the weaknesses in other interpretations – even those as bizarre as the lunatic fringe who believe in extra terrestrial interventions to account for Stonehenge or the Nazca lines – be refuted? In particular, the issue of who owns the past was raised. Archaeologists soon found that governments were more often swayed by political minorities when deciding on who had access and control over sites, landscapes and objects. The archaeologists lofty claim that they were investigating a segment of the cultural heritage of humankind did not always win either at the ballot box or in the corridors and lobbies of power.

When the dust had settled a bit Hodder (1991: 1) identified three results from this work that might be taken as the post-processualist platform for the 1980s:

- material culture was meaningfully constituted, by which he meant that it has an active role to play in how we make social relationships. It is not just a simple reflection of how society was organised;

- the individual needs to be part of theories of material culture and social change;
- archaeology has its closest explanatory ties with history.

Interpretive archaeologists have continued to build on this foundation.

Interpretive archaeology: points for and against

Will interpretive archaeology ever become the default setting of what archaeologists do? Possibly yes, though most will not realise it has happened because it will probably bear little relation to the current position. There is still a lot of hard work down by the riverside for the four apostles. When it was a critique of other approaches it evoked strong passions for and against. Now much of it has seeped into general practice, particularly the reflexive stance. Once the archaeological imagination got out of the bottle marked 'science', it could never be the same again. Diversity of theoretical interests combined with many different dialogues are, like it or not, now the canon (Preucel and Hodder 1996: 15).

Archaeology has, since the advent of interpretive approaches, been overtly politicised, the World Archaeology Congress being a prime example. Many other groups than archaeologists now have an interest in the past. Issues such as the return of museum collections to their original owners will not go away. Archaeologists now have wider responsibilities than making sure they die with no unpublished backlog.

On the less positive side, what has interpretive archaeology really achieved apart from a critique and getting us to find out what other academic subjects have been doing? Feminist archaeology has gone further faster for the simple reason that its objectives and focus are much clearer. Marxist approaches have greater maturity and more to say about change. The excavations and analyses seem very similar to the demands of processual archaeology for sampling, quantification and explication of research designs (Chapter 3), which are the lasting inputs from processual archaeology. As Tim Darvill has pointed out to me, interpretive archaeology still relies on field methods designed to achieve quality culture history. One response has been Hodder's

(1999) innovative experiment in excavation and interpretation which gives everyone on the project at Çatalhöyük, a prehistoric town in Turkey, a voice through video, the Internet (http://catal.arch.cam.ac.uk/catal/catal.html) and long discussions into the night. The business of too much subjectivity worries many archaeologists – partly because of the authority challenge but also because the past, through its surviving objects, exists for them as a reality rather than as an artificial, narrative exercise. Where are the boundaries to the shared archaeological imagination?

Neo-Darwinian archaeology

True to its label, my final approach within anthropological archaeology is evolving. It owes much, as do Marxist and interpretive archaeologies, to a wider intellectual debate, but this time in the biological rather than the social sciences. In the broader scientific field neo-Darwinians acquire their 'newness' because of the science of genetics, which was unknown to Darwin. As part of this scientific movement archaeologists aim to apply the principles of neo-Darwinian evolution to the past. This concerns not only human physical evolution but also cultural evolution.

Biological and cultural transmission

In 1859 Charles Darwin provided a very powerful mechanism to explain change. Natural selection works because individuals within a population vary. Without that variation there can be no evolution, since there would be no expression through natural selection of either the differential survival of offspring into the next generation or of their evolution through mutation (Box 9). What happens is that biological information, in the form of genes, is transmitted between generations. The key point about this transmission process is that it is undirected. The social Darwinists of the nineteenth century ignored this basic point and instead turned human history into a catalogue of progress and a celebration of Western achievement (Lubbock 1865; Spencer 1876–96). As a result they gave social and cultural evolution a bad name in both archaeology and anthropology.

Box 9: Key concepts in Darwinian evolution

Natural selection is the differential contribution of offspring to the next generation by individuals of different genetic types but belonging to the same population (Wilson 1975: 589).

Selection pressure is any feature of the environment, both physical and social, that results in natural selection (i.e. food shortage, predator activity) and can cause individuals of different genetic types to survive to different average ages, to reproduce at different rates, or both (Wilson 1975: 594).

Archaeologists are well aware of such historical pitfalls. If avoided, then Darwin's immensely powerful theory can be harnessed to the explanation of cultural change. For example, cultural transmission is likened by Stephen Shennan to a system of inheritance (1989b, 1993). The information contained and transmitted by imitation and teaching through the many media of culture (language, performance, gesture, ritual, material) therefore affects what an individual looks like and does. It is, if you like, another part of our individual phenotype – what we see, for example skin colour or stature, as the expression of the invisible genotype.

Where the neo-Darwinian part comes in is in considering the population of ideas, or representations, that are available for transmission (Sperber 1996). It is these ideas that make up that all-important pool of variation for natural selection to get to work on. This involves us in *population thinking* (Box 10).

Applying such principles is all about how ideas and representations, what archaeologists would usually call styles and types, are distributed within the populations of objects we are studying. What is their frequency? Why will natural selection favour some and not others as the generations roll by? Shennan's approach investigates the conditions under which we expect transmission to occur and in what directions it will drift, change and 'mutate'.

Box 10: What is meant by population thinking

In basic terms, any aspect of culture that is imitated is either more or less common in the population of cultural representations. The result of the copying process is either to decrease or to increase variation between groups, depending on the frequency of the item being copied. Of course, very faithful copying of the frequencies would lead to stability in cultural representations. This does not imply that natural selection is not working, only that selection pressures (Box 9) are constant.

Neo-Darwinian archaeology: points for and against

The neo-Darwinian approach to cultural evolution has great potential for archaeology. But it is not a unified field (O'Brien 1996: 4). There is currently little agreement on which units, such as the individual or the human population, should be used to measure the effects of selection. Alison Wylie (1995: 208) has also raised doubts about the hopes of some of the practitioners which are pinned on the power of biological explanation. Does this necessarily make the inferences based on archaeological evidence with all its problems any more secure?

Moreover, so keen are some neo-Darwinists (Dunnell 1978; O'Brien 1996) to drive out what they consider to be unscientific concepts such as *intent* from the explanatory process that they seem to me to produce an automaton view of human sociality, more akin to the sociobiologist for whom social life is mandated by natural selection as played out by our genes. But as Shennan has pointed out:

> Assumptions about individuals are in fact behind any attempts at understanding past socio-economic change, or indeed social evolution. The basic ingredients required are *social actors* with *intentions*, who may or may not stand for more than themselves; *conditions of action*, acknowledged and unacknowledged; and *consequences*, intended and unintended.
>
> (Shennan 1993: 56, my emphasis)

The point about humans is that we negotiate what the social structure will be. It is not, and never has been, specific to our species. Therefore intent, while difficult to measure, is part of the explanation.

Neo-Darwinism, if interpreted broadly, does allow those all-important processes that integrate the micro- and the macro-scale of human activity, such as individual and society, village and civilisation, a year and a millennium, to be explored. It is a strong explanation which will be very powerful when used, as Shennan proposes, as a biological metaphor for cultural stability and change (Chapter 7). It is also the case that the co-evolutionary processes that led to language (Deacon 1997) and domestication (Rindos 1985) have been very important in human evolution (see Chapter 7). A good case of question and theory being adapted to each other.

Summary

At the end of his 1962 paper Binford warned archaeologists that 'we cannot afford to keep our theoretical heads buried in the sand' ([1962] 1972: 31–2). Part of the process of removing them has been to recognise a diversity of views, aims and ambitions for the study of archaeology. The position almost 40 years later is that no consensus exists on theoretical perspectives, which is a healthy sign for the archaeological imagination.

I have shown in this chapter that there are as many archaeologies as you can count but that basically there are two. There is the archaeology of dates and data, culture history, which has been with us since Thomsen in the nineteenth century. Then there is the archaeology of ideas and imagination which has many forms but is, at most, only 40 years old, following the widespread appearance of an anthropological archaeology.

Both approaches need data. Both need ideas and theories. However much you might want to, it is not possible to break with past traditions of doing archaeology for the simple reason that we have to incorporate existing facts into our on-going syntheses. Just because we might not like the theories and excavation techniques employed by archaeologists a century ago doesn't mean that we can ignore their data. Archaeologists do not start afresh. Rather they add to what is already known. Those facts, those objects, are patinated with the theories that give them significance to archaeologists. We need to recognise that archaeological fact just as we now need to scrape some of that patina away.

The point about anthropological archaeology is that it has actively encouraged archaeologists to be theoretical. Hence Marxism, which has a much longer history in archaeology than the scientific methodology of processual archaeology, has been extended to consider global issues in the ancient world (Chapter 6). Feminist approaches have successfully challenged entrenched ways of thinking and by focusing on gender have added to our understanding of the active role of material culture in creating power (Chapter 8). Interpretive approaches may have more adherents in Europe than anywhere else. However, the social theory they draw on has wide significance and provides archaeologists with an entry to debates other than those of science. Finally, the neo-Darwinians, a diverse bunch ranging from the hardest of hard scientists to those wrapped in a thin coating of biological metaphor, remind us that we need to develop our own theory and methods rather than be simply borrowers.

So, the archaeological imagination is now developing on several fronts. This can be seen in the different approaches that define the nature of what we study, the archaeological record (Chapter 3), in a variety of ways (Patrik 1985). Even so, while drawing the lines between approaches I have been very aware in this chapter of just how overlapping rather than territorial the position really is. Although frowned upon by some (Johnson 1999a: 118), what is emerging is a more eclectic, rather than evangelical, approach to the use of theory. For example, recent prehistoric case studies by Christopher Tilley (1996), Alasdair Whittle (1996) and Richard Bradley (1997) combine the synthesis of data favoured by culture history with many of the techniques advocated by processualists, to produce strongly interpretive accounts. I have found this in my own work on Palaeolithic Europe. What began as a processual description full of adaptive, functional solutions to capricious and repeated climatic conditions (Gamble

1986), a game played by groups against their environment if you like, has now become a story of individuals creating social networks in well-trodden landscapes of habit (Gamble 1999). Much still remains of my earlier approach. But the addition of insights from novel theoretical perspectives has allowed me to expand the range of evidence that is normally used and to suggest fresh ways of looking at old data and reasons for acquiring new data.

Within archaeology many of the basic concepts, methods and principles remain very familiar, as I will show in the next chapter. What is changing is the archaeological imagination that uses these tools for purposes other than those already tried and tested.

Chapter 3

Basic concepts

It is now time to meet the archaeology. Exposure to the data is the most important aspect of doing archaeology. However, I resisted opening this book with an account of how we go about finding things and, once found, how we organise them for a good reason. Until I had given you a taste of the varieties of archaeology, which includes both themes (Box 4) and theories (Figure 2.1) there was no point in discussing how we handle data. There is nothing more silent than a piece of archaeological evidence. Pots, stones, bronzes and bones do not speak to us. They make no sense by themselves. They only acquire significance when interpreted. To interpret the themes and theories, questions and problems are necessary before any sensible answers will be forthcoming.

We now have some of that basic framework. What I have shown is that there are many ideas about the past, usually several interpretations of the same data (see the changing views of Sutton Hoo in Chapter 1) and definitely more than one answer to the same question. What all this is telling us is that archaeologists

can disagree because they have developed ways of gathering and organising data that allow them to differ. Fieldwork and analysis run to a set of conventions. To participate in the excitement of archaeology requires a knowledge of the concepts that underpin those conventions. In this chapter I will look at those that deal with data gathering and analysis. Later chapters will expand on other themes. In the present chapter I will concentrate on a framework for practical archaeology which will lead us into a consideration of the nature of the archaeological record.

Starting out with a research design

Doing archaeology starts with questions. As we saw in Chapter 1, with the latest campaign at Sutton Hoo, these are now formalised into a research design that sets out what we want to know, the methods we plan to use and the contribution the answer is expected to make. This is all part of being explicit about the business of archaeology, stripping away, if you like, some of the mystery that surrounds the process and that often amazes visitors to excavations who ask 'How did you know to dig here?'.

Explication – setting out what we plan to do, why we want to do it, how we will do it and what we expect to achieve – lies at the heart of a research design. Put like that some research designs sound very obvious. Too obvious for many, which is why few were written down before the appearance of processual archaeology in the 1960s. Of course, prior to this, the culture history approach had research designs, but they were rarely very elaborate. Usually they involved selecting a region or site for survey, excavation and recovering data. This recovery usually was, and in many cases still is, to sort out issues of dating, sequence and the relationship between archaeological cultures.

For example, questions at a regional scale might ask what relative impact did each of the contemporary cultures Hohokam, Patayan, Anasazi and Mogollon have on each other during almost 9000 years in the Southwestern United States (Willey 1966: figures 4.1 and 4.6). Regional survey and excavation would then be employed to get the answers. At a site scale the question might be about the constructional history of York Minster in England. Did the layout of the cathedral follow the earlier town plan for the city as established by the Romans and the Vikings?

Answering these questions, which are posed at very different spatial scales, undoubtedly adds to archaeological knowledge. A lot of very good archaeology and many excellent syntheses have resulted from answering similar questions that deal with local and regional culture history.

However, the criticism mounted by processual archaeology was that in many cases such approaches were often unsystematic. While data were recovered, the question was how *representative* of past activities were they? This is what was meant by the new archaeology's call for explication in the 1960s. Research designs had to be stated, goals set, procedures outlined, methods detailed, and then samples could be recovered.

There was a lot of fuss when this strategy was first proposed (Binford 1964). Comments such as 'we don't know what we will find until we start digging' were matched by a reluctance to set down all those ingrained, internal procedures, the experience and knowledge of being an archaeologist. Some of them just seemed too obvious to commit to paper. It was tantamount to revealing hard-won trade secrets. It has also become apparent since, that writing down a research design does not necessarily make for good archaeology. Research designs do, however, expose poor questions and ill-conceived methods very quickly.

Research designs are now standard. In fact you will not get funding without one. The scientific model that Binford and others were following now dominates to the extent that it is a professional fact of life. As a result we do have a much better idea of what we are doing and why. The rise of contract- and developer-funded archaeology has also made explicit research designs essential. Business as well as government wants to know what it is paying for, and why. Accountability has led to the formal management of archaeological projects (Andrews and Thomas 1995; Cooper *et al*. 1995), which seems a far cry from earlier approaches (Wheeler 1954). But archaeology then was still predominantly a pastime rather than the international profession it is today. The jargon of performance indicators, project milestones, value for money, assessment and evaluation are a very necessary part of securing funding at a scale that 50 years ago would have seemed inconceivable.

The representative sample

The shift that research designs typified was to dig in order to answer questions rather than to dig for things. The objective was the recovery of a representative sample of material so that the questions about site function and organisation and any changes they underwent could be reasonably answered. Sampling theory was needed. This was not just because archaeologists lacked the time and money to dig and analyse every site or to survey and record every valley. It was needed to meet the criteria of the representative sample.

The culture historians' complaint about research designs included a good point. We do not know exactly what we are going to find. This is clearly a problem for systematic sampling, where a representative sample usually depends on knowledge of the population being sampled. This is why opinion polls and market surveys have an acceptable degree of accuracy. The number of voters is known. Moreover, the larger the population and the greater our knowledge of its size and structure, the smaller the samples can be to get at that representative result. Pollsters do not have to ask every voter about their intentions. They sample.

Archaeologists do not know before they start how many sites they will find in a valley survey. Neither do they know how many potsherds, and what frequency of types, will come from an excavation. If we cannot specify our populations beforehand, how can we recover anything but a grab or haphazard sample?

FIGURE 3.1 A sampling strategy. The Cycladic island of Melos was systematically surveyed using fieldwalking transects. A 20 per cent sample of its surface was covered (lower). The choice of sampling design took into account topography and vegetation. The new sites that were found are shown. For comparison, an alternative strategy using a random set of quadrants is also shown (upper). In both cases the sampling strategy can be extrapolated to the areas not surveyed and a representative island-wide picture of prehistoric settlement built up (after Cherry in Renfrew and Wagstaff 1982)

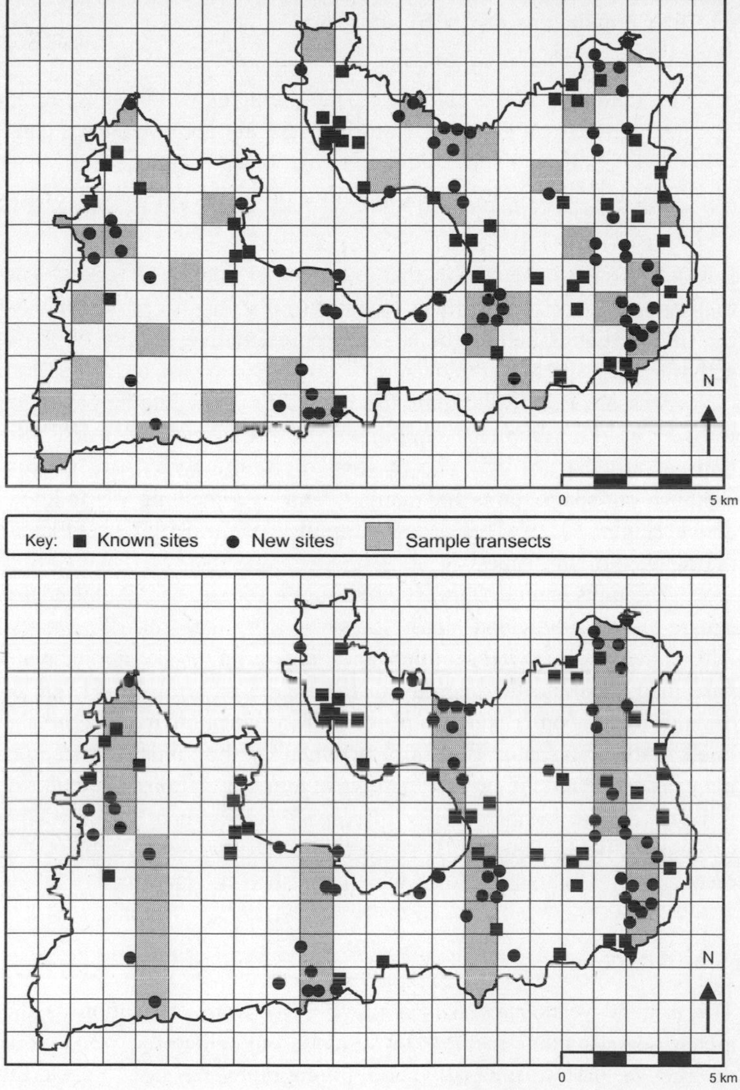
N
0
5 km
Key: Known sites New sites Sample transects
N
0
5 km

Space is the answer. Binford (1964) broke the problem down into four populations that need sampling:

- cultural items (artefacts);
- cultural features (buildings, pits, temples within sites, etc.);
- ecofacts (in his terms culturally relevant non-artefactual data, e.g. animal bones, sediments, carbonised seeds);
- sites (as activity foci containing the three populations listed above).

Beyond these lay the region that contains populations of sites. The region, as will be discussed in Chapter 6, also has to be larger than the past activities being studied if a representative sample of those activities is going to be recovered.

So space is the solution to the catch-22 of only finding out about what we want to sample by sampling it. Before we walk that first field transect, lift the turf or make the first dive on a wreck site we can establish our spatial units and sample them as something we do know about (Figure 3.1). This can be applied to most archaeological materials and landscapes.

The units can be arbitrary: a 50 metre square, or a 20 kilometre square grid subdivided into transacts for the surface survey. Alternatively a *stratified* sample can be drawn up to take into account base map soils and the geology of the region or prior knowledge of the site from geophysical prospection or aerial photographs. But the point is that the spatial grid is determined by the kinds of questions being asked. Within it the material, those four populations listed above, is being *cluster* sampled. Therefore space rather than the objects it contains is being sampled. It is on that basis that we systematically recover representative samples which can then be quantified.

Survey and excavation

The past 30 years have seen a move away from excavation as the archaeologist's main method for finding out about the past. Non-destructive survey, principally aerial photography, has been a powerful tool for over 80 years and is now backed by satellite remote sensing. Indeed, with the pace of urban expansion, the dewatering of wetland areas and, most importantly, changes in forestry and farming practices, such as widespread deep ploughing, the aerial record is now an immense archive of what has been lost in the second half of the twentieth century. Landscapes from all periods, with their settlements, fields and cemeteries, have been obliterated and continue to be under threat. Non-destructive techniques, particularly geophysical survey and other methods such as ground penetrating radar and the controlled use of metal detectors, now allow the rapid (by the standards of excavation) plotting of buried features. Computer enhancement of the results can produce plans of buried cities and landscapes that are very accurate. These serve as a basis not only for finding out about what's there, and analysing it, but also for deciding on a strategy for excavation designed to answer questions about the date, relationships and sequence. Systematic field-survey, where transects are selected according to a sampling design and then walked to recover artefacts from the ploughed soil, has also been instrumental in building up a wider picture of settlement and its changes through time. In many cases material discovered on these surveys is no longer brought back to the lab but recorded on computer in the field and left where it was found. The geographical information systems (GIS) revolution provides a framework for integrating both on-site and off-site data. It grants rapid access to computer-recorded data and allows archaeologists to change their field and excavation strategies, ideally on a daily basis.

Excavation is costly and is increasingly seen as a last resort, particularly in the contract- and developer-funded arena. Often mitigation will change the plans for the road or building so as to preserve the archaeology in situ, as in the cae of the Rose theatre (Chapter 1). Preservation by record, which is what excavation boils down to, has to be a well-argued case.

Recovery

Total excavation is nowadays rarely either an option or desirable, and for a very good reason: the archaeological record is highly repetitive. There is a great deal of redundancy in terms of aspects such as what was made, how people used their landscape and where they buried their dead. Such repetition makes sampling for the representative possible.

Sampling will not guarantee the recovery of either the rare or the unique. Some wonderful find may well be in an undug pit that was set aside when a 10 per cent sampling scheme was applied to a site. This reflects contemporary archaeology's interest in the general rather than the unique. Of course we all like to find gold torcs or the oldest bone of a mink. In the early days of the subject when that was all archaeological diggers were after what suffered were the ordinary pots, bones and stones, which were simply thrown away. Rare finds grab the headlines and they do no harm. But archaeologists need to concentrate their marketing skills on generating excitement in the less-newsworthy small Roman villa, medieval farmstead and prehistoric stone quarry.

Recovery is something that we can control (Figure 3.2) or at least be systematic about. In the quest for the representative sample the use of sieving and the broader consideration of preservation has received much attention. The recovery of small elements such as the foot bones of sheep or fish remains is something that can be addressed, so that their absence can be attributed to excavation procedures, inimical soil conditions or past human activity.

Archaeological entities

What we discover and recover from our spatial grids still needs to be organised. These are the entities that we spend a great deal of time analysing, reassessing and shifting around the museum, work-room and laboratory. There are three basic entities that allow us to examine a key archaeological question of why cultures vary in time and space. In ascending order they are: attribute, artefact and assemblage.

Artefact types are classified by the attributes they possess: shape, colour, material, decoration, etc. Assemblages are defined by the frequency of artefact types, itself an attribute of that entity, and cross-checked through stratigraphic context and dating. At a higher level of classification we will encounter archaeological cultures, culture groups and technocomplexes (see Chapter 6).

Attribute, artefact and assemblage have of course been around since the start of systematic archaeology with Thomsen and Montelius

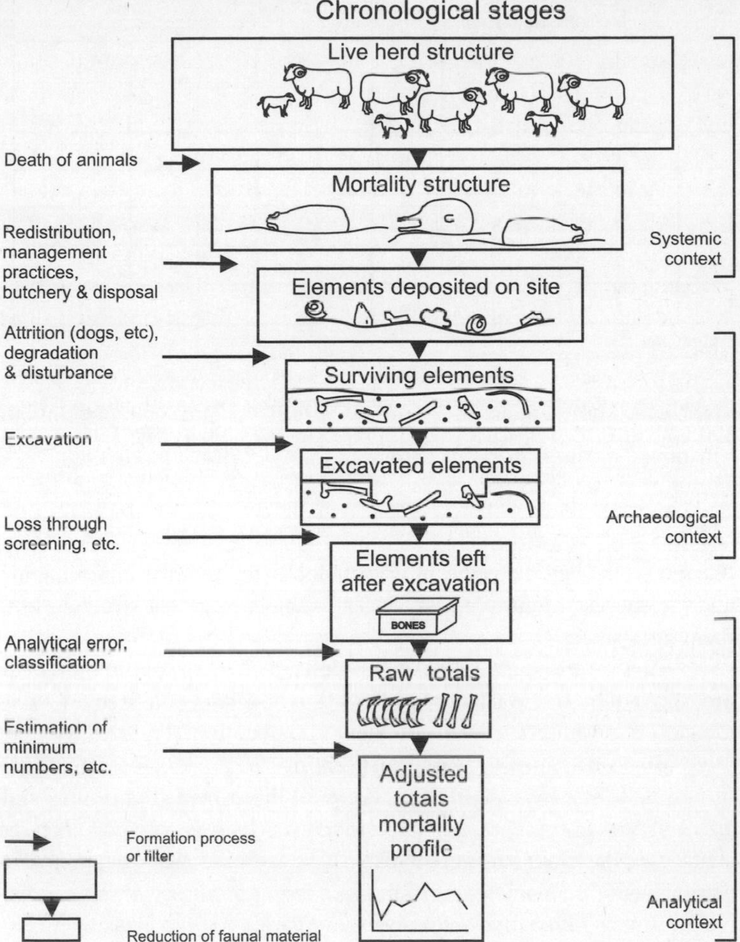

FIGURE 3.2 Recovering samples. This diagram shows what happens to animal bones at each stage in the archaeological process. Similar diagrams have been produced for other materials. The point of this visual jargon is to remind us that what we do, as much as what happens in the ground, affects how representative our samples will be

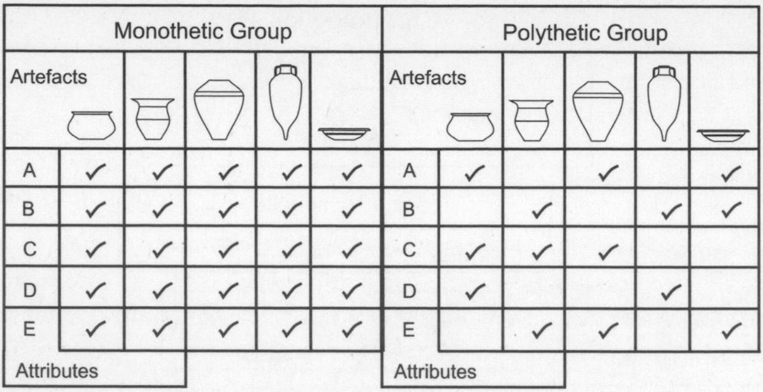

Monothetic Group					
Artefacts					
A	✓	✓	✓	✓	✓
B	✓	✓	✓	✓	✓
C	✓	✓	✓	✓	✓
D	✓	✓	✓	✓	✓
E	✓	✓	✓	✓	✓
Attributes					

Polythetic Group					
Artefacts					
A	✓		✓		✓
B		✓		✓	✓
C	✓	✓	✓		
D	✓			✓	
E		✓	✓		✓
Attributes					

FIGURE 3.3 Polythetic and monothetic systems of classification. The top row of pots are respectively always or partially present as attributes in the culture, or assemblage, A–E (after Clarke 1968: figure 3)

(Chapter 1). They were the building blocks for relative chronologies and the success of culture history. The subject has been structured by them ever since.

They were comprehensively defined for an anthropological archaeology by David Clarke (1968: 37), who also formalised a fundamental observation for archaeological classification (Figure 3.3).

When it comes to using such entities in archaeology it is rare to find that they are *monothetic*, where all the expected attributes and artefacts are always present like students at a nine o'clock lecture. Rather, as the class register reveals, it is the case that attendance is variable as in the *polythetic* group. This is important because we must expect fuzzy rather than clear-cut boundaries to our classifications. Archaeologists spend much of their time deciding how many aspects determine membership of such a group, and in what frequency, as though this was our major problem. This is an aspect of the principle of popularity (see Box 2 and below). Usually the preservation and haphazard recovery of the data are blamed as the usual suspects. However, the data are the data and like children should not be blamed for being difficult. Neither should we get too hung up searching for ultimate classificatory units as a monothetic approach requires. They will remain elusive. Classification only exists to help answer questions and is not an end in itself, although to read much archaeology you would have to conclude otherwise.

Attributes

Artefacts are examined through their attributes. These can be observations on composition, raw materials, form and decoration as well as the techniques of manufacture and the contexts in which the artefacts were found – a pit, a house or a burial, for example – and what they were found with – bodies, animals, other similar or dissimilar artefacts. Quantity is also an important attribute as is independent dating evidence.

Attribute analysis is also applied to higher-order classifications such as Childe's urban revolution or the neo-evolutionary stages of chiefdoms and state (Chapter 7) proposed by Ellman Service (1962). Here a checklist is drawn up and the attributes of the archaeology of Minoan Crete or Mississippi Moundville compared to it (Box 18). The purpose of investigating such archaeological correlates is purely descriptive and classificatory.

Artefacts

Artefacts can range in size from a glass bead to the continent it was exchanged for. They range in number from the isolated potsherd to the contents of the city of Teotihuacan or the Roman Empire. The term 'artefact' embraces a wide range of objects, many of which are not traditionally thought of as artefacts. The familiar would include hand-held and human-scale objects, for example knives, beds and houses. This also extends to the built environment of towns and cities, with monumental architecture, sculpture, bridges and factories. The less-familiar usage of artefact includes landscapes and worlds used and lived in by people. Many wild areas much loved for their natural beauty turn out to be human artefacts. In southwest England, Dartmoor, a National Park, is seen by many as wild, untamed moorland, in contrast to the farmlands that fringe it. However, the Dartmoor we experience today was created in the Bronze Age when an elaborate system of boundary banks was laid out and the forest cut down. Subsequent exploitation for sheep, tin, granite, tourism and as a military training area have added to, and preserved a prehistoric artefact.

Dartmoor is therefore a large piece of material culture. But the artefact scale can get still bigger. Consider Australia, the continent of hunters and gatherers. Erroneously, such lifestyles are thought to be shaped by nature rather than to affect it (Chapter 8), a view that owes everything to the evolutionism of the eighteenth and nineteenth centuries when Australian Aborigines were thought by some not even to possess society.

Fifty years of archaeological research has totally reversed that passive view. Long before Captain Cook the continent was a cultural landscape. Stone artefacts, the oldest of which date back some 60,000 years, are found everywhere, even in southwestern Tasmania where nobody lives today. The widespread practice of burning the country, traced archaeologically through charcoal deposits, transformed the vegetation in favour of the fire-resistant eucalypts. Many animals, especially the megafauna marsupials became extinct either through habitat change or human predation. Finally, Australia is one giant canvass of rocks which have been painted, engraved and pecked with signs and representations of animals and humans – artefacts which depict artefacts which contain artefacts.

Assemblage

The third level in the basic classification of archaeological entities is the assemblage. This was defined by David Clarke as an associated set of contemporary artefact types (1968: 188). It is also a small step from there to a type list that defines an assemblage excavated from a stratigraphic level or chronological unit.

The most celebrated debate concerning the interpretation of archaeological assemblages has used Palaeolithic data. It involved, among others, François Bordes and Lewis Binford. It was based on the interpretation of stone-tool assemblages excavated from stratigraphic layers in the many caves and rock shelters used by Neanderthal people 100,000 to 40,000 years ago in southwest France. One of the most famous is the rock shelter at Le Moustier, after which the widespread Mousterian culture, based on distinctive tools and techniques, is named. The assemblages were studied by François Bordes, who devised a type list with 63 elements such as stone scrapers, points and borers and a series of technical indexes that described the method by which the tools had been knapped (Bordes 1972). Each assemblage contained different proportions of types and variable application of different flint-knapping techniques. What he discovered surprised him. Bordes wrote later that he had expected a spectrum of variation. What he found from his analysis were only five assemblages, or variants, of the Mousterian.

The Mousterian debate, as it is known, revolved around explaining that clustering. Were these assemblages the ethnic markers of five different Neanderthal tribes, as Bordes claimed, or functional toolkits as Binford proposed (Binford and Binford 1969)? Or instead, as others argued (Mellars 1970), stages in a chronological development? Similar assemblage studies based on type list and type frequency abound in studies of archaeological ceramics and metalwork.

Archaeological cultures

Cultures, like the Mousterian, are the next brick in the wall of entities. They are traditionally, and for the foreseeable future, the archaeologist's basic building block. They form both the thing to classify and the thing to explain. Two classic definitions emerged from very different philosophical and political backgrounds. The earlier comes from the ultra-nationalist, and racist, Gustav Kossina, whose settlement archaeology was enthusiastically applied after his death in 1931 by supporters of the Third Reich:

> Clearly defined, sharply distinctive, bounded archaeological provinces correspond unquestioningly to the territories of particular peoples and tribes.
>
> Kossina (1926, in Veit 1989: 39)

The second, and better known, was penned by Gordon Childe, an Australian who spent most of his career in Edinburgh and London.

Childe wrote about the past with a Marxist perspective. He defined the archaeological culture concept in the following classic manner:

> We find certain types of remains – pots, implements, ornaments, burial rites and house forms – constantly recurring together. Such a complex of associated traits we shall term a 'cultural group' or just a 'culture'. We assume that such a complex is the material expression of what today would be called a 'people'.
>
> Childe (1929: v–vi)

Childe's innovation was to pave the way for a social account of the past. His 'culture = peoples' hypothesis took into account the mosaic-like character of the archaeology of Europe. He disagreed with Kossina, who put everything good and innovative down to his own ancestors, the northern Aryans, but agreed with the Swedish typologist Oscar Montelius in his acceptance of diffusion from the Near East. The *ex oriente lux* ('from the light of the east') direction also provided Childe in his early work with an explanation of change within Europe.

Anthropological culture

The definition that Childe gave us describes the archaeological reality of pots, stones and house types. But culture has a much broader meaning than this within anthropology. E. B. Tylor mapped out the field in the nineteenth century:

> Culture, or civilisation . . . is that complex whole which includes knowledge, belief, art, law, morals, custom and any other capabilities and habits acquired by man as a member of society.
>
> Tylor (1871: 1)

It is acquired and transmitted:

> Culture . . . refers . . . to learned, accumulated experience. A culture . . . refers to those socially transmitted patterns for behaviour characteristic of a particular social group.
>
> Kessing (1981: 68)

It can be viewed in very adaptive, functional, terms:

> By culture we mean an extrasomatic, temporal continuum of things and events dependent upon symboling. . . . A mechanism whose function is to make life secure and continuous for groups and individuals of the human species.
>
> White (1959: 3, 78)

For Leslie White culture was our extrasomatic (literally outside the body) means of adaptation. Although he referred to symbols he did not mean, as Clifford Geertz later proposed, that culture was a network of interpretations:

> Believing that . . . man is an animal suspended in webs of significance he himself has spun, I take culture to be those webs, and the analysis of it to be therefore not an experimental science in search of law but an interpretive one in search of meaning.
>
> Geertz (1975: 5)

These poles-apart positions are one of the reasons that the concept of culture is regarded as highly problematic by many anthropologists, even though it is historically their core concept. Recent discussions are provided by Michael Carrithers (1990), Tim Ingold (1994), Christoph Brumann (1999) and Adam Kuper (1999).

Two principles

The entities attribute, artefact, assemblage and culture are the basic bricks in the archaeological wall. They are used to build classifications and to present interpretations. As we saw in the Mousterian debate, these interpretations might differ. But even here the major protagonists agreed that assemblages exist. They only disagreed over what they signify. Two principles help us to understand why such different archaeologists are agreed on the bricks in their wall. These are:

- popularity, and
- stratigraphy.

The principle of popularity

Much of what I have so far described in this chapter depends on the principle of popularity. This has been applied to items as well as types and to styles or traits of manufacture, decoration and use. Fluctuating popularity both identifies a change in the archaeological record and explains it by invoking either the diffusion of peoples or the spread of ideas. Popularity changes with time and across space. The principle of popularity also supposes that things are similar because people share the same ideas and cultural premises. This sharing is presented as a basic aspect of all humans. It started in the Palaeolithic and continues today. For culture historians like François Bordes a stone-tool type is therefore as understandable as a Frenchman's beret or an Englishman's bowler hat. They are all expressing the same cultural imperative whereby sharing norms of behaviour establishes group identity. But this imperative is never analysed, rather it is assumed as the basis for understanding why archaeological units vary and why they changed? It was this lack of clarity that led some, such as Binford, to a serious rethink about what popularity was measuring.

The principle of stratigraphy

Popularity and stratigraphy are two principles that go hand in hand. Stratigraphy turns 'walls of mud' into a record of time and past activity. Most importantly, thinking stratigraphically makes you *look* at time vertically, stacked-up like so many different-coloured bricks and laid down like sediments in a lake. You need to add that *vertical* dimension to your everyday experience of time as *linear*, minutes turn into hours into days, and as *cyclical*, when your birthday comes round once a year (Chapter 6).

The essence of stratigraphic analysis is determining discrete, superimposed layers or features and then examining their contents. A very systematic and thorough analysis is provided by Edward Harris (1989). His logical matrix analysis (Figure 3.4) is a widespread convention in field archaeology. It is an example of visual jargon.

Stratigraphic differences may be geological – variation in soils and sediments that appear as textural or colour changes – or they may

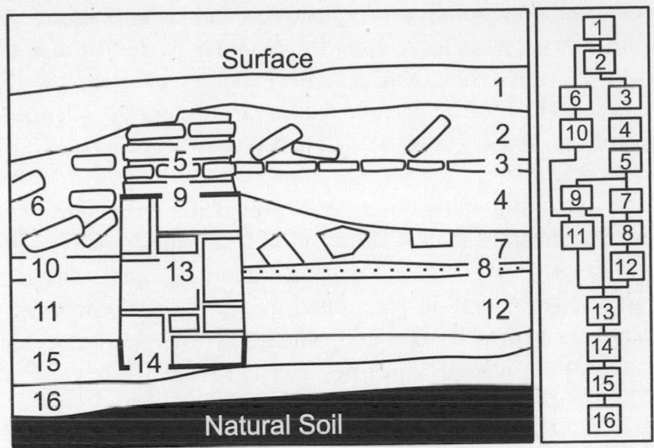

FIGURE 3.4 A Harris matrix for a section in an excavation. This would be combined with all the other sections in the trench as well as with the plans as the excavation proceeded

be features of human activity – the digging of pits and ditches, building of walls and dumping of waste material. Stratigraphy is therefore about the building up of layers and features, as well as their cutting away and reworking as a result of human occupation. A stratigraphic analysis unravels the sequence of that creative process of living in the landscape over periods of time.

Stratigraphic excavations began in the middle of the nineteenth century and some of the best exponents were J. J. A. Worsaae, who excavated prehistoric sites in Denmark, and Giuseppe Fiorelli, who applied a stratigraphic approach to Pompeii in 1860. Not everyone followed suit and not all stratigraphic excavations were well recorded. Moreover, the breadth of interests that Worsaae pursued in his excavations, including the recovery and analysis of organic evidence to reconstruct the environment and subsistence economy, was often lacking. Most digs were just that – digs – with the sole aim of recovering pots, metal, art and burials. The exceptions stand out, such as Ferdinand Keller's pioneering work in the well preserved Neolithic Swiss lake villages which he started excavating in 1854. In England the military training of General Pitt-Rivers and his unshakeable belief in evolutionary science led to a model of good practice (Bowden 1991). He both excavated sites and published the results from his Dorset estate (1887). In 1882 he became the first Inspector of Ancient Monuments for the country after Parliament passed legislation protecting some important sites.

Sound stratigraphic observation provided archaeologists with a means of comparing their results and building their relative chronologies. Exactly when each regional tradition went through its stratigraphic revolution differs around the world. In North America it took place later than Europe and centred on work in the pueblos of the southwestern United States between 1915 and 1927.

Seriation dating

Combine popularity and stratigraphy and you arrive at seriation (Chapter 1), a standard archaeological procedure that sorts series of attributes and artefacts and then interprets them. One of the best examples of seriation comes from the southwestern United States.

The main question that faced archaeologists investigating the prehistory of this region, with its monuments such as Pueblo Bonito in Chaco Canyon, New Mexico, concerned relative dating. The answer as developed by the anthropologist A. R. Kroeber in a ground-breaking paper in 1916 provided a chronology using frequency seriations of pottery. He made the distinction that variation in the proportion of types could be due *either* to time *or* to geography. Remember, this was a sequence not a scale and no seriation can indicate how long any phase lasted. That would come first from dendrochronology (tree-ring dating) in the southwestern United States and universally through radiocarbon dating after 1945 (see below). The underlying principle in seriation is that change is analytically visible through the shifting popularity, or frequencies, of artefact, usually pottery, types (Figure 3.5).

Kroeber was not alone in developing such techniques but appears to have made the breakthrough independently (Lyman, O'Brien, and Dunnell 1997: 55). Nels Nelson, Clark Wissler and Leslie Spier also produced seriation chronologies for the American

Site	%	%	%	%	%	%	%	%
A	4.1		6.4		85.4		4.1	
B	3.8		5.7		86.7		3.8	
C	4.1		6.2		85.4		4.3	
D	6.4		14.4		75.2		4.0	
E	7.7		18.5		71.2		2.6	
F	18.4		48.0		29.8		3.8	
G	23.3		53.8		20.0		2.9	
H	32.3		48.2		5.2		14.3	
I	38.7		43.1		0.4		17.8	
J	49.0		29.6		0.2		21.2	
K	61.5		20.3		0.0		18.2	
L	87.5		3.1		0.2		9.2	
M	89.5		0.8		0.0		9.7	

FIGURE 3.5 Battleship curves. This seriation reflects changing popularity among the four pots over time. Each row adds up to 100 per cent

Southwest. The excavations in the Pecos pueblo by Alfred Kidder during the 1920s, using natural rather than arbitrary stratigraphic units, confirmed that these shifts in the frequency of pottery types were indeed chronological. The battleship curves which present a seriation analysis are another piece of visual archaeological jargon.

Absolute dating

Stratigraphy provides a sequence; B came after A but before C. Popularity, when used in a seriation elaborated the process of culture change. You could now ask 'Who came from where?, based on the popularity of types. However, what archaeologists, and especially prehistoric archaeologists, wanted was a way of measuring time not through changes in relative frequency but in terms of absolute years. How long did those battleship curves last?

The absolute measure of time beyond written records and king lists was first achieved by counting annual lake varves and tree rings. Such continuous records are extremely valuable. They provide very accurate dating but of course depend upon either the preservation of suitable materials, such as wood, or the deposition of artefacts in lake muds. What was needed was a technique that could date items that were found on most archaeological sites – charcoal, bone and shell.

The major breakthrough came after 1945 with the development of isotope-decay methods. Radiocarbon was the first, soon to be followed by a number of related techniques which used different isotopes associated with the elements uranium, potassium, argon and thorium. Now there are also dating methods using geomagnetism, thermoluminescence, electron spin resonance and amino acid epimerisation. Different techniques have different time spans and apply to a range of materials (Figure 3.6). Box 11 lists the materials upon which each technique is based. A full account of this very important but highly technical branch of archaeology can be found in Aitken (1990).

The absolute measurement of time by scientific methods is undoubtedly one of the great achievements of interdisciplinary research. It was primarily a combination of physics, chemistry and archaeology. Willard Libby working in Chicago pioneered the radiocarbon technique in the immediate post-war period. His breakthrough was recognised by a Nobel Prize in 1960. Older techniques such as tree-ring dating and varve counting were later used to refine and calibrate the results when it was realised that some of Libby's original assumptions about the stability of carbon in the atmosphere did not adequately allow for variation over time. A review of the power of dendrochronology and its importance in calibrating radiocarbon is provided by Michael Baillie (1995).

Radiocarbon (C^{14}) dating is very useful for archaeologists

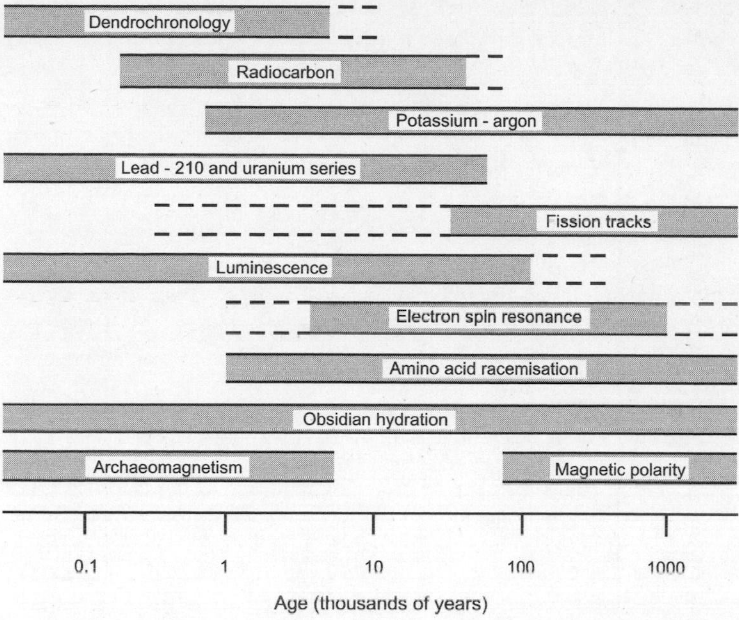

FIGURE 3.6 The age ranges of dating techniques (after Aitken 1990: figure 1.1)

because carbon is so widespread. Charcoal, wood, bone, fibre, shell and seeds can all be dated, though the chemical pretreatment of samples varies and different laboratories prefer different materials. The applicability of this technique worldwide allowed archaeologists to compare global cultures and processes. Archaeological findings were incorporated into global history and the scene was set for a generalising, comparative approach. Science-based dating such as radiocarbon dating was part of the quantitative revolution in archaeology after 1950. It is quite possible that without it the anthropological archaeology of the 1960s (Chapter 2) would have been delayed. I believe it would still have happened but probably not quite in its original form as a hard-nosed, scientific and processual investigation of the past.

Box 11: Some of the most important science-based dating techniques, the materials they date and the ages they cover

Dating technique	Materials	Upper limit (years)	Lower limit (years)
Potassium/argon (K/Ar)	Volcanic rocks	30,000	All of human evolution i.e. 5 million
Thermoluminescence (TL)	Burnt flint, ceramics Unburnt sediments	Present 5,000–10,000	100,000–500,000 50,000
Electron spin resonance (ESR)	Tooth enamel	Present	> 1 million
Uranium series	Stalactite, stalagmite	5000	350,000
Radiocarbon (C^{14}) using accelerator mass spectrometry (AMS)	Bone, charcoal, shell, fibre	Present	50,000, possibly 70,000 in the future
Radiocarbon (C^{14}) conventional methods	Bone, charcoal, shell, fibre	Present	40,000

The archaeological record

I have now described some of our basic units. I have also shown how archaeologists used the principles of popularity and stratigraphy to order their materials, prior to absolute dating, into sequences. The study of change is then possible.

However, the absolute measurement of time did not make the archaeologist's job of interpretation any easier. Instead it contributed to a major debate starting 30 years ago, concerning the composition and nature of the archaeological record: 'What exactly is it, how was it formed and how should it be investigated?'

After 1969 Binford, as he recalled later (1983), became disillusioned with his new archaeology. He was concerned that all that had happened was that archaeology had become a more statistical, and increasingly computer-literate, culture history. Archaeology might have been recast as an anthropological inquiry with a concern for real-life processes, but this still left a yawning chasm that needed a bridge of inference to span it. Quite simply, how could you go from the static facts that could be dug up to the dynamic but invisible behaviour that produced them? The new archaeology, for all its insistence on testing hypotheses, the deductive method, and collecting samples in a more rigorous manner to enable such testing to occur, had difficulty with this crucial methodological point. It had to be addressed if a scientific approach was to succeed. But how?

Middle range theory

Binford's answer was to set out principles that could act as a bridge between the statics of the archaeological record (those bones and pots) and the dynamics of past human behaviour (the now invisible actions that produced and organised them into spatial and temporal patterns). He called this a *middle-range theory* (Box 6). In practice it was based on experiment and on the observation of people and animals doing things in the modern world, which would allow us to learn about how patterns are created.

Binford undertook his own studies among the Nunamiut hunters of Alaska and the Alyawara people of central Australia (Binford 1983).

Box 12: What is taphonomy?

Closely related to both middle-range theory and site formation processes is the field of taphonomy, literally the laws of burial (*taphos* = burial; *nomos* = law). It is the study of a subset of the archaeological record which deals with organic remains (Lyman 1994: 1). Taphonomy has therefore been particularly important in studies of animal bone assemblages, crop residues and other environmental evidence such as geoarchaeology in sorting out the varied agents and processes, natural and cultural, that have contributed to and shaped archaeological samples.

Box 13: Doing middle-range theory

- Understand the dynamics of behaviour by undertaking a detailed ethnoarchaeological study of a modern hunting society to learn about the decisions they face and how the archaeology they create is organised in time and space ([1978], Binford 1978a,b, 1980).
- Hone the skill of recognising relevant patterns in the data. Build a middle-range theory to form the bridge between data and the behaviour, now invisible, that produced it (Binford 1983).
- Compare human hunters with carnivores. Examine how carnivores regularly feed on a carcass and carry food back to their dens. Since the behaviour of wolves and hyenas has remained the same, while humans evolved new adaptations during the Palaeolithic, they provide a yardstick for measuring those changes (Binford 1981a).

He also studied carnivore feeding and denning behaviour in Africa and North America to try to understand how they use and pattern bones (see Box 12). Similar taphonomic studies became common.

In all of this Binford's aim was to determine the range of potentially relevant causal processes for his chosen area, the study of prehistoric hunter gatherers. His strategy was threefold (Box 13).

Not everyone followed Binford's strategy because not everyone was interested in hunters and gatherers. What use were hyenas and modern hunters to the study of sedentary farming societies? Ethnoarchaeological studies have certainly been carried out among agricultural, horticultural and urban communities. But these have started from rather different premises. Modern material culture such as the Tucson garbage project (Skibo, Walker and Nielsen 1995) and Hodder's Baringo work in East Africa (Hodder 1982) are just two well-

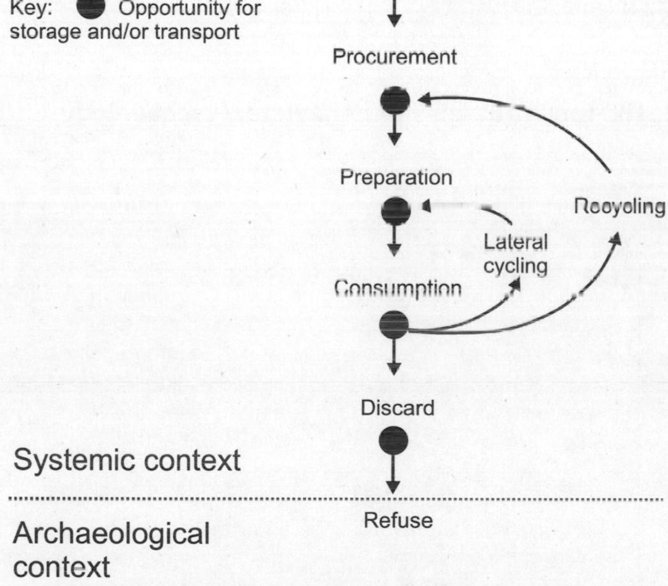

FIGURE 3.7 Making archaeology. The formation of the archaeological record with the passage of materials from a systemic into an archaeological context (after Schiffer 1976)

known examples that raise challenging alternatives to how we think culture works in time and space and how such patterning reveals people consuming and interacting through the medium of material culture.

Site formation

Michael Schiffer, once a Binford student, developed an approach that privileged the study of human behaviour – especially making, using and discarding artefacts. Schiffer (1976) was interested in making explicit the multiple role of laws in archaeological research. For Schiffer it was not middle-range theory as much as the study of how the archaeological record was formed. These formation processes were of two types; natural and cultural. 'N' and 'C' transforms affected objects and their associations in predictable ways as they moved from the past, systemic context into the present archaeological context, where they became refuse (Figure 3.7).

Box 14: The four strategies of behavioural archaeology (Schiffer 1976)

Human behaviour	**Material culture**	
	Past	*Present*
Past	Archaeology and the study of *particular* past cultural systems, e.g. rise of palace societies in the Aegean Bronze Age	Ethnoarchaeological studies to inform *general* archaeological interpretation, e.g. hunter-gatherer settlement patterns
Present	Archaeology's contribution to understanding *general* aspects of contemporary as well as past behaviour, e.g. population pressure as a cause of cultural change	The study of *particular* industrial societies, e.g. the Tucson garbage project as an investigation of material consumption

If a difference exists between Binford's middle-range theory and Schiffer's formation processes it lies in the broader archaeological goals they are pursuing. For Schiffer and his colleagues 'the subject matter of archaeology is the relationships between human behaviour and material culture in all times and places' (Schiffer 1976: 4). They identify four strategies which nicely illustrate what they hope to achieve (Box 14).

The purpose of archaeology for Binford (1983), however, is to understand evolutionary transformations such as that from hunting to farming, the replacement of Neanderthals by modern humans and, most recently, asking under which conditions do low-density populations among hunters and gatherers become high density. Further differences between their positions are explored in the next chapter.

Summary

In this chapter I have gone from research designs to the archaeological record. Both of these concepts represented a major shift in the way archaeology was conceived and practised. At one time the archaeological record was not seen as a problem. Indeed it is still sometimes claimed that getting the stratigraphic facts right is our goal (Harris 1989: xiii). But, as we have seen, the archaeological record is more than just an offshoot of geology and its laws of superposition. Instead it provides an active, interpretive problem that begins in Hodder's phrase 'at the trowel's edge'. In the same way being explicit about research designs is another means by which we came to grips with our samples. Obtaining a representative sample has nothing to do with the principles of stratigraphy. Instead it has everything to do with our assumptions about, and approaches to, investigating human behaviour and action through material remains as they are distributed in time and space.

Consequently I have introduced some of the entities, such as attribute, and principles, such as popularity, that archaeologists commonly use. I have provided you with definitions of culture, taphonomy and many other terms. I have acquainted you with these conventions because they structure the practice of archaeology and so make it intelligible to initiates. These conventions are the shorthands that you will find in site reports, conference papers and textbooks. Suitably armed, it is now time to see what we can do with them.

Chapter 4

People

Getting at people is the core activity of archaeology. Finding objects, and then analysing and interpreting them, is what we do most of the time. What we must never lose sight of amidst the excitement are those people. It is all too easy to find both dispirited and perfectly content archaeologists who, like Arthur's knights in search of the Holy Grail, have either given up or forgotten that they were even trying to look for them. As a result the people, individuals or collectives, can very soon get lost in the detail – the necessary report writing, the catalogues of coins and carp's tongue swords, the syntheses by region and period, the textbooks by topic and theme: the grist but not the grail.

In the last chapter I examined the entities archaeologists use and the concept of the archaeological record. Now the spotlight falls on people in the past. This all important focus requires that we ask three basic questions:

- Who do we want to know?
- What can we know?
- How do we know?

To answer them we will need to examine the use of analogy and the way we build inferences about people in the past either by using a scientific method or as an exercise in spinning a cable.

Who do we want to know?

Throughout the history of archaeology there has been a shifting argument about the relative importance of the individual and the group to understanding the past. This reflects wider trends in the debate over individual responsibilities, power, freedoms and psyches and the role of society and the state in constraining and shaping them. The study of the past is one way to continue this debate and is a form of self-knowledge about who we are and why we act in so many different and similar ways.

However, at a practical level, can we study the individual without written documents which give us that sense of the person – of his or her thoughts, feelings and intentions? Must we always look to an aggregate such as the culture, the system or society to study people in the past? What role did the individual play in making decisions and so push forward the idea of urban living, imperial expansion or just what to eat for dinner?

The individual

In prehistory the individual is usually regarded as a shadowy figure lost in the long corridors of deep time. Even though prehistoric villages may have had few inhabitants and the campsites of hunters and gatherers even less, there is a prejudice against looking too hard for them. This may seem strange given that there are many archaeological instances, stone knapping would be one, of well-preserved, individual actions and, by inference, individual decision making. In fact I suspect that the earlier prehistoric record has rather more snapshots where we can easily see the individual at work than in the later text-assisted periods.

For example, records survive that chart the changing ownership of properties for many of the medieval streets in English towns. Inventories of house contents were often made when an owner died.

From these a picture of comparative wealth and status arising from the trade practised in the house or shop can be built up. This is information about the individual. An archaeological excavation of one of these houses, probably deeply buried by subsequent renovations and rebuilds, usually fails to add much more than the size of the living room, how it was built and the contents of the latrine pits in the back garden. This is not the fault of the archaeology, with its coarse-grained time signatures (Chapter 6). Rather it is the error of expecting the material record of the past to furnish information in the same form as the more familiar text-based evidence. Room size and pit-contents, as we shall see in Chapter 8, can be every bit as illuminating of wealth and status as an inventory written down for probate purposes. Furthermore, in his study of eighteenth century Bristol, Roger Leech (1999: 30) shows how changing architecture and the ordering of space within houses permits a different identification of individual lives than most text-based accounts allow. He shows that rather than pursuing status by the numbers and size of rooms in houses, it is instead possible to trace distinct lifestyles through separate and peculiarly urban genealogies of architectural form.

The individual and the system

The question is rather what do we mean by the individual? For culture historians it is still the identification of the historical person. Who was buried in the Sutton Hoo longship? Was it really Raedwald, who died around AD 625? And if it was, what do we know of him from the few texts that survive? Very little is the answer. Not even that he was buried in a ship on dry land with a silver spoon in his mouth.

This game of spot-the-individual was rightly criticised by Colin Renfrew, who observed that we don't want to know *who* was top dog, but *what kind* of dog he was (1973b: 12). However, rather than teaching the dog new tricks many processualists only let it run with the pack. Kent Flannery's statement is typical:

> Obviously individuals *do* make decisions, but evidence of these individual decisions cannot be recovered by archaeologists. Accordingly it is more useful for the archaeologist to study and

> understand the system, whose behaviour is detectable over and over again.
>
> Flannery (1967, in Leone 1972: 106)

The system rather than the individual governs what happens. Systems have their own trajectory and cannot be deflected by individual action. Raedwald, whatever personal qualities he might have had, was irrelevant to the process of change that was soon to sweep paganism from his kingdom and replace it with Christianity. Systems, as I examined in Chapter 2, are said to run according to basic laws and principles, such as those of thermodynamics or natural selection. These cross-cut prehistoric and historic periods and uncovering them is the aim of a scientific archaeologist such as that of Flannery.

With this outlook individuals become nothing more than the servants of systems. An example from elsewhere reiterates the point and should warn neo-Darwinian archaeologists (Chapter 2) to be cautious with their dismissals. The biologist Richard Dawkins maintains that individuals are just a means by which genes and their cultural counterparts memes, replicate themselves (1976). This view of the system as paramount has been nicely parodied by the philosopher Daniel Dennett. He points out that from a library's point of view a scholar is just a way to make another library (1991: 202). Taken to its logical conclusion systems reproduce themselves through the unthinking actions of individuals. If we follow this line then we can abandon the individual among the dusty stacks of unreadable time.

Thinking people, dumb systems

Happily the argument continues to shift. The individual, correctly in my view, is currently seen by some as the unit of selection, the locus of change (Chapter 7). The argument that we can't see individuals' actions or decisions in archaeological evidence has been tackled by Steven Mithen. He uses an evolutionary approach to decision making among prehistoric hunters. He ascribes to the individuals he studies a knowledge of the world and a capacity to plan and make decisions. In addition they are able to respond creatively and intelligently to the challenges of their social and physical environment (Mithen 1993:

396). Without these attributes there can, in his opinion, be no satisfactory explanation. Emphasising those basic systems, as advocated by Flannery, involved steam-roller explanations for change such as group selection and population pressure. The study of the individual never had a chance.

Mithen's description harmonises with the interpretive approach, although its adherents would probably fault him for filling up the individual with *essence* (Chapter 1) in order to get them to make up their mind. Post-processualists are very keen to reinstate the individual in archaeological studies (Shanks and Tilley 1987b). But at the same time this is not just swapping the system for the individual. The interpretive twist is to insist on the influence of an individual on the creation of the wider social structure *and* the importance of that structure on the creation of the individual.

In this approach, giving Raedwald a name and elevating his elaborate ship-burial to the status of a historic event is unimportant. 'Raedwald' and all his fine accoutrements are instead an object (Chapter 5), influencing the structure of his society and in turn being influenced by it. Raedwald the 'person-thing', rather than the 'king-person', is both material action and a symbol for action by others. But then so too was every other individual and artefact in his kingdom and outside it. Here is Renfrew's dog howling a new tune.

The individual in archaeology

Does this mean that individuals will only be found archaeologically where preservation is good and time signatures fine-grained? I would answer no. We should not confuse precision in our methods with knowing people. Neither should we expect our knowledge of individuals to be accessible in similar ways through either the object- or text-based record of the past. We know about individuals through interaction and involvement. We engage with others in all the varied activities of our daily lives. That involvement comprises material culture as well as flesh-and-blood people. We utilise the full set of our senses to live in and with that experience.

We use those same senses and rules of social engagement when we go about investigating the past *with others*. But those others, trowelling next to you in the trench, sitting across from you in class or the library, or walking around the museum, are not the individuals of the past. We cannot engage with the Minoans in the same way that we can with fellow tourists at the Palace of Knossos. That is patently impossible. But what we can do is to credit them with actions, make them knowledgeable, as Mithen suggests and before him Grahame Clark, who declared that just because prehistorians cannot identify individuals is no reason why they should ignore their existence (1957: 248). The critical point to emphasise concerns change. With the individual correctly identified as highly variable, and hence the unit of selection, we make change an internal, human process. The alternative is to rely on an external steamroller to iron out our historic wrinkles.

How to get on in primate society

Society is a difficult word. It is very imprecise yet easily understandable. Mrs Thatcher, when in power, famously declared that 'There is no such thing as society. There are individual men and women and there are families', and she still fails to realise that she was booted out of office by what she claimed did not exist. However, with typical political canniness she points us to a tension that has occupied many social theorists over many centuries: what exactly is the relationship between the individual and the wider social structure that we all must live within? Opinion swings between the importance of the individual and the primacy of the state, the micro- to the macro-scale. How we conceive of the problem is very important for getting at those people in archaeology.

Let me come at the problem by examining what we make of the societies of apes and monkeys, our primate cousins.

One reason for drawing the comparison is that monkey watchers have had, like archaeologists, to work out the structure of a society (in this case the primate society) for themselves. They cannot converse with their subjects and they definitely have no written records to guide them. They take either a bottom-up or a top-down approach (see Chapter 7, neo-evolution) to society, those collections of individuals who associate with one another (Figure 4.1). Appropriately for primate

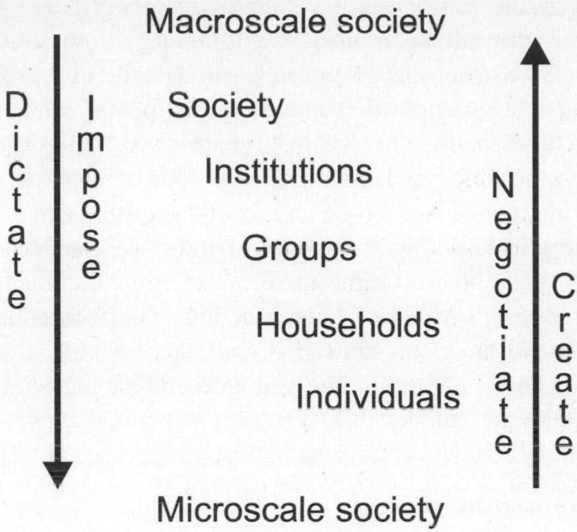

FIGURE 4.1 Top-down and bottom-up approaches to the study of society

societies, a bottom-up approach to explain how society is created is currently the most popular.

This model sees the individual baboon, chimp or vervet monkey as negotiating and performing society into being. They do this through building alliances where you find out who your real friends are when fights break out. These are finger-tip societies. The ties that bind are literally groomed into existence. Many primates spend up to 25 per cent of their waking time grooming each other and through this mechanism establishing long-lasting emotional bonds.

The main point, however, is that these individual apes and monkeys are active agents in the construction of their social worlds. The intensity of grooming may to some extent be predicted from their genetic relationships to each other, but it is by no means solely determined by that blueprint. Social life is neither biologically determined, as sociobiologists have claimed, nor inherited in finished form. Moreover, read any primate-watcher's study (Waal 1982; Goodall 1986) and you will be impressed by the personalities, biographies and sheer individuality of the 'animals' they are studying. This is not crude anthropomorphism. It is, however, a major change in the way we conceive of society, from one based on pre-ordained rules and roles to one open to active participation and interpretation. Of course there are limits, but there is not a hard-wired, innate structure. And of course it is all done without words and normally without material culture.

The alternative is a top-down view of society. Here institutions precede the actors. You are born into a society. You inherit its culture. You act out your life according to rules determined collectively and somehow existing outside of human action. The institutions of the state, the law, business and education continue, unlike you and I who are their temporary stewards. The system therefore *seems* to be more important than the individual, as Flannery explained above.

Institutions and social archaeology

Now in practice both bottom-up and top-down approaches must be considered. We may negotiate what sort of society we want, but we do not have a completely free hand. Karl Marx pointed that out. Mrs Thatcher might still be in power if she had read and understood what he was saying. Individuals are part of wider groupings and those institutions do carry on, many of them beyond the lifespan of an individual. It is this reciprocal relationship, the give and take of social life at the micro (individual) and macro (society) scale that needs to be appreciated (Figure 4.1).

The dominant model in social archaeology has emphasised the top-down, institutional approach. Examples would include Renfrew's early state modules (1977), equal polities locked together in competition for prestige. Closely allied are the chiefdoms of the neo-evolutionists. They use their checklists of attributes to distinguish chiefs from states and tribes (Kirch 1984). Then there is the 'institution' of hunting and gathering, which is treated as different in essence from farming or horticulture (Service 1966). Finally, there is the condition of being a modern human as opposed to a Neanderthal or any other of the myriad early hominids (Stringer and Gamble 1993).

Such models have been very useful in pointing archaeology towards big questions (Chapter 7). This social archaeology exploits the dimensions of time and space to discover repeated regularities that then need explanation.

The bottom-up and top-down approaches must work together (as shown in Figure 4.1) and so long as it is recognised that only a matter of emphasis privileges one over the other, the situation is tenable. More importantly this contrast between the individual and the institution is important to archaeology as anthropology. The distinction raises the question of how do we think society works? Without such a model we can hardly expect to get at those people who are the core of archaeological enquiry.

Agency: an alternative thought

This contrast is important for archaeologists because it returns us again to units of analysis and contexts to explain change. Let me make a suggestion.

The individual may be a red herring. In fact if we are not careful the individual may only be a small institution, filled with essences, like free will, and attributes, such as the right to bear arms, that we believe are, or at least should be, universal. If that is the case, then what has to be avoided is putting the individual forward as another ideal type or cipher. Rather than make a checklist of those attributes, it helps to follow the social theorists and attribute individuals with agency, the act of doing (Dobres 2000; Dobres and Robb 2000). With agency comes that all-important capacity for involvement. If that did not exist, then there would be nothing to talk about. Therefore agency can be universal without being one of those unhelpful essences. A historical discipline like archaeology can use a universal property like that.

Networks

Network analysis provides another pointer to help us round the conceptual problem of society. As Charles Orser argued (1999: 280), in his discussion of the components of modern-world archaeology (Box 3), network relations that cover groups and individuals define humanity in a much more satisfying manner than our often vague notions of culture.

Moreover, it is more immediately applicable to the archaeological record. Individuals – both human and primate – are all concerned with building social networks. These change throughout our lifetime, for example as we pass from childhood to adulthood. By old age we might have created huge webs of interaction based on many connecting ties involving such activities as politics and economics as well using symbolic codes and constructing gender. Not surprisingly, therefore, we vary enormously in our skill to build and maintain networks. Network size and the types of relationship they contain differ from person to person.

One way to understand this variation is through the three resources available to construct your own social networks – emotional, material and symbolic. Network analysis shows that most of us use emotional networks to build small, intense and long-lasting networks of between three and seven members. Material resources expand that number to about 20, while symbolic resources – sending someone a card as a token of acquaintanceship or friendship – can extend to over 500. You can check this out from your own experience. Count up the names in your address book, then see who you designate as best friends on your telephone tariff and compare how many people are on your Christmas card list. You will see that this fits the model of an intimate, effective and extended network which *you* build, negotiate and maintain. Welcome to your very own bottom-up society.

The explanation of why we can identify three major but overlapping networks could be given to us by any baboon. It is largely a matter of time. Baboons are limited in the amount of time they can spend per day grooming each other: too much and they die happy but very hungry – so too with us. Therefore the number of other baboons they can groom into their intimate network is limited by the means that makes it such a powerful bond. Emotional resources are expensive, concentrated and exhausting. Maintaining 500 ties at a highly emotional pitch would wear us all down very quickly. So we have devised other ways to perform socially, to engage with that number of people, to construct action and make it predictable. Material resources, food, marriage partners and raw materials are one means. Symbolic resources, that elision between style and social technology, provide an even more plastic and extensive mechanism (Gamble 1998).

Networks are relevant to the archaeological record because they vary enormously from person to person in terms of size and scale. Potentially networks flow in all directions and could go on for ever. The trick then is to discover how we cut networks down to size. The answer according to anthropologist Marilyn Strathern (1996) is through transactions. These of course can be of material and symbolic kinds.

The existence of limits does not imply that once negotiated networks are fixed for all time. We can change the members of our networks, promoting some, divorcing others. Very little of this is based on genetics and almost all of it on action and involvement. The result resembles the overlapping figure of cultures (Figure 6.1). We all construct overlapping social fields. These are defined not by institutions but by the web of networks we spin, which in turn spin us.

Back to essence

You might argue that this is just a vague universal function supported by a large dollop of essence. After all what is a relationship if not the essence of something we express as friendship, love, altruism, hate and indifference? This is partly true. Networks are only useful in exposing the flows of action in society. What to my mind overcomes the problem of essence and universalism is the sheer variety of experience that this formal structure, rather than just a loose blanket term like 'society', allows us to encompass. Without variation, as Darwin pointed out, there can be no change. If individuals and populations were identical there would be nothing for natural selection to get to work on. No people to get at. Networks tell us what we know but have difficulty expressing: that our social powers are limited though we strive to overcome them.

What can we know?

My second question is basically about where ideas come from. These ideas are what makes our archaeological imagination tick. To answer it we need to examine the issue of analogy. This will involve a brief examination of some of the pitfalls that surround its use.

Many of these are so deep that they create to many people's minds limits to inference – boundaries to archaeological knowledge about people.

Analogy

Analogy is basically about using the present to interpret the past. The first step is to recognise a similarity between two entities. These could be artefact styles, site layouts or settlement systems within a region. The similarity is then measured in space and time. I would call this *pattern recognition* that only comes from a knowledge of the data and a sense of problem (Chapter 6).

The next step is to infer the relationship. That can be deceptively easy. I notice that the first domestic plants and animals in Mesoamerica and Mesopotamia coincide with the expansion of villages in both regions. I infer a common process of population pressure on resources to account for the intensification of subsistence in the first place and the continued growth of settlement size once turkeys and sheep, maize and wheat are available.

So far so good. That analogy seems reasonable based on a supposition, believed to be universal, that population pressure is inevitable and will only result in growth if carrying capacity can be boosted. The backing for such an inference stems from how we see the world working.

The problem comes when you are asked to justify that inference. Why should the past run according to the present? Should the past be interpreted in the light of the present because we can measure some similarity? (Hodder 1991: 148)

Ethnographic analogy

This brings us to a pitfall into which many have fallen because of an injudicious use of ethnographic analogy. The misuse of the ethnographic parallel is something that the founding fathers of the discipline have never been forgiven for. Wilson (1862) and Lubbock (1865) illustrated their works on prehistory by drawing parallels with the customs and morals of modern peoples. The lesson they drew was a living archaeology, where examples of the European Neolithic could still be found in the nineteenth century Pacific or among the Native peoples of the United States.

The most famous example was published in 1911 by an Oxford professor of geology W. J. Sollas. His book *Ancient Hunters and Their Modern Representatives* illustrated the three stages of the Palaeolithic (Old Stone Age) with the Tasmanians as the Lower Palaeolithic, the Australian Aborigines as the Middle Palaeolithic and the Bushmen (San) and Eskimo (Inuit) combined as living examples of the Upper Palaeolithic. For Sollas the superficial similarity of the stone tools was enough to draw the analogy. His inference was no doubt based on a ladder of progress where the simpler your technology the lower down the scale you were placed.

The reaction to such rampantly progressive schemes would, you might have thought, been total. They do live on, however benignly they are now presented, in neo-evolutionary models (e.g. Johnson and Earle 1987). Here simple and complex hunters are arranged in ascending order towards the 'goal' of becoming an agricultural society. The Tasmanians serve as examples of the former and the Inuit of the latter (Keeley 1988; Woodburn 1991).

Ethnography with a shovel

Ethnographic analogy cannot provide insights unless the relationships that are implied by the similarity are thoroughly understood. Robert Ascher tried to narrow the field by limiting analogies to cultures that manipulate similar environments in similar ways (1961: 319). This was still too broad for new archaeologists, particularly Binford, who were rightly concerned about the subtle power of analogy to simply recreate the past in the shape of the present. If this happened, then there would be no independent place for archaeology. The past would be what we said it was, justified by what went on in the present.

If broad categories such as habitat and economy were to be used, then why they produced similar cultural responses had to be understood rather than assumed. The fact that the temperature was the same between a modern and an archaeological situation did not by itself justify the use of an analogy. The best warning of this pitfall came from Martin Wobst (1978). He coined the phrase 'ethnography with a shovel' to warn us against the problem and advised us to backfill the pitfall before we fell into it. He was very clear about what we were throwing away if we continued to wield the shovel. This was the opportunity to examine data on human behaviour in all its many dimensions, people, space and time – from single individuals in private to the largest groupings, from the smallest catchment area to continent-wide spatial distributions, and from single events to millennia.

Ethnographic clues

But once aware of the dangers we can also be aware of the importance of ethnographic analogy for our archaeological imagination. Gordon Childe pointed the way:

> Ethnographic parallels in fact afford only clues in what direction to look for an explanation in the archaeological record itself.
> (Childe 1956a: 49)

This is how I interpret Ascher's approach. It was also the guiding principle that sent Binford on a learning experience to work with the Nunamiut in northern Alaska. From this came his exercise in building middle-range theory (1978a) (see Chapter 3 and Boxes 6 and 13).

We would of course be unwise to ignore ethnography with the variability and action it contains just because of some inappropriate uses (for a full discussion see Wylie 1985). What we have to remember is that the ethnographic variation we can see today is only a tiny fraction of all that has gone before. This includes objects. It also includes the structure of relationships and society. This was a point the new archaeologists were very clear on. The end product of archaeology was not interpretations or even syntheses of interpretations, but rather generalisations. These concerned how cultural systems operated and why they evolved. As Binford observed (1972: 49), you will never find this out by observing the present. Ethnography suggests ways of thinking, not the answers to such questions.

Direct historical analogy

There has always been a division between the use of analogy in the prehistoric and historic periods. Ascher (1961: 319), and many others, pointed to the comparative logical ease of drawing analogies when the time gap is short and space, in the form of common geography, is constant. As soon as these gaps widen, as they must in prehistory, the job of the archaeologist changes. The key word in applying direct historical analogies is continuity. Where prehistory grades into recorded history or ethnography, as in the pueblos of the Southwestern United States or among the Australian Aborigines or from the British Iron Age to Roman occupation, then, according to Ascher, interpretation proceeds by analogy to living or historically recorded groups.

Christopher Hawkes (1954) had previously gone much further. He identified two modes of thinking that he believed strongly conditioned archaeological interpretation when there were texts about. These were the *distinctness* and *proximity* of the recorded history to the prehistoric world (1954: 159). Hawkes was an expert on the pre-Roman British Iron Age, which explains his interest in ascertaining how the few lines about the British in Julius Caesar's *Gallic Wars* could help in the interpretation of hill forts, burials and tribal boundaries. In this instance distinctness is well attested by the contacts between Julius Caesar and the British when he invaded for a few weeks in August 55 and a couple of months in 54 BC. By invading and jotting down a few notes for the benefit of those in Rome the proximity factor is catered for in a direct historical analogy.

Never underestimate the power of text, especially for the culture historian. Take one example, Strabo's throwaway comment that pre-conquest Britain produced much grain and hunting dogs for export. Notwithstanding that we do not know which part of this large island he was referring to or the quantities involved, this line has been used to summarise all of British agricultural production before the Romans arrived. On the other side of the scales the analysis of several million animal bones and thousands of carbonised grains from many archaeological excavations seem to count for nothing. All this confirms is the primacy that some archaeologists traditionally give to the authority of the written word, a curious view that the past becomes interesting only when put down on paper.

Hawkes' onion

A much-quoted paper by Hawkes (1954) is often held up to indicate how difficult some inferences are for archaeologists. His ladder of inference, as it is usually called, is really better described by the analogy of peeling an onion with four skins (Figure 4.2).

Inference became progressively more difficult as he peeled from skin one through skin four. The core of his concern lay with the relative difficulty of inferring activity in the absence of texts. Each peel brings tears to your eyes as you realise what has been lost because it wasn't written down. Getting at religion was the hardest of all, unless aided by texts that keyed you into the minds and beliefs of the people who built the temple and buried their dead.

And then just when you think the worst is all over and you can put your handkerchief away you reach the heart of the inferential onion. The move from techniques to spiritual life represents to Hawkes the move from the animal to the human. Therefore our real object of

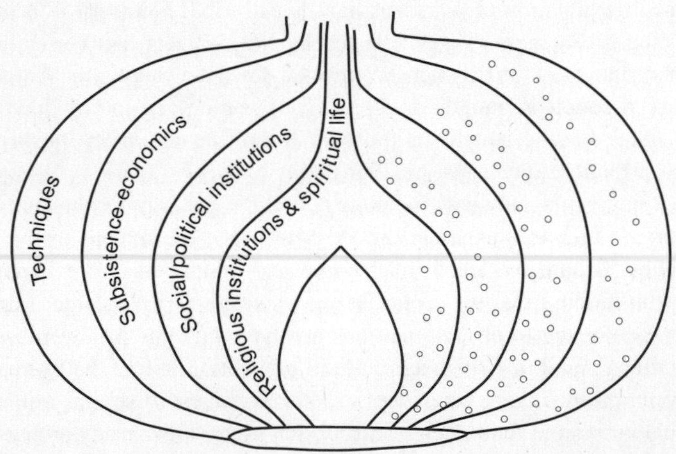

FIGURE 4.2 Hawkes' onion. The layers of archaeological inference

study – people – is the most difficult. As Hawkes put it 'the more human, the less intelligible' (1954: 192).

These limits to inference have been very influential. Hawkes' onion has been peeled many times and his ladder propped against many theoretical walls. The limits he identified confirmed the primacy of text-aided archaeology. They still confirm to many culture historians that processual and interpretive approaches are just speculation, unfettered by analogy and therefore best not attempted. Having dug the ditch around their onion fields they could return to collecting and describing data.

Objects, essence and inference

The big problem with Hawkes' onion was that it accepted only one source of authority for interpreting *all* his skins of activity contained in archaeological evidence. These were texts. To a much lesser extent the environment and ethnography could provide analogies for his first two skins, but this just confirmed to a classical scholar why the study of hunters and gatherers was best left to others. In the absence of direct historical analogies (an impossibility for the Palaeolithic of even 20,000 years ago) could they ever be brought into the human fold? As a result Hawkes' ladder of inference was also the familiar ladder of progress. Texts tipped you into being human because only texts allowed you to get to the heart of the matter and deal with the most human bits of being human.

I would counter this by returning to our earlier discussion of essences (Chapter 1). For many culture historians, especially those nestling close in time to recorded history, texts have the power to animate. What they breathe life into is by definition human, its human essence being defined by those very same attributes and properties contained in the texts. They have an authority like a magic wand, transforming what they touch.

The same could be said of the organisational system that formed the framework for the processualists. These had essences such as self-regulation and cyclical patterning. The mistake they made was not to abandon the authority of texts in order to peel the onion but rather to trust so blindly in the universal qualities of science. Generalisation allowed processualists to abandon such notions as distinctness and proximity and to argue instead for those repeated basic functions of the system. Patterning, they argued, was so strong that it must refer to repeated solutions governed by understandable processes of adaptation and change. This is the line that some neo-Darwinian approaches have continued to investigate, underpinned by the biological structure of change and variation.

Pickling the onion

I believe that the answer to the difficulty of analogy is to recognise that this is an onion that has passed its sell-by date. What is at fault is the very idea of layers of human activity or subsystems within an overall systemic structure. Instead the social is bound up with the technical, just as the religious is part of subsistence. It may be an analytical convenience to divide up human action in this manner, but not if all it does is to close off large chunks of the past to interpretation. So, don't peel the onion. Either eat it whole or pickle it in a jar labelled history of the subject. I think you will find that the limits to inference suggested by this analogy will then become less of a problem.

The analogy of chains and cables applied to explanation

Onions and ladders are only two of the analogies used to help us understand how we infer and explain human action from archaeological remains. The process is also commonly described as forging links in a chain of logic (Figure 4.3). The strength of the link is usually based on a scientific approach to hypothesis testing and one where the method of deduction (see Box 15) is often preferred.

However, methods and explanation do not necessarily need an explicitly scientific framework, particularly if we now accept that the archaeological record is much more complicated than we once thought (Chapter 3). Part of this complication is the problem of what survives, but more important is the question of how the archaeological record preserves human action. If these issues remain unresolved within the subject (Patrik 1985), then just how appropriate are scientific methods for their investigation?

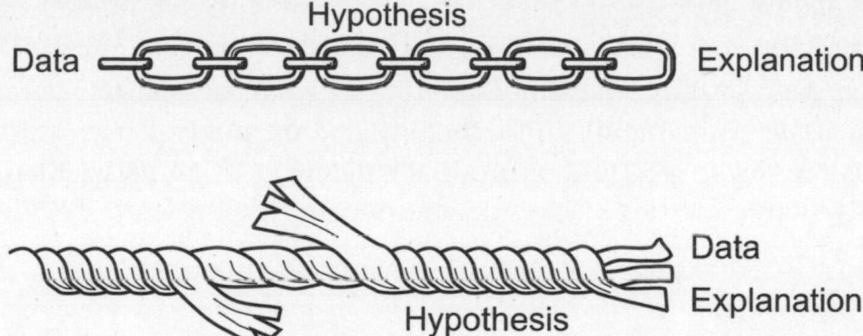

FIGURE 4.3 Links and cables: two approaches to building explanations

Is there an alternative? In particular can we capitalise on the combined insights of the traditions and approaches beneath the archaeological umbrella (Figure 2.1) and by entwining them produce greater strength in our methods and explanation?

I think we can. As we integrate these approaches in order to enhance our archaeological imagination we are witnessing a very positive development, described by Alison Wylie (1993: 24) as a cabling, or tacking, exercise. The way we construct theory in archaeology cannot mimic the links in a well-forged chain, where each link is logically joined to the next by the strength of the hypotheses we are testing (Figure 4.3). Instead, we build theory in a historical discipline such as archaeology by spinning many-stranded cables. This way we do not have to have cast-iron links but rather more flexible explanatory structures that depend for their strength on many frames of reference rather than just one.

Tacking is another way to describe the process, and at the same time retain the nautical analogy. The analogy is with a yacht tacking into the wind; between problems and theories, data and interpretation (see also Figure 7.2). The result is very much the same: a many-stranded cable of explanation. Tacking also acknowledges the spatial- and time-scales with which we deal as we infer action from our inert data. We tack from immediate, small-scale, individual actions such as eating or making stone tools, which might have taken minutes, to the layers in which they are contained, which might represent a thousand years and ten thousand people. At the same time we are often tacking between the individual and the group and between the site and the region. Recognising that this flexibility is what we do, and how we compensate for variation in the quality and quantity of our information, allows us to steer a course through the rocks of the archaeological record.

How do we know?

My third question brings us back to basics. With some of the approaches discussed above we might have begun to drift away from archaeology being about people but concerned only with objects. Somehow we have to return to that rich texture, those unimagined worlds of ethnographic variety, which the processualists wanted. Contextual archaeology might provide this. The fusion is well described by Ian Hodder:

> Without the general theories there would be few questions asked of the past and fewer answers given. Without a contextual approach, the present and the past become reduced to an assumed sameness.
>
> Hodder (1991: 149)

Two detectives

Hodder's point is so basic to the future development of archaeology that I will illustrate it further with my own analogy: archaeologists are often likened to Sherlock Holmes, the master of induction and deduction (Box 15).

No clue is too small or insignificant for the trained observer to see how it leads to an inescapable conclusion. To Holmes the mud on the boot of one of his visitors to 221B Baker Street is a guide to his or her travels around London. His cursory inspection of trusty Watson's family watch is an opportunity to diagnose that his brother, now dead, was an alcoholic. Holmes has a fine archaeological imagination and an ability to tease out the system from a detached description of the facts, rather like someone watching a play.

Box 15: Three approaches to building a theory

Induction: a generalising approach to understanding the world based on a number of specific observations. *Bronze metallurgy always precedes iron*. This statement could of course be contradicted by new discoveries.

Deduction: a truth-preserving approach that begins with a premise which, if correct, must mean that the conclusion is also true. *Bronze metallurgy is a less complicated process and this is why it always precedes iron*. Complex is a difficult premise. It could well be redefined as the wider notion of progress is rethought. It could be falsified by replication that showed that in fact bronze metallurgy was the more complicated process. In both cases it would lose its ring of truth and fresh deduction would be needed.

Abduction: the construction of theory. The leap of faith from the data to the theory that explains it. *Bronze age artefacts embody the principle of individualism over collective social action*. Such leaps of faith have a short half-life but move the subject onwards much faster than induction and deduction.

Contrast Holmes with another detective in another continent and another city, Philip Marlowe. Not for him a seat in the stalls, more a view from backstage, if not the backstreets. Stuck in his empty office with a large bluebottle, he ignores the clues to trouble sitting in front of him when Orfamy Quest (the perfect name I always think for an archaeological project) comes to hire him. The reason is that Marlowe is not detached from the world, he is fully involved in it. Through his involvement he has a moral sense which acts as his guide in unnavigated waters. Marlowe, if he thought about it at all, which he doesn't, has an abductive approach to problem solving. His leaps of faith are not based on probability and that sense that night will always follow day. Rather they are based on understanding how people work – that curious co-ordination in collective human action which works because of some implicit contract that exists between us. This allows us to guess what other people will do and most of the time get it right. The alternative, working it out step by step every time we encounter someone, does not bear thinking about unless we have the brainpower of a Holmes.

Furthermore, Holmes starts with an inductive model of how the world works. He knows intuitively what the system should be because he is by his class and upbringing the product of a top-down approach. Marlowe, by contrast, is very often in the gutter because he didn't see the sap coming. There is only one way for him and that's up. Both are successful even though their methods are so different.

Holmes represents the general system. It is significant that his exploits are related to us through the eyes of another, Watson. The observer, observing the great detective. Marlowe stands for that contextual richness. A lived-in experience that he passes on to us in the first person.

As an archaeologist you basically decide what type of detective you want to be. But sensibly, as Hodder indicates, you learn from both. 'Am I right, or am I right?', as the singing detective, with the same name as Raymond Chandler's hero, once sang.

From the present to the past

If Marlowe and Holmes had become archaeologists these differences would probably have surfaced in the way they made use of the present to study the past. Holmes would have been in his deductive element proceeding from the known to the unknown by carefully researched steps. The remains of the past are static. In order to reconstruct the behaviour that produced them and the variation in time and space they posses requires some careful inferential steps. These are steps to the archaeological imagination that we need to make explicit.

The principle of uniformitarianism

Such an approach recognises two main procedures. The first is the principle of uniformitarianism, long recognised by geologists, where the key to the past is contained in the processes we can observe in the present. The processes of tectonics, weathering and sedimentation are assumed to be uniform between the present and the past. The laws of physics, chemistry and geology remain the same. Explanation is to be sought in the repeated workings of these processes to explain drifting continents, mountain building, ice ages and all the varied landforms studied by the geologist.

Uniformitarianism has also been applied to the historical sciences including archaeology. The principle has been most successful when dealing with absolute limiting factors such as the need to eat and reproduce. Failure to do both results in no archaeology, as Eric Higgs pointed out to me when I was an undergraduate in the 1970s. The application of models developed in evolutionary ecology that recognise the selective imperative of reproductive success provide an example of the principle in action (Bettinger 1991; Kelly 1995). By contrast uniformitarian assumptions about the details of ritual or social life soon start cracking like a bad analogy.

Living archaeology

Actualistic studies provide insights into the complexity of living systems. These may be ethnoarchaeological studies examining boundaries, the use of technology, patterns of mobility or the arrangement of settlement. Termed living archaeology by Richard Gould (1980), they have transformed our understanding of the most unfamiliar societies to Western city dwellers, those of hunters and gatherers. In Binford's (1978a) classic study of the Nunamiut people of northern Alaska he revealed the complexity of the decision-making processes that a small group of people are involved in when it comes to tracking, killing, processing, transporting and consuming their staple food, caribou/reindeer. More than any other work this study confounded the idea that hunters and gatherers are simple and easily explained by common sense.

Archaeologists have also studied how other species exploit and interact (Box 12), and Binford has once again been instrumental in such work (Binford 1981a). Attention has focused on those species that create their own archaeological record in the form of bone accumulations in caves and under overhangs. These include hyenas, leopards, wolves, porcupines and owls, and once again the interest has been in earliest prehistory, where such studies have unravelled the various agencies that contributed to a bone deposit (Brain 1981; Stiner 1994). Very often it has been found that the human component from these Pleistocene sites is comparatively small. In much of Europe, for example, glacial climates produced both rich grazing conditions but also severe penalties for failure. We find in many regions in this continent that the dominant species, as revealed by the consistent accumulation of bones in caves, were hyenas rather than humans (Gamble 1986). This discovery should not be regarded as wasted effort. It was Binford's insight that by learning about carnivores in the present we could sharpen our observations about the people we really wanted to study. The competitive relations between carnivores and humans is one route to describing more accurately the capabilities of early hominids such as the Neanderthals.

Reading the record right

But what sort of data do we ideally want? The problem is that generally speaking, ethnoarchaeology and living archaeology seek to understand the system. They search for systems rather than individuals. For some this colours the way they interpret the archaeological record and the people it contains. In his critique of Schiffer's formation processes Binford (1981b) returned to a comment by Robert Ascher:

> In a certain sense a part of every community is becoming, but is not yet, archaeological data. The community becomes archaeological data when replacement ceases. What the archaeologist disturbs is not the remains of a once living community, stopped as it were, at a point in time; what he does interrupt is the process of decomposition.
>
> Ascher (1961: 324)

Archaeologists who thought they were obtaining a snapshot of the past, like watching a shark swim past the glass window in an aquarium, were guilty of what Ascher called the 'Pompeii-premise'. Human history is not arrested and preserved in the archaeological record like a giant jar of pickled herrings. Neither should we necessarily try to strip away the taphonomic overprint from our samples, to remove all those hyena-chewed bones and owl-introduced rodents. Diane Gifford (1981) pointed out that to do so would in fact remove information. We learn about the selective forces on humans by seeing the full constellation of agents with which they were involved. Taphonomic overprinting is good, like removing the pumice from Pompeii. The record is not blurred by these other agents but rather put in context.

To understand what we have in the archaeological record we need another analogy. To rework Ascher's words the archaeological record is constantly in the process of becoming. There is no single point of view. A better analogy would be Dennett's multiple drafts of a book (Chapter 1). As I know only too well, there is a timeline to their production. There is a history to their development. They only become fixed, i.e. published, when, as Ascher pointed out, replacement finally ceases. So too with the archaeological record. Each new field project expands and changes our understanding of it. Every new analysis and synthesis alters what we thought we knew. The archaeological record is about the most unfixed thing I know. And even as I write that, it has changed.

Summary

Getting at people through archaeological evidence will always need more than digging. In this chapter I have examined some of the terms and contrasted various positions such as group and individual, networks and systems, analogy and inference. The two fictional detectives Holmes and Marlowe remind us that there is always an alternative way to crack a case. What I have identified here is that we need to adopt an anthropological approach to the task of getting at people. This does not mean that the key lies in more ethnoarchaeology. What we need to consider instead are the questions we want to ask and the approach to change that we take. This will be examined in Chapter 7. We also need to return identity to these people, whether it is as individuals, groups or nations. This will be my task in Chapter 8.

Archaeology as anthropology has been with us in several guises for about 40 years. It has proved an immensely productive way of investigating the past and has fostered the development of several alternative approaches. It transformed and broadened the archaeological imagination. New questions were devised and methods were developed to answer them. This is an ongoing process and replacement has not yet ceased. However, as we will now see as we turn to objects and material culture, the approaches can be as different as a deer-stalker and a trilby hat.

Chapter 5

Objects

We have now seen that there is nothing self-evident about the past. The enterprise of archaeology is not simply confined to the things of the past but, more importantly, deals with questions, approach and interpretation. Archaeological debates and disagreements are not just about the dates of *this* pot and *that* city. Rather they are more fundamental. They concern approaches to gaining knowledge about human action in the past. The outcome produces expectations about what is known, and can be known, of activities in the past. Because such activity is invisible, objects are crucial to all our debates. The way we investigate and interpret objects is therefore important and I will now explore these issues.

Objects and the archaeological imagination

In Chapter 1 I introduced Julian Thomas' idea of the archaeological imagination – the aspect of our everyday lives that makes the investigation of the past possible. The simple example he gives is finding crumbs in a

cake tin (1996: 63). From this we infer not only that once there was cake, and even what sort of cake it was, but also that someone, or something, has been there before us. The only alternative is that the cake was beamed-up onto a passing spacecraft, which requires an imagination that is definitely not archaeological!

Material culture

Thomas' cake tin is an example of material culture, which can be defined as the objects, environments and worlds with which we interact and that surround us. The world we are born into is very much a material one that shapes and creates us. We will also contribute to it by, in our turn, creatively adding, arranging and subtracting elements within it. And that is the point. We are both created by and creators of material culture. As Randall McGuire puts it:

> material culture not only exists in a context, but it also helps form that context. It is not just backdrop; it is instead the stage and props for human action.
>
> McGuire (1992: 104)

Neither is there any reason to suppose that this relationship has not been going on for a very long time. As a result these objects, this material culture, has a history. That cake tin endures. It began life as part of a *production* process. It might change *function* and become a box in which to store your photographic memories. Its *context* of use might also alter as it moves from the kitchen to the living room. It might be *exchanged* for another as an act of *consumption*. It could *transform* into an heirloom and then become an antique, its value judged by attributes other than function alone. It still remains a tin box but now it is supporting a raft of possible social relationships and activities. The crumbs it contained, and the activity, eating, that we infer took place, are less important than its history and its personality.

The key words: production, function, context, exchange, consumption and transformation will be examined later in this chapter (The biography of objects). For the moment notice that when treated separately they sum up our common-sense attitude to material culture – 'It must mean or do something, otherwise what's the point?'. Individually, they represent our usual approach of conceptually breaking down the object we are studying into discrete parts and analysing them separately before the mental task of reassembly takes place and conclusions are drawn. In this sense the process resembles the much larger project of systems analysis (Figure 2.2) where whole societies were reduced to their component subsystems. While this proved a useful device to tackle a complex problem, somehow Humpty-Dumpty never quite got stuck back together again.

Archaeologists are not alone in breaking eggs and scrambling the result. Many other disciplines are also object-centred, rather than solely text centred. They also employ the customary definitions to analyse their objects, as provided here by a distinguished art historian:

> Material culture is just what it says it is – namely, the manifestations of culture through material productions.
>
> Prown (1993: 1)

The goal, he goes on, is to uncover the thoughts and beliefs in peoples' heads. Why did they make a tea-pot with a short rather than a long spout? In silver rather than china? Plain-brown instead of covered in flowers?

Now this is only one view of material culture and, as we saw in the last chapter, a rather traditional one. It attempts to explain culture *by* culture. The shape of the things we make (material culture) is to be explained by the shape of the beliefs (cultural norms) that we all have in our heads, and share, so long as we come from the same culture.

Mental templates

These norms are the mental templates that Binford so effectively criticised in the 1960s new archaeology (Chapter 2). The sharing of culture represents the normative view. Thirty years later he might have used a computer metaphor to beat them with, perhaps describing culture as hard-wired into the brain. Certainly the French archaeologist François

Bordes, with whom (as was mentioned in Chapter 3) Binford debated the meaning of variation in stone-tool assemblages made by Neanderthals more than 40,000 years ago, would have argued in this way. For Bordes cultural choice was non-negotiable (1950: 419; 1973). This is the classic view of the culture historian. For Binford, culture was our adaptive process of survival (Binford and Binford 1966; Binford 1973). It was therefore under selection and would vary as environmental conditions, rather than minds, changed. Cultures varied not because people shared similar cultural values and expressed these in terms of material culture, but because they participated in culture in different ways. Culture, as the principle means of human adaptation, was not spread evenly over the geographical range covered by either a person or a group. Ecological circumstances resulted in local variation as different survival responses were made.

Interpreting artefacts

In Chapter 3 I reviewed the basic entities, the building blocks, that archaeologists use to recognise repeated patterns in the data. Now we can begin the task of interpreting such regularities in time, space and form. But remember, these patterns are theory-laden.

Artefact classes

Processual archaeologists have recognised three behavioural realms that artefacts serve. These are:

- material – artefacts coping with the environment;
- social – those dealing with social organisation;
- ideational – artefacts that addressed ideas, values and belief systems.

Binford originally referred to these as technomic, sociotechnic and ideotechnic artefacts and stressed how they primarily functioned in different contexts (Binford 1962: 23–5). In fact all artefacts cross-cut these three classes, though they may appear to play a more significant role in one than the others. Take, for example, the crown a monarch wears. It is possible to interpret this object in all three classes.

Technomically it is a hat which keeps the head warm or, depending on design, it might equally make a crash helmet for a cyclist. Socio-technically it is an item of display which communicates information about status and rank. Furthermore, how it is displayed, on the head, privileges the 'head' of state above the 'body' politic. Ideotechnically the crown is a symbol of the abstract concept of monarchy and the rites and duties of allegiance and obedience owed to it.

Partly in recognition of this blurring, James Sackett later reduced the three classes to two (1982: 70). These are the *utilitarian*, which include tools and weapons in the material realm, and *non-utilitarian*, such as ritual paraphernalia and artwork which are suspected to have expressed social relationships and beliefs. A function is therefore implied.

Artefacts and meaning

The phrase 'symbols in action', which was also the title of Hodder's ethnoarchaeological study of culture (1982), neatly summarises the emphasis a post-processual, interpretive approach attaches to artefacts. Hodder's great complaint is against imposing universal functions on data just because they look the same. Hence a tea-pot or a crown, a lamb or a tiger may have very different functions in very different settings.

However, Hodder readily admits that some functional meanings are inescapable. Hammers are intended to pound and doors to shut. But these are regarded as trivial, 'So what?' meanings.

Artefacts escape from the mundane to become symbols in action in specific historical contexts. The density of meanings contained either in a medieval city street or in the contents of a rubbish pit are so great as to defy universal description and comparison, one street with another, pit by pit, layer with layer. Furthermore universal meanings quickly run into the cul-de-sac of the single hermeneutic (Box 8).

Hodder's original solution for the material culture in the archaeological record was to treat it more like a 'text' waiting to be read (1991: 125). 'Text' and the double hermeneutic, backed by Giddens' notion that we have a dual position in the world (1984), were designed for each other (Box 8). Moreover, the reading that takes place depends on data, not theory. The more data, the better, for such a contextual approach.

But there is a contradiction here. On the one hand Hodder is highly critical of universal functions being attributed to artefacts and vociferous against universal measuring devices as proposed by middle-range theory and its bridge from statics to dynamics (Chapter 3). But on the other hand he is nonetheless entirely happy with universal principles of meaning as contained in notions such as the *habitus* and power (see Chapter 8), while at the same time insisting on the importance of examining specific contexts on their own merits (1991).

Artefacts with personalities

However, we can move on from these normative, processual and post-processual statements and a lead is given by Marxist and feminist approaches. Once again I return to Thomas' idea of the archaeological imagination. It is because we interact with the material world today that we have an in-built appreciation of how objects and people interacted in the past. We do not have the people. They are long gone. But we do have the artefacts, sites, monuments, landscapes and even worlds. These may only be partially recovered and much has been lost. But what remains is intelligible. Not by lifting that pot to your ear and listening. Nor by standing in a street in Pompeii and empathising what it must have been like to be a Roman citizen on the day before the volcano went up, but through the understanding that comes from making, using, interpreting and interacting with objects. As anthropologist Daniel Miller has written:

> Artefacts are a means by which we give form to, and come to an understanding of, ourselves, others, or abstractions such as the nation or modern.
>
> Miller (1994: 397)

Karl Marx made the point much earlier with his notion of objectification, the process by which objects and things become components of social relations (McGuire 1992: 103). This is a crucial point for an object-centred subject such as archaeology. It is also one that keeps being rediscovered. As Roberta Gilchrist (1993: 15) puts it, the great contribution of post-processual archaeology in the 1980s was to return to this position by reaffirming that material culture is *active* in social relations rather than just a *reflection* of society. She continues 'material culture can be seen to construct, maintain, control and transform social identities and relations' (1993: 15). This is very different to Sackett's utilitarian and non-utilitarian classes described above or even Binford's three behavioural realms. Grasp this point and you will appreciate what some of the long standing disagreements between different archaeological schools boil down to.

However, before we get too carried away, Hodder (1991: 69) makes the point that material culture, while a type of social reality, is not the only one. We may have 'love affairs' with Lamborghini's and talk to the cat as a member of the family, but what we cannot do is read off those relationships by just looking at the car and the cat. We have to interact with those artefacts and that is the problem that faces the archaeologist (see Chapter 3, The archaeological record). You and I can interact with artefacts when we visit rock-art sites; during excavations, when we carefully lift that Anglo-Saxon glass claw-beaker from the ground (and then view it on display in the British Museum); and by walking the landscape of any city or monument-strewn countryside. But that is our experience and just the latest page in the biography of those artefacts as we interpret them. What remains hidden is their previous lives, apparently the very subject matter of archaeology.

This raises two issues for the study of objects in the past: dualistic approaches and the archaeological concept of style.

Dualisms

One problem that has dogged material culture is the familiar dualism, or oppositions, that separate out the constituent essences of objects. The most prevalent is the dualism between natural and cultural objects and you will be familiar with others such as subject and object, internal and external.

Nature : culture

In practice this dualism may seem straightforward. A railway engine is a cultural thing, while Australia's Great Barrier Reef is natural. In practice such oppositions only work in extreme cases, which, being extreme, are of little value. Most distinctions are decidedly fuzzy. A domestic sheep is obviously a cultural object even though it has credentials for being considered a natural thing. A wild sheep may seem more natural, but if it is part of a hunter's world then it is also cultural because it is available for exploitation. And consider that most durable of natural things, stone. When nicely shaped into masonry and used to make cities it is cultural. But what about all the unmodified stone that makes up Neolithic tombs, the ballast in ships, or just litters the landscape as named rocks and places? Nothing we touch remains natural. Nature is what we say it is. It is an unhelpful concept, impossible to define.

Subject : object and the Cartesian theatre

The division between subject and object is a foundation of Western analytical thought, usually traced back to the French philosopher and mathematician René Descartes (1596–1650). The notion divides the world into inanimate (rocks) and non-sentient (sheep) things, and humans who are animate and sentient. It also divides a person into mind and body, thereby detaching thought from action. We become thinking machines, applying our subjective reason to the objects of the world. This conjures up the unlikely picture, known as the Cartesian theatre, where your mind sits in the audience, analysing your body performing on the stage. You may also find you are sitting next to Sherlock Holmes analysing a case (Chapter 4).

In terms of material culture what the subject : object dualism promotes is the separateness of things from people. What is denied is the full inclusion of objects in our individual and collective worlds. All that can be achieved is a single hermeneutic (Box 8), a one-way street to understanding.

ıternal : external and the essence of things

The last dualism I mentioned, internal: external, continues this division. When applied to objects it proposes hidden meanings and different levels of understanding (Tilley 1993: 5). Traditionally it has placed limits on the inferences we feel safe in making about the past (Chapter 4). For example, it is supposed that an object like a teapot has an external appearance and a hidden internal essence. On the outside we can read the shape and form, the teapot's style (see below), as a functional thing. A teapot functions as a teapot – everyone knows that, even the Mad Hatter. The internal essence is, like the doormouse, harder to tease out because not everyone knows, or can be bothered to consider, that a teapot is also a symbol of global consumption, imperial ambitions expressed through production and exchange of an exotic crop, and a local way of life. Teapots can also trigger strong emotions, as Bill Bryson records in his travels (1995), when he discovered that the English can get genuinely excited about the prospect of a hot beverage. The eagerness for regularly consuming a tropical product was a result of colonialism related to the transformation of the world under capitalism. British workers now drank a mild, hot stimulant to have the energy to stand at their looms (Mintz 1985). And all this inferred from a small pottery object.

Style

You cannot go far in your archaeological reading without coming across the concept of style (Box 2). Very soon, however, you will wonder why something so basic has to be so complicated. Opinions are sometimes contrary and a marked lack of agreement exists about what style is, and what in fact it does. Let me give you some examples (Box 16), in their proponents' own words, from the archaeologies we looked at in Chapter 2.

Some common concepts emerge, indicating that there might be more common ground than at first meets the eye. These are 'similarity' and 'variation' in forms and types which were so skilfully exploited by Thomsen and Montelius. But, as the few quotes show,

Box 16: The many faces of style

Culture history

'A style is a norm' (Hawkes 1954: 158)

'A highly specific and characteristic manner of doing something which by its very nature is peculiar to a specific time and place' (Sackett 1982: 63)

'What do I mean by style? The configuration of a single object is its form. When groups of objects share formal characteristics, those resemblances or resonances constitute style . . . When style is shared by clusters of objects in a time and place, it is akin to a cultural daydream expressing unspoken beliefs' (Prown 1993: 4–5)

Processual

'The working definition . . . equates style with that part of the formal variability in material culture that can be related to the participation of artefacts in processes of information exchange' (Wobst 1977: 321)

'Formal variation in material culture that transmits information about personal and social identity' (Wiessner 1983: 256)

'Style from a unified perspective [is] a means of non-verbal communication to negotiate identity' (Wiessner 1990: 108)

there is much more disagreement in the definitions over function, information and the individual and social aspects of style.

Robin Boast sums up this confusion and points to its source:

> I have not resolved the question of style because it is not resolvable. It is a social categorisation of the world, one among many, that grew out of a set of assumptions about how the world works. It exists as part of our social and intellectual tradition, an 18th-century western tradition that has become doctrine.
>
> Boast (1997: 191)

Box 16 *continued*

Interpretive

'Style must concern structure as well as function' (Hodder 1982: 205)

'Style is defined here as: "the referral of an individual event to a general way of doing"' (Hodder 1990: 45)

'In order to understand style – more broadly, the meaning of material culture-patterning – we have to understand the social conditions of its production' (Shanks and Tilley 1987b: 144)

'Style is a form of social rather than individual practice' (Shanks and Tilley 1987b: 155)

'Style is not a characteristic of material culture, but is a result of a contemporary way of conceptualising material culture' (Boast 1997: 174)

Neo-Darwinian

'Style denotes those forms that do not have detectable selective values. Function is manifest as those forms that directly affect the Darwinian fitness of the populations in which they occur' (Dunnell 1978. 199)

The doctrine that supports the archaeological concept of style is the Cartesian separation of the world. Without dualisms such as external : internal there is no place for style. As Boast also shows, what stems from these divisions is the idea that objects have an inherent social character. In other words there is a basic purpose to things *before* they become social (Boast 1997: 174). We are back to essentialism, which I highlighted as a basic concept of archaeology in Chapter 1.

The problem we face is that such ways of thinking about the world are so ingrained that we regard them as entirely reasonable and natural. That's fine. But unless challenged our archaeological imagination will never escape from its chains because they cannot be seen. The reason why style is so complex is not only because we are blind to the causes but also because the major approaches, as shown in Box 16, cross-cut four archaeologies, making simple pigeon-holing difficult. Style is eclectic and so is its interpretation and explanation. Let me now sketch the chains that bind.

Isochrestic and iconic style

Polly Wiessner (1990: 105) tries to unravel the spaghetti by pointing out that you can't ask 'what is style?' without asking 'what is stylistic behaviour?' This moves the issue away from definitions, where I think everyone is agreed that there will be no general agreement, and back to the all-important aspect of style as 'doing', as action. The key question then is 'what is understood by such action?' Is this in turn functional behaviour, being ethnic or a notion of human agency (Chapter 4)? Adherents of the different approaches have all argued their corner at length in order to answer the following question:

- How does this action, variously described, relate to artefacts and material culture generally?

The answers are numerous but dominated by the conclusion that at its heart style is linked to identity and in particular to ethnic identity (Chapter 8). This is of course what Childe (Chapter 3) played on in his famous definition (1929: v–vi) of an archaeological culture, recognised through repetition and similarity, and his translation of that entity into a people. James Sackett is very clear about the reasoning behind this equation when he accounts for similarity in style by intensity in social interaction. The most important aspect producing similarity is propinquity in time and space (1982: 74).

Sackett has developed this concept of style further by asking where style resides in the formal variation of artefacts. Which elements of shape and form can be said to be the result of stylistic behaviour? To answer it he has explored the choices open to anyone making and using artefacts. In many instances there are several, often many, ways to achieve the same end result. Think of the variation in styles of toothbrushes, screwdrivers, cars, books, houses, etc. Not all of this variation is dictated by functional requirements alone. So, according to Sackett, the artisan has a choice of equivalent alternatives for the finished product, each of which will still be able to brush teeth or drive down the motorway. He calls this an *isochrestic* approach to style, a word he coined and which means equivalent in use. This approach provides an answer to his question where does style reside in those pots and toothbrushes? Whenever isochrestic options exist, which is most of the time, then factors allied to ethnicity dictate the choices that are made (1990: 33). Such choices may be based on habit – they are probably largely made unthinkingly in what might be simply termed tradition. In other frameworks they would be regarded as aspects of practical consciousness or *habitus* (Chapter 8).

Set beside these is Sackett's *iconological* approach to style, where choice is purposeful and style is consciously added-on (known as adjunct style) to reinforce identity. Designs are added to clothing, pots, bronzes and sculpture in order to make the point that we are who 'we *look* we are' as much as 'who we *say* we are'. Once again, in another interpretive framework this would be seen as a discursive, thinking operation.

Information and style

Sackett is at pains to be clear that he is not providing a theory of style but only showing where it resides in the shape and design of artefacts. Wiessner and Martin Wobst are more explicit in their discussions of the role style plays in the visual exchange of information that turns out primarily to concern identity. Wobst's model (1977) was based on the principle that since information contributes to survival, then style, which expresses that information, will be under selection. Choice is therefore determined by transmitting messages efficiently and unambiguously so that social encounters generally pass off successfully. This is in marked contrast to Dunnell's view, quoted in Box 16, where style is presented as superfluous to Darwinian evolution. It is 'noise' rather than 'information' because it is not under selection.

Wiessner, using her ethnographic study of projectile points in the Kalahari, bases her explanation on the psychological benefits that accrue from belonging to social groups. She proposes two styles:

assertive, where individuals express their individuality and skills, and *emblemic*, where group identity is expressed. Both will be under selection from the social domain. Sackett regards approaches such as those of Wobst and Wiessner as stressing the *active* voice of style (1990: 36–7). Style does something, it has a function. It is an add-on, as in his iconological approach. By contrast Sackett is a supporter of the *passive* voice of style. Signalling still takes place but it does so as a set of habitual isochrestic choices where ethnicity acts as the unseen selective force.

Expanding style

The link between style and ethnicity satisfies some as an explanation. Among the interpretive archaeologists, however, ethnicity is too narrow a concept to account for style. Instead style connects in different social and historical circumstances all those social, political and ideological relations (Shanks and Tilley 1987b: 144), and not just to who 'we *look* we are'. This aspect has been explored by Siân Jones (1997: 119) who, in contrast to Sackett and Wiessner, emphasises that all material culture is active in the process of creating those social relationships that we label ethnicity (see Chapter 8).

And this raises another very pertinent question:

- To what extent are these actions which create style more than just the shapes of artefacts? How big a concept is style?

Sackett again provides an important lead (1990: 35). Style for him is not just the finished, hand-held artefact, the city plan or the landscape littered with tombs and monuments. The term must incorporate the choice of raw material, the techniques of production, the tradition of apprenticeship by which these are learned and what he calls the 'themes', for example the standardisation, specialisation and efficiency that guide all these choices. The latter may sound rather like shared norms but it is his inclusive approach to the thoughts and actions as well as the objects that is important. In broadening this analysis he is also proposing a unified approach to style. Instead of making the distinction that evolutionary archaeologists such as Dunnell insist upon as a basic dichotomy, that between style and function among artefacts,

Sackett brings them together, which is a view that most interpretive archaeologists would support.

Chaîne opératoire and style

It does appear, however, that this unification could have occurred much earlier. The French archaeologist André Leroi-Gourhan provided a theory of technical processes which, in 1966 when his book *Le geste et la parole* ('Gesture and speech'), appeared, achieved just that (Leroi-Gourhan 1993). His ideas came from a very different tradition of thinking about technology and style than his Anglo-Saxon contemporaries. His influence outside France remained confined to his seminal analysis of cave art and excavation of well-preserved Palaeolithic hunting camps, until his book was translated in 1993.

The basic idea in *Le geste et la parole* is that technical acts are at the same time social acts. Calling on the French anthropological tradition most closely associated with Marcel Mauss, he emphasised the importance of the human body as a source of meaning, power, symbol and of course action. He used the term *chaîne opératoire* (operational sequence) to examine how actions can, literally, speak louder than words.

Learning through the body

A good way to illustrate Leroi-Gourhan's concept is to consider how we learn to make things. He would say that it is through attention to the gestures of manufacture and doing, for example watching potting, stone knapping, weaving, butchering animals, threshing grain, ploughing fields, and then trying it for ourselves. It is by seeing the body in action, imitating and copying these rhythmic gestures that we learn to walk, eat, embrace and indicate moods. Much of this, Leroi-Gourhan pointed out in advance of either Bourdieu or Giddens (Box 8), was part of habitual, unconscious action. As put by Thomas (1996: 19), we don't 'live in' our bodies as those dualisms would suggest. Rather the body is an aspect of the self that we 'live through'.

Our life's routines do not take up much of our conscious thought. The trick to learning is to eventually throw away the rule book and fully enter the activity. Walking is a good example. Think about it and you will probably fall over, as can happen when you are faced with crossing a high, narrow plank and vertigo kicks in, making you unsure of what you normally take for granted.

Learning in a social context

Now the context in which this learning takes places is a social one. Learning how to use the body and disciplining it to act in customary ways is a style every bit as indicative of who you are as a coloured shirt or a fancy spear point. Artefacts are therefore extensions of the body, the result of sequences of gestures applied to material, and so truly social as well as technical. The opportunity to dispense with a dualistic approach to understanding what we do and why is therefore presented.

Let us now consider an alternative and more familiar view of learning by going back to that Cartesian theatre. Remember, in this theatre mind and body are split. Thought is applied to materials which are also separate from the body. Here the mental template comes back into its own. The potter starts with a mental image of the pot he or she is going to make and then works towards that goal. The apprentice potter is instructed in that image and tries to copy it. The finished pot is very much an object, external to the person who made it, as a good dualism requires. What has been forgotten in this scenario is the sequence of gestures, the rhythms of the *chaîne opératoire*, which link act and object in a continuous flow. Far from separating action into cognitive and technical domains (or material, social and ideological domains as above), everything becomes social. Thus the *chaîne opératoire* is more than just a suite of muscle memories about how to do things without thinking about them. It is the acts themselves and the linkages they provide across time and space that matter.

Randall McGuire provides the Marxist perspective, which nicely sums up the position:

> Material culture entails the social relations that are the conditions for its existence. It is both a product of these relations and part of the structure of these relations.
>
> McGuire (1992: 102)

The biography of objects

I will end this chapter on archaeological objects by considering their biographies through those six keywords – production, function, context, exchange, consumption and transformation – that I promised to return to. The point of a biographical approach is to animate those objects through inquiry and interpretation. Remember this is not an autobiographical approach where these same pots, temples, shipwrecks and tin mines speak to us eloquently about their pasts. Rather it is, as Thomas pointed out, an approach that acknowledges just how important artefacts are in creating us. He writes:

> Ways of engaging in the world are not simply stored 'in the head': they are immanent in the relationships between people and things.
>
> Thomas (1996: 19)

Artefacts have histories just as we do. They have life cycles. They participated in other lives. Their analysis provides an example of cabling and tacking between data and ideas (Chapter 4). These points are well illustrated by one of the commonest forms of archaeological evidence: pottery.

The life of pots

The example could come from anywhere but I have chosen a modest rescue excavation in a quarry in the heart of England (Hearne and Heaton 1994). The Shorncote Quarry site is Late Bronze Age in date, which puts it in the ninth to eighth centuries BC. Several timber roundhouses once stood on the site and there were some large pits containing broken potsherds which added up to at least 31 vessels, a clay weight probably used in making textiles with a loom and a few fragments of clay moulds for bronze casting. A small collection of animal bones and crop remains was also present. Elaine Morris studied the pottery (in Hearne and Heaton 1994: 34–44).

Production and manufacture

The evidence for production is lacking. There is no obvious potter's workshop or even workspace. Artefacts used in smoothing and finishing the pots – bone spatulas for example or ornamental stamps – were not recovered. Neither is there any evidence for pottery kilns, not even a simple bonfire firing, at this small site.

Absence of evidence, however, is not always evidence of absence. The pots themselves are all handmade, built up with a distinctive slab and coil technique. The microscopic analysis of each potsherd's fabric, the clays and the mineral inclusions they contain, point mainly, however, to local production. Most of the clays and temper, which stops the pots cracking, are found within 7 km of the site. This distance matches those in a global ethnographic survey of local pottery production by Dean Arnold (1985).

Not a single complete pot was found at Shorncote. Nonetheless a variety of shapes and forms were present in the collection. These were determined by making comparisons with complete examples from elsewhere in the region and reconstructing complete profiles from the fragments. As a result we know that jars dominate the collection. Bowls and other forms such as dishes are rare or non-existent. The lack of bowls among the fewer than 1000 sherds could be a result of sample size, since larger collections from nearby sites do have this additional form. Alternatively, the lack of bowls could be a clue to the activities performed at the site.

The pots have one of three types of decoration: none, finger tipping (which produces little indentations) and the application of cordons or strips to their surfaces. Of the 31 pots 24 had no decoration.

The different shapes, manufacture and decoration all point to something more than pots being functional or constructed according to some cultural template only found in the Late Bronze Age. Ethnography can help here to open our eyes to the possibility of variation. In her study of traditional potting in Northern Cameroon, Judy Sterner (1989) found that contrary to expectation the most decorated pots, large jars, were the most rarely seen, being kept in houses and compounds. She also found that the shape of the pot was more important for making a visual statement than the decoration it carried.

It seems that, as with much material culture, it is the overall features of the object rather than the fine detail that has significance.

Function

The fine wares, highly burnished forms, are very rare in the collection but do seem to have been used for holding acidic liquids, as shown by pitting on their interior surface. Most of the pots fall into the archaeological category of coarse wares, even though some of them are decorated. The jars could have been used to store many things. Food residues were found as sooty deposits on the inside of pots, and elsewhere these reveal products such as milk, honey, fish and pig fat. At Shorncote, Morris found that the frequency of such evidence correlated with only three of the ten fabrics, or wares, analysed. These accounted for over 50 per cent of the sherds and were likely to have been the cookpots. From sites nearby we know that cookpots at this time are usually medium to small in size, whereas storage jars are medium to large.

Context

The potsherds were clustered in significant areas of the site. The overall pattern was of low density but Morris found that there were concentrations in the top layers of the big pits and in one circular gully feature. The two roundhouses had no pots. She put this patterning down to three factors. The roundhouses may have been built for different functions and used at different times. The big pits were closer to one house, making it easier to throw broken pots away rather than leave them in the gutter. We don't know for sure, but simple explanations of refuse disposal, a theory-loaded term at the best of times – one person's dust heap is another's fortune – probably miss the mark. Potsherds at Shorncote might have been intentionally deposited in selected parts of the site as they were on many other settlements in later prehistory, a social action that was just as significant as the more familiar ritual of sweeping a broken jar out of the home.

Exchange

Interestingly when Morris analysed the fabrics in the potsherds she found that some of the rarer forms in the collection had different raw materials, hinting at different production centres. Not everything was locally produced after all. This was expected since prehistoric pottery in this region has been known for many years to have been exchanged over distances of up to 100 km (Peacock 1968). This was not in the form of commodities, like us buying mugs that were made in Taiwan at a petrol station. Rather such exchange was based on creating social relations out of social relations (Chapter 8). To exchange or trade a pot was to exchange or trade a part of yourself.

Consumption

Pots can hold more than just water. For example, the Middle Bronze Age (fifteenth to eleventh century BC) is well known for its elaborate cremation urns. It is known that these started life as domestic pots and only later became used in burials. Sterner (1989: 454) found in her ethnoarchaeological study that individuals had their personal soul pots, empty but brim-full of meaning. These pots embodied and brought to life the underlying beliefs about the living and the ancestors and the relationships between these categories. Christopher Tilley (1996: 323) goes further, arguing from his case study in Neolithic southern Scandinavia that pottery was metaphorically related to the corporeal aspects of human existence. The soft, malleable substance of clay and water have to be built up and shaped. The parallel with the soft outer flesh of the human body and how it is shaped over the skeleton is striking. Skin can be decorated with tattoos, paint, cicatrices and pierced for ornaments, which may explain the frequent decoration of pottery surfaces. Then fire makes the clay hard. Fire also reduces the body when it is cremated to its final hard components.

These contexts, Tilley reminds us (1996: 323), show that the process of production is a relation between people and objects rather than a cause. It is through production, exchange and consumption that people establish relationships with other people and so negotiate the form and meanings of their world (Miller 1995). As Mary Douglas and Baron Isherwood (1978: 72) point out in their study of consumption 'goods that minister to physical needs – food or drink – are no less carriers of meaning than ballet or poetry'. Just because it is common, and survives well, does not make the consumption of pottery a mundane, functional activity. At Shorncote the potters and pot-users were just not meeting a need, making a container to cook barley in. Instead the potters were the facilitators in a *chaîne opératoire* (see above), where the properties inherent in the clay and water were cross-cut with analogies drawn from bodily processes. These included growth and decay and technological processes involving shaping and building-up those jars from the material in hand.

Transformation

Finally, the Shorncote pots incorporated a deeper past into their fabric even as the wider world of the Bronze Age changed. Morris found that some of the temper, or filler, that was added to the clay to improve its mechanical properties during firing was not simply ground up shell or limestone but ground up Bronze Age pottery as well. This is known as grog-temper. There are two explanations for its use. The first emphasises practicalitics. The potters needed some temper so they ground up some pots there and then. Alternatively, as Sterner (1989) found, the decision is deliberate. The pot you are grinding into grog is a person, an ancestor. Pots are repaired with other pots. New pots are made which include older pots in the constant cycle of social reproduction. In the Middle Bronze Age, before Shorncote was built, large food vessels were often turned into cremation urns. These pots contained people, or at least their ashes, just as today in Cameroon soul pots contain souls. By the time Shorncote was built the burial rite had shifted from cremation to excarnation, the exposure of the dead body to the elements. But during this transformation of a key ritual the older tradition of regeneration survived. Those pots Morris analysed contain grog, other pots. But rather than seeing this just as pots within pots it is instead another way of putting a person in a pot, just as previously the large urns contained the ashes of the deceased.

During the simple act of pottery production some of the vessels at Shorncote took on the attributes of persons dead and persons living. Grandmothers, uncles and great aunts, all gone, but still incorporated into the everyday activities of the living such as cooking and the storing of food and drink which makes life continue. Thus the individual pot became a sort of family tree, reworked by each new generation. A ceramic-tape of social memories and a reminder of ancestral obligations.

The incorporation of the tradition of regeneration through the medium of pottery manufacture, repair, and the process of cooking and consumption serves, as Morris reminds us, that simple functional explanations only deal with one aspect in the lives of even the scruffiest of pots, from the smallest and most forgotten of excavations.

Summary

In Chapter 1 I defined archaeology as basically about three things: objects, landscapes and what we make of them. It is quite simply the study of the past through material remains. I have shown in this chapter how archaeologists have used their analyses of style to make something of the material they study. Style both orders and interprets the differences in architecture, stone axes, bronze pins, burial rites and the layout of towns and fields. But I have indicated that although style is one of our most trusty methods for recognising patterns among archaeological evidence, it is also one of our most slippery terms. We have relied upon it because it produced understandable results in the great scheme of looking at and interpreting the world as a set of oppositions; for example, nature : culture, internal : external. However, such great schemes have their own history of popularity and like a battleship curve in a seriation chart they come and go. Much of what is presented as theoretical forment in archaeology is due to changes in the way that the world is now conceived and analysed. The certainty of style, however defined, is one of the casualties in that change. As a result we can never look at objects, including the human landscape which I have only so far touched on only briefly, in the same way. The next step is to broaden the enquiry and look at the all-important frameworks of space and time which provide our main route to the interpretation of the past.

Chapter 6

Time and space

Time is the big one for archaeologists. Or at least you would think it should be. Until recently time as a concept, rather than a technique of dating, hasn't been at the top of our list of things to sort out. Indeed, our other dimension, space, has received far more attention both conceptually and as a framework for measuring and comparing archaeological data. In this chapter I will examine these two basic dimensions. We shall see how different concepts of time are every bit as important, if not more so, for understanding the past as getting the age of the Pyramids right by developing a new science-based technique to accurately measure how old things are (see Chapter 3).

Time and space are in fact inseparable. To think of one is to suppose the other. In line with earlier chapters I present you with a basic choice. Time and space can be used as the struts in an external framework – something that people today, and in the past, rattle around in and bump up against, like the wall of the set in *The Truman Show*. Or you can see them as created by human activity. Space and time are examples of

those everyday rhythms described by Leroi-Gourhan (1993). They emerge through our involvement with the world rather than as pre-existing conditions on our actions.

Contexts and entities

In order to understand the alternatives on offer we need some further entities to add to the list of attribute, artefact and assemblage discussed in Chapter 3.

In the first place there are *contexts*. This term can mean different things to different archaeologists. I define them below. Then there are *entities* or classifications that cross-cut contexts and are built up piece-meal from their contents. These depend on space and time for their definition. The most important are the, by now, familiar archaeological culture as well as some newcomers *culture group*, *technocomplex* and *world system*.

Context and preservation

When excavating, a context has both a spatial and a temporal meaning. This is what stratigraphy (Chapter 3) is all about. The context from which finds come could be a pit or a grave, a temple or a granary. It can be disturbed, containing items deposited at different times and for different reasons, thus upsetting the ideal which, for most excavators, is undisturbed, in-situ preservation of the evidence. This situation is an *ideal* because it would produce a closed find-group. From such contexts come precise associations of artefacts which can be used for dating purposes as well as for the reconstruction of events and activities. These can on occasion involve very short-lived activities, for example the 15 minutes it took to make a flint biface half a million years ago at Boxgrove, West Sussex, England.

Contexts, like time, can be vertical as well as horizontal. The stratigraphy of a tell mound or deep urban excavation is built up through the changing picture of the contexts that excavation reveals. Pieced together these might refer to new neighbourhood functions with alterations in settlement size and its cultural demography. Thus several hundred or even thousands of years of continuous occupation in one place is built up as a record of intersecting contexts. These are represented in a piece of visual archaeological jargon (see Figure 3.4).

Time capsules

Precise, in situ information is not rare in archaeology. On occasion there are even time capsules such as the Tudor warship the *Mary Rose*, which sank, with all hands on board, off Portsmouth in 1545 in front of Henry VIII and the invading French fleet. Another warship, the *Vasa*, toppled over on her maiden voyage in Stockholm harbour on 10 August 1628. These are precise time capsules, storehouses of material culture and habits, to be compared with Tutankhamun's tomb, the Copan burials or the town of Pompeii – sealed by what happened in the space of a day.

But not all in situ time capsules yield easy answers. The contents of the dry-land ship burial of Sutton Hoo in Suffolk, eastern England, have been much discussed (Carver 1998). They are an eclectic group of local, continental, eastern Mediterranean, Pagan and Christian items. Some of them were antiques when they were put in the ground, thus blurring the notion of contemporaneity. Moreover, perhaps the most significant artefact, the body, was either never present or just not preserved. In this instance an in situ context has led to much disagreement over the date, whether it is a burial or a cenotaph, and the identity of the person who was either buried or commemorated. This is partly due to the very scrappy textual evidence which most commentators try to tie the find into. I suspect that if the fates of the *Vasa* and the *Mary Rose* had not been written down at the time, similar, rather unproductive debates about whose ship it was and which reign it sank in would have followed.

Archaeological time signatures

Contextual integrity, the in situ ideal, is rather different to the notion of signatures. A *fine-grained* time signature provides a very good match between what went on at a site and what was left behind. It is the archaeological equivalent of the Polaroid snap. Typically a group of mobile hunters might catch game, gather plant food and use local stone which they turn into artefacts. If they do all of this locally and then leave the residue behind, it can become a fine-grained signature even if it is later disturbed by geology, ploughing or any other transformational process (see Chapter 3).

A *coarse-grained* time signature is much more common. Here there is a lag in both space and time between activity and deposition. It is like film editing: starting and stopping, shooting out of sequence and splicing together later. The wheat that went into the granary was grown many kilometres away. It sat in the storage jars for a long time. It was then redistributed, perhaps to people who never grew or processed it. Only then was it turned into bread, after which it began to trickle into the archaeological record. Those wheat grains that fell on the fire and became carbonised might still be lying exactly where they fell 6000 years ago. The integrity of their preservation is not the issue. Time signatures record the temporal rhythms of the behaviour that left something behind.

Meaning = message + context

The other use of the word context is concerned with a rather different set of meanings. Rather than simply recording objects by aspects of their space–time dimensions, a contextual analysis also looks to interpret their meaning. But what is meaning? I define meaning quite simply as message + context. Message was touched upon in Chapter 4 through the complicated issue of style in material culture. It is difficult to interpret but we made some headway in dissolving the dichotomies between style and function, social and technical. Can we do the same for context?

Contextual analysis

Context has been defined by Hodder as the totality of the relevant environment in which entities such as attributes, artefacts and assemblages are found (1991: 143). This 'relevant environment' refers to a significant relationship that will help unpick an object's meaning. The questions being asked by the archaeologist will also shape that context.

What the archaeologist is saying is actually quite simple and follows the basic rule of how to systematically sample the unknown (see Chapter 3, The representative sample). To get at meanings, contexts must be bigger than the entities being studied. If an artefact is under the interpretive lens, then the context has to be the time and space dimensions from which it comes and from which other similar or dissimilar artefacts might come. If meaning is the goal, then the artefact, the culture or any other entity cannot be abstracted from this framework, what Hodder calls the 'relevant environment', and studied in isolation. If it is removed, then the message is lost.

A contextual analysis seeks to unpick those strands of symbolic references that signify the context and give the object meaning within their well-spun webs. Hence a contextual analysis, to go back to the 'text' metaphor, depends upon many readings. It thrives on a high density of data, the richer the better. And while meaning is specific to a particular context, it may be repeated elsewhere.

Conjunctive approach

Several of these points were made 40 years before by Walter Taylor in his conjunctive approach, from which Hodder traces his contextual perspective (Hodder 1991: 189). The conjunctive approach stressed analysing cultures from the inside, identifying affinities through associations and relationships, similarity and difference, item *to* item, attribute *to* attribute (Taylor 1948: 95–6). It was contrasted with the then dominant comparative approach that looked for correspondences outside the entity being studied, which was usually culture *by* culture. Taylor, like Hodder, warned against the attractions of the comparative approach with its interest in universal meanings such as function (Chapter 4).

Contextual and conjunctive analysis also share the basic belief that culture explains culture and that the meaning of objects is contained within them and revealed through their context. They would also agree that:

> Much of an archaeologist's work consists in judging relative similarities or differences between material remains, whether at the level of artefacts, assemblages or whole complexes.
>
> Doran and Hodson (1975: 135)

Archaeological culture and culture groups

Childe's classic definition of an archaeological culture was set out in Chapter 3. It combines recurrence in time with distribution in space. David Clarke updated it slightly and added a higher grouping, the culture group. Culture was a 'polythetic set [see Figure 3.3] of specific and comprehensive artefact-type categories which consistently recur together in *assemblages* within a limited geographical area', while a culture-group is 'a family of transform cultures; collateral cultures characterised by assemblages sharing a polythetic range but differing states of the same *specific multistate artefact-types*' (1968: 188, original emphasis).

What Clarke is saying in the language of the time is that culture groups are weak cultures. We can see that patterning exists but it is not very robust. There are contradictions with the culture model, where greater correspondence is expected in the popularity and presence of artefact types within and between assemblages excavated and recovered from different sites.

Clarke's important point about the polythetic structure of artefacts establishes that culture groups will have less overall affinity. He suggested about 30 per cent affinity for specific artefact types, for example particular forms of pottery beakers or clothing pins, but about 60 per cent affinity among the larger sets of artefacts, graves and pots. A culture would, by contrast, have much higher percentages of both types and sets of types.

Fuzzy taxonomy

The overlapping, fuzzy-bordered nature of these entities, as could have been predicted from the polythetic set (Figure 3.3), can be shown spatially (Figure 6.1). The lesson is that human activity is continuous. It is overlapping and blurred in the present. It is also blurred in such

FIGURE 6.1 The overlapping character of archaeological entities. These could be spatial or temporal distributions. They could refer to single artefact types as shown here by the four pots or to the many items that make up an archaeological culture. They could also be webs of relationships and practices in a landscape of habit or a social landscape (after Clarke 1969: figure 58)

representations of the past. We impose the edges, or cut the continuum, in order to break down complexity so that we can manage, analyse and re-experience it.

This fuzzy reality is the hard part for the archaeologist as taxonomist. Where do you start to carve this turkey when you can't even see its joints clearly? We are left with the question of whether more work,

Box 17: The size of archaeological entities
(Clarke 1968: 331)

	Estimated range Radius (km)
Culture	30–300
Culture group	300–1200
Technocomplex	1200–7500+

more data, would turn culture groups into cultures by boosting the level of affinity. Then we believe we would know where to put our taxonomic knife. Clarke's intuition was that the structural bones would be seen spatially. He even suggested guesstimates (Box 17), which I don't think are far wrong, to guide us.

Technocomplex

Clarke proposed another term, 'technocomplex', for the even vaguer entities beyond the culture group. It has been widely used, particularly in the study of stone artefacts. In North and South America it is broadly equivalent to the term 'tradition' as in Paleo-Indian, Old Cordilleran, Desert, Archaic, Northwest Microblade and Arctic Small-tool traditions/technocomplexes.

Technocomplexes are characterised by general *families* of artefact types. If plotted out, the assemblages in a technocomplex might share only 5 per cent of the artefact types but up to 60 per cent of these families, such as hunting tools, transport technology and storage equipment. This suited the rather unstandardised but broadly similar sets of stone tools widely distributed across Europe and Africa and thought to cope with common environmental problems at a regional and inter-regional scale. Clarke's use of terms such as 'family' indicate his adherence to a biological model for drawing up an archaeological taxonomy. It is very functional, highly systemic and ultimately adaptive. While we need to classify, we must also recognise that revealing natural taxonomies cannot be the sole task of the archaeologist. That way lies a degree in stamp collecting.

World system

A problem that has faced archaeologists is thinking big. Not in terms of ambition, something that archaeologists have never lacked, as demonstrated by excavating the Ziggurat at Ur or clearing the rainforest from Ankor Wat, but rather in thinking about the scale of human interaction. The temptation has always been to think local, be parochial, with just a whiff of diffusionism to paper over the unexpected.

When studying the ancient empires there have been surprises such as the extent of the Inca road system down the spine of South America or the discovery of coins, minted in Rome, from excavations in Laos. The problem has always been considering the impact of these indications of contact. One of the achievements of archaeology in the past 40 years has been to expand the scale at which we commonly think people interacted from the Palaeolithic to the industrial eras.

Archaeology has played its part in demonstrating that well before Columbus and the European world-empires life everywhere was equally international. A useful model in such a mindset change is provided by the Marxist historian Immanuel Wallerstein and his analysis of the modern world system (1974, 1980). He deals with the cyclical accumulation of wealth and power between dominant centres and their tributary peripheries. The spatial notion of core/periphery struck a chord with archaeologists, who expanded their studies of the earliest states to include, as part of the civilising process, those neighbouring prehistoric societies (Frank 1993; Kristiansen and Rowlands 1998: 222). Such analyses soon went beyond the rather general expectations of world-systems theory. Sometimes these imply nothing more than chaos theory at its most banal, where everything is related causally to everything else (Chapter 7); a Roman emperor stamps his foot and the tempest of world religions are the result.

One world

However, the real value of world-systems thinking is to confirm the subject matter of archaeology as globally interconnected. No one is left out of this world, especially those, like hunters and gatherers, whom the nineteenth century consigned to stagnation and primitiveness. For example, even those hunters at the 'uttermost ends of the earth' to Europe and eastern North America were influenced by, and had some reciprocal influence on the centres. The transformation of Siberian and Alaskan Inuit society through indirect contact with the Amur civilisations 2000 km away is an example. We know from the excavation of their graves that these prehistoric warrior-hunters went into local battle protected by whale-bone armour made to a Chinese pattern far to the south. Much later their descendants would supply that same whale-bone for the corsets of London and Paris. A good example of the power of material culture to constrain and transform the shape of society.

The lesson from world-systems theory is think big. Basically, do not always expect local answers to local questions, especially those that involve change (Chapter 7). Never underestimate the scale of the 'primitive' world.

Time

The discussion of contexts and entities has been necessary because, like action in the past, time remains invisible. Certainly we experience it but we cannot grasp it. We use metaphors to describe those experiences – 'time is like an arrow', 'time is cyclical' – and the rate at which it seems to happen – 'how time flies when one has fun', 'time on my hands' and 'how time drags'. The way we experience time in the past is not, I maintain, by chronologies alone, but through entities such as artefact, technocomplex and archaeological culture, which we have now examined. These are, if you like, congealed lumps of time. The difference is that we can grasp these archaeological entities because we created them and we can even change their shape by changing our mind about them.

Temporality

This raises the important issue of temporality, which I define as the varied activities and processes that occur within time. Since the flow of experience is continuous, what we are looking for are those temporal structures that we use, often arbitrarily, to make the process meaningful. At the same time by chopping up time we acknowledge that different activities have different temporal structures. Some may well fit the metaphor of the arrow, with its hint of progress and direction to the process, or the wheel that comes round every year in the ritual of Christmas or every generation in births, marriages and death. Other activities may better fit the process of ageing, as with ruined, ivy-covered monuments, symbolic of time passing and the eventual decay of all things, even the Pyramids.

But these metaphors are predictable and rather reduce the flow of time to analytical chunks that often come to be disembodied from the people who generated them. It is possible to compare one arrow with another (Chapter 7), for example the rise of civilisation in the Near East and in Mesoamerica or the development of metallurgy in China and in Africa. It is also possible to contrast different cycles, such as the annual subsistence rounds of hunters and gatherers (this can be done on a truly world scale) or the solar and lunar inspired rituals of the Neolithic monuments of Knowth and Newgrange in the Boyne Valley, Ireland. Valuable as these comparisons might be I would agree with the conjunctive approach (see above) that we need to get beneath the surface and see if we can't address the issue of temporality rather than the comparative classification and measurement of units of time (see Box 11).

A and B series time

The anthropologist Alfred Gell (1992) neatly dismissed the idea, once held by many, that the cultures of the world experience time differently. This is important since we can then assume a similar state of affairs for the peoples of the past (Chapter 4, The principle of uniformitarianism). Gell concluded that we all basically have a choice when it comes to time concepts. These boil down to the following difference:

A series time = past/present/future
B series time = before/after

In A series time, the present is wafer thin, just a fleeting moment. It is a drop in the stream of consciousness and cannot be tied down or adequately described. Adherents to this view have to spend a lot of time referring to the past and the future in order to fix what is going on in the present. B series time, on the other hand, is congealed by being mapped on to space. It occurs between dateable events.

That is the choice. In practice, Gell argues, the two series work together. A series time provides us with internal representations of what external, B series time, is like. Those B series representations in turn inform the way we think about time in the instant of the present. How does this help the archaeologist? The answer is through objects. They endure (B series time) and they continue to change because of our relations with them (A series time).

Timescales and time perspectivism

It should by now be clearer why time concepts, as opposed to time measurements, never count for much in culture history, neo-Darwinian or processual archaeology (Chapter 2). As Geoff Bailey has shown, we spend a great deal of our resources on measuring time but very little on the concepts of time (1983). Perhaps, ironically, time is not seen as a resource that built or shaped the past. It is only seen as something, in the guise of decay, that stops us receiving the full picture in the present. Moreover, given *enough* time, which obviously archaeologists have never lacked, change by diffusion, natural and cultural selection or systemic transformations could be assumed.

Within this barren time-vortex there have been some considerations of what an archaeological perspective offers to our understanding of human time. Time perspectivism, as discussed by Bailey (1983), looks at the issue of the very long timescales we have at our disposal in the long run of human evolution. Geologists refer to this as 'deep-time' and archaeologists have emphasised the long-term perspective that our studies bring to questions of adaptation, survival, stasis and change.

The long term, measured in thousands of years, is indeed an archaeological way of thinking. When faced with dates as long as telephone numbers many people wonder how archaeologists can think in those time spans.

Contemporaneity

The answer is that we don't. In the same way that the distance to the stars is mind boggling, so too is the fact that Chauvet Cave in southern France, with its fabulous paintings of rhinos, horses and lions, dated by radiocarbon to 33,000 years ago, is about the same distance in time from the very famous cave paintings of Lascaux, executed 17,000 years ago, as the latter are from Michaelangelo's Sistine Chapel. All three were painted by people with modern capabilities, but the first two by a long tradition of activity in the landscape governed by the rhythms of hunting and gathering.

Here is an example of enough time by anybody's standards. To comprehend it we don't think of ten thousand individual years. Nobody can. Neither do we even think in more manageable spans of 500 or a thousand years. Both of these scales our outside our ken. You might as well try to imagine each byte in the gigabytes in your computer. What we do is crystallise time, like honey on the end of a spoon. We average it in order to manage it.

But that is only part of the process of understanding time. What we also need to do, as outlined above, is to make time more human, more personal. This is done by treating the crystallising process as one that respects the archaeological record and the way time has always been experienced.

Time averaging

Time averaging, that process of crystallisation, is how we deal with a common question, contemporaneity. Historical records are apparently well suited to dealing with this aspect of time. With a bit of digging in the archives we could probably find out what the other European monarchs were doing on 10 August 1628, when the *Vasa* sank. Laughing probably. It would be even easier to compare what was going on in Sweden, England, Massachusetts or China in that year and that decade. This would be regarded as pretty good control over contemporaneity, slotting into a human life span.

Thirty-three thousand years ago that precision of course escapes us. We could compare what was going on in Tasmania, South Africa and Europe at around that time, but nobody could claim contemporaneity on the scale of a human generation, 20 years. But then why would you want to? The questions relevant to 33,000 years ago are not going to involve the foreign policy and military ambitions of King Gustavus II Adolphus, whose flagship sank on that calamitous day. Although the cave paintings might have taken the Chauvet artists a single week, a month or repeated visits to the cave over 20 or a hundred years, we just do not know – the issue of contemporaneity is meaningless. What we have are some precise events and large blocks of time represented by a palimpsest (or jumble) of times, places, landscapes and objects. In the Lower Palaeolithic such time averaging means that 'contemporary' is often a block of time 70,000 years in length. By the Neolithic that comes down to between 700 and 1000 years. By the medieval period contemporary time units of 100 or 50 years are common.

So, don't expect the past to behave like the present, especially when contemporaneity is at issue. Instead, celebrate that part of our cultivated archaeological imagination that allows us to think beyond our normal restrictions and to recognise that our experienced time frames (yesterday, today, the news breaking now in all the capitals of the world) are not the only way to reckon contemporaneity in human action.

Micro- and macro-timescales

The discussion of contemporaneity has highlighted an issue I have already returned to several times, micro- and macro-scale. Archaeology has plenty of temporal data to examine this important issue. In any excavation you will come across evidence of very brief micro-episodes of time. How long does it take to tip food refuse into a pit? Those same plant and animal remains as well as the pot that got thrown away with them can be inferred to represent longer periods of time. That leg of pork came from a three-year-old pig, the charred wheat grains from a season's crop, the pot maybe lasted a generation. The pit they were all found in might, however, be dated to no finer than 150 years in the early Medieval period.

When micro-timescale activities are also preserved in situ, then our archaeological imagination really feels a frisson. The main archaeological horizon at the 500,000 year old site of Boxgrove, West Sussex, England, lasted for probably no more than a human generation, 20 years. Over this time people regularly visited the place, made stone tools, hunted and butchered animals, and left the remains behind. Fifteen minutes to make a biface, a few hours to butcher a horse, contained within a stratigraphic envelope of 20 years and all half a million years ago. Here the micro- and the macro-timescales are neatly embedded in each other.

Place and landscape

The reason for worrying about the time concepts we use comes down to that other archaeological dimension, space. The entities and scales I have previously described above (e.g. technocomplex), in Chapter 3 (e.g. assemblage and culture) and will shortly describe below (e.g. site and region) largely need time as a measure of their duration. In spatial terms they are made up of popular artefacts and repeatable combinations which are left behind as solid markers. Their message is clear: people were here, they did this, they lasted this long, they went and others came in their place.

The alternative is to think rather differently about seemingly ordinary terms such as 'place' and 'landscape'. The trick is to realise that they are not alternatives for those archaeological journeymen terms 'site' and 'environment' that people either built or played games against as part of their adaptive survival. Instead places and landscapes were constructed from the act of living. These terms are about time and temporality.

The key word is human *involvement*, with its implication of a continuous activity stream. As Christopher Gosden has insisted, we start by understanding that the times those activity streams generated *is* the landscape (1994: 193). Place in this context can be defined by:

> the experiences it affords to those who spend time there – to the sights, sounds and indeed smells that constitute its specific ambience. And these, in turn, depend on the kinds of activities in which its inhabitants engage.
>
> Ingold (1993: 155)

Places are not distinct from the landscape but part of that continuous involvement. The activities that occur there do, however, structure the temporality of the landscape and inscribe it with meaning. The landscape also acquires its own history through the superimposition of traces of human activity that can range from erosion of the soils to the building of a ceremonial centre, from throwing away a bone to burying a loved one.

In the light of this understanding we can now rewrite the meaning equation from

meaning = message + context

to

meaning = object/style + place/landscape

Landscape of habit , taskscapes and the social landscape

Three further terms will help to make the point. The first, the *landscape of habit* (Gosden 1994: 182) summarises those habitual, taken-for-granted, actions by which we live most of our lives. The landscape of habit is constructed by the actions that normally get things done but which don't really concern us unless something goes wrong – the axe breaks, the snows stay late or the harvest fails.

The second, the *taskscape*, has been suggested by Tim Ingold (1993). Actions speak louder than words. We hear activity as much as see it or infer it by using our archaeological imagination. Attention – attending to others, attending to the task in hand – is a very important social activity. Our ears confirm that we are surrounded by creative action which we respond to.

Habit, like the distinction between practical and discursive consciousness, lies within our third term, another landscape, this time a *social landscape*. Here the choices are more deliberate, more creative in terms of negotiation with others and with things. Both landscapes influence each other and are firmly embedded in each other. The parallel is obvious with the practical and discursive consciousness that all of us has, which is indivisible but allows distinct ways of acting. An excellent example is provided by Richard Bradley's (1997) study of rock-art sites in Atlantic Europe. The composition and siting of the art is conditioned both by everyday, habitual actions, such as tending livestock, as well as by a wider social world.

During the course of human evolution there have been significant changes to our social landscape (Chapter 7). Objects and our relationship to them have been central to these changes. With those objects comes an in-built time. It is through these objects that place and landscape come to symbolise time and space as a result of human action. The concept of *habitus* provides another formulation of these issues, which I shall discuss in Chapter 8.

Space

On the face of it space seems much more straightforward than time. The distance between two points can be measured as can the size of towns or the quantities of goods found away from their source of manufacture. Archaeologists like distribution maps and at a smaller scale excavation plans will always be an essential record of what we do. The quantification of spatial data and systematic sampling based on a spatial framework were two of the great steps forward made by processual archaeology. These advances will now be examined through another of the lasting products of processual archaeology, the research design.

The new geography of the 1960s (Haggett 1965; Chorley and Haggett 1967), which like the new archaeology also dealt with laws, hypotheses, models, sampling, quantification and statistical analysis, provided the impetus for a spatial archaeology (Clarke 1972a, Hodder and Orton 1976). It was more enthusiastically pursued in Britain and Europe partly because the quantification seemed to fill the gap left behind by the lack of ethnography in that continent. 'Archaeology as anthropology' in North America became, for a short

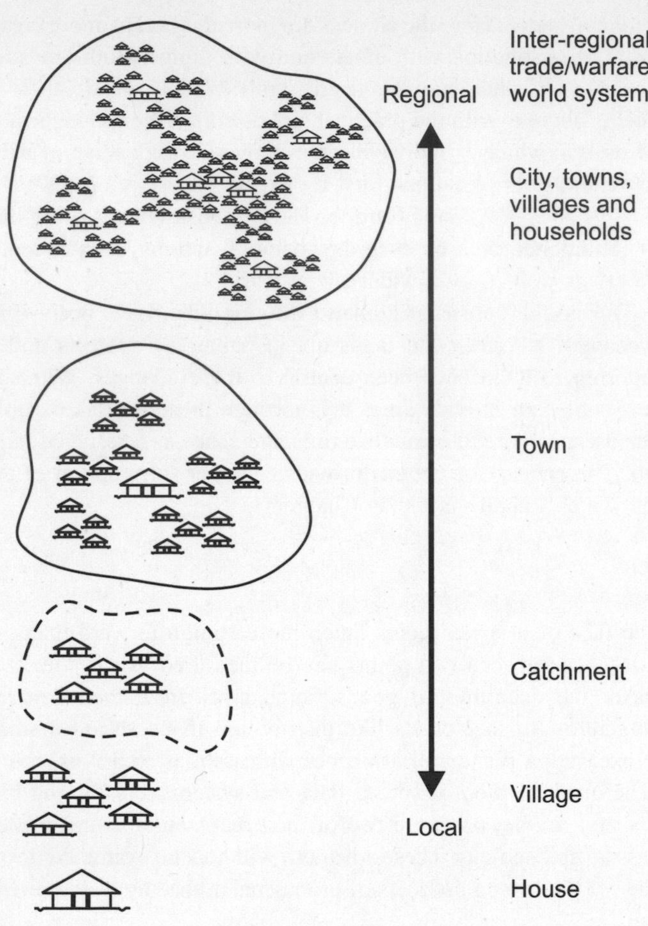

FIGURE 6.2 From the micro to the macro. Fitting the spatial scales into this nest of concepts allows us to analyse human action at a variety of scales while keeping sight of the whole picture. The example comes from the Iron Age of southern England (after Clarke 1972)

while, 'archaeology as geography' in Britain before the lack of human content in such approaches was fully realised (Gamble 1987).

Scales of spatial analysis were thoroughly investigated from the micro to the macro (Clarke 1977). The blending of research design, methods and analysis came together in the intra-site to inter-regional model that has been very influential as a framework for investigation and interpretation. Two early and classic examples are illustrated by Flannery's work in Mesoamerica (see below) and Clarke's (1972b) study of an Iron Age settlement system (Figure 6.2).

But space is not just about research designs, systematic sampling and nested levels of enquiry. In the first place it is about *pattern recognition* where the levels in the nest are, at a minimum:

- intra-site,
- site, and
- region.

Then secondly there are at least four *analytical approaches* to space which need to be briefly reviewed because of what they have contributed to archaeology. They are:

- central places and polities,
- the attrition of distance,
- Geographical Information Systems, and
- the social use of space.

Pattern recognition

As accurately described above by Doran and Hodson (page 128), archaeologists spend a great deal of time recognising patterns in their data. This is done at a number of scales. Three are very important: intra-site, site and region.

Spatial scales

Analytically these three spatial scales form, like Russian dolls, the tiers in a nested hierarchical structure.

Intra-site

The first level in the *nested hierarchy* of spatial scales lies at the intra-site level. This combines many of the aspects of contexts that we have discussed above but with an important difference. Intra-site analysis looks for spatial patterning among connected groups of contexts and features recognised during excavation. It may be based on the distribution of finds and their quantitative frequency as gridded out rather than necessarily related to a definable context. This is a common strategy in field walking. Intra-site patterning is very strongly linked to specific questions about activities and aspects of the built environment.

Site

Sites are the stock-in-trade items for archaeologists. They are what we excavate and are the repositories for information. Successful careers can be built on their excavation alone. Increasingly, however, our information comes not from excavation but from various forms of non-invasive techniques (Chapter 3). These include geophysical prospection, aerial photos, and the surface survey of artefacts, for example when we systematically pick up finds from the surface of ploughed fields. Excavation is not the way to answer all our questions.

Sites are described in many ways. Functionally we have among many others: villas, towns, forts, monasteries, pueblos, camps and shell middens. These are described quantitatively by such factors as size, contents, age, duration and complexity.

But sites, like culture groups, can also be difficult to define. Sometimes the boundaries are difficult to discern. Where there are ditches, walls and banks the category seems clear cut and comparisons can be made on size alone. But very often where one site ends and another begins is a problem, especially for a vast category of site, the unenclosed settlement, often represented by a scatter of materials across the landscape. Within such find scatters there may be chronological indicators provided by some distinctive flints and pots, but very often there are not.

Region

The last level in the nested hierarchy of spatial scales is the region. These too can be difficult to define. They can be period specific such as a hunting territory or any of the ancient empires. They may be delimited by the similarity of particular artefact categories. Flint, pottery and coins are the normal items used. But this is unsatisfactory and often difficult for reasons shown in Figure 3.3. In cases where rich linguistic and anthropological data exist, as in the southwestern United States and Australia, these have been used to draw up regional boundaries. The archaeology is then compared between such ethnographic regions to investigate issues of time-depth. This approach can run the risk of re-creating the past in the form of the present (see Chapter 4).

The regional scale of investigation and analysis, as established by processual archaeology, is an important archaeological concept. When behaviour is being studied, the unit by which it is studied must be larger so that a representative selection of that behaviour can be recovered for study (Chapter 3, Sampling strategies). That has always been a problem with earlier approaches where one site was taken to represent much more widespread aspects of cultural behaviour when in fact it could be atypical. Moreover, the size of regions will vary depending on the mobility and scale of inter-group contacts. This is why regions are often set arbitrarily by a grid, whose size might vary depending on the mobility and range of contacts the system being studied is thought to have, and then the contents of each cell systematically sampled. The alternative is to delimit natural regions. This carries some weight when the questions being asked are ecological, for example sampling the annual subsistence round of hunters and gatherers. It makes less sense when the focus shifts to more abstract instances of power, exchange or identity.

Regional thinking

An excellent example of this nested approach is Kent Flannery's (1976) investigations of the archaeology of the Oaxaca Valley, Mexico. This influential, as well as entertaining, study of the rise of civilisation also stands as a parable of the archaeological times. Interspersed with systematic, quantified fieldwork linked to testing dynamic, rather than providing purely descriptive, models is a dialogue between three fictional archaeologists. The points of view of Flannery's Great Synthesiser (GS, who relies on other peoples data), Real Mesoamerican Archaeologist (RMA, who is a culture historian interested in the Formative period) and Sceptical Graduate Student (SGS, who is strongly quantitative, processualist and a 'pain-in-the-ass, but at least he's my little pain-in-the-ass' according to the RMA) do not disguise the fact that they are all part of one archaeological personality. The parable is not about which one gains ascendancy but rather that after years of either silence or single points of view a debate is now taking place.

Flannery's approach to regional analysis was to build from the bottom up. He starts with the household, then goes to the village and on to the region, and finally the inter-regional scale in Mesoamerica. This model has been very influential. Rather than start with a grand theory or law, it begins with the recovery of information about how people lived their daily lives. Such a nested hierarchy of analytical techniques, changing questions and behavioural inferences shows how a processual archaeology can be built rather than assumed. This same methodological structure can be found in Clarke's analysis of Iron Age Britain (1972b, 1979) and in Colin Renfrew and Malcolm Wagstaff's (1982) study of the town of Phylakopi, on the Greek island of Melos, and its place in the Bronze Age Aegean.

Analytical approaches to space

Space provides many strong patterns in the data and a framework for archaeological investigation. But what do we then make of space and what principles apply? I have selected six models and techniques that illustrate how important space is for archaeology. In particular, the study of social relationships and the construction of gender depend on space.

Central places

The link between space, settlement and social organisation has been important in synthesising archaeological data at both a site and regional scale. Central places have particular functions, such as a market, and often geographical explanations for being there, for instance proximity to the richest soils in the region or good water communications. But natural advantages are not always self-evident. Why was Sutton Hoo on that little backwater in Suffolk? Will someone please explain to me why Stonehenge is on windswept Salisbury Plain?

Central places are about people and the flows of goods and information. The concept has been applied to all periods of archaeology. Glynn Isaac (1978) proposed a central place foraging model for hunters and gatherers based on his archaeological fieldwork in East Africa and ethnographic work by Richard Lee among the !Kung San, mobile foragers in the Kalahari desert. Isaac's model for hominids 2 million years ago had them radiating out from a home base on a daily basis as they foraged for food. He expanded his model to consider such issues as the spatial extent of foraging activity, the division of labour between the sexes, and the transport of food. From this he developed his food-sharing hypothesis to account for human cultural origins.

These properties of centrality were used by Claudio Vita-Finzi and Eric Higgs (1970) in their model of site catchment analysis which amalgamated the principles of urban economic geography and the foraging of the !Kung San. They applied a territorial analysis to hunting and agricultural sites. Circles were drawn around sites based on the economics of walking. These had a radius of 10 km for hunters and 5 km for farmers. Beyond these distances returns dropped-off in a predictable manner. More calories, or energy, had to be expended than could be acquired. Hence a sort of territorial threshold, or sphere of operations, was established. These thresholds could be established by walking the radii from archaeological sites and noting soils, slopes and the terrain. The catchment of the site was linked to its economic contents, which included animal bones and carbonised cereal grains. Site catchment analysis therefore provided, in an appropriately circular fashion, the explanation for site location. People made camps or built villages to exploit nearby resources.

The notion of centrality has also been widely applied to later monuments and settlements. Here Colin Renfrew's studies of the palace economies of Minoan and Mycenaean Greece have been influential (1972). Palaces such as Knossos and defended citadels such as Mycenae were analysed for their size and functions. In particular, the presence of granaries at Knossos led to its interpretation as a redistributive centre. Furthermore, central places had central people whose status and power stemmed from their ability to organise redistribution of agricultural and craft surpluses.

Polities

The relative sizes of these central places has been a powerful tool in characterising the demography and attendant power structures of early state polities. In Mesopotamia there is usually a marked difference in the size of the largest site, for example Warka or ancient Uruk (Redman 1978: 255), when compared to its neighbours. This is known as a primate distribution, where one centre dominates the regional settlement picture. In the later stages of state formation this disparity in site size levels out and the graph shows a continuous distribution for urban sites and villages. At the same time there are changes in the means by which power was concentrated in the hands of the few in a single centre.

The interest in political formation has been investigated as much through the spatial dimension as the artefactual (Renfrew 1977). The attraction of such an approach lies in the comparative basis that space provides. Comparing site size and density and examining differences in a settlement hierarchy is often easier than assessing the comparative complexity of early states on the basis of the number of gold masks they produced, the size of their pyramids, or the intensity of their agricultural production. Space contains relationships because distance carries costs as well as opportunities.

Islands and archipelagos provide a good example of how space has been used to investigate polities. They often combine a clearly bounded regional approach with an imperative for exchange. This has been done for Hawaii (Kirch 1984) as well as for many of the Mediterranean islands. The framework is reminiscent of a world-systems approach but in this case delimited by natural boundaries and related to objects.

The attrition of distance

By quantifying the spatial distributions they have always plotted out archaeologists have revolutionised their study of trade and exchange. This has been combined with advances in sourcing where the raw materials came from that were used in the manufacture of common items such as pottery and stone, and bronze and iron tools. As a result it is possible to examine systems of production, distribution and consumption (Chapter 5). For example, Palaeolithic archaeologists have shown that stone tools from hunting camps are invariably made of materials that come from less than 5 km away (Geneste 1988). Furthermore, if distant stone sources, those from between 30 and 80 km, are being utilised, the archaeological evidence will be in the form of retouched implements rather than waste flakes. In other words we are seeing the movement of finished items, presumably carried by individuals.

Pottery also provides a quantified measure of the difference between local and distant. In his ethnoarchaeological survey of central America, Dean Arnold (1985) found that potters obtained their clays from within 7 km and usually from within 1 km. Of course, this local procurement has to be set beside the long distances over which some pots were subsequently traded. Examples in Europe include Roman wine amphorae and fine table wares, such as Samian pottery, which were traded around the empire.

The quantified evidence exploits the geographical observation known as the attrition of distance. As a general rule a fall-off in the popularity of objects is expected the further one goes from their place of production. Distance in this instance represents a cost, especially when translated into transporting heavy, bulky items. This was the model underpinning site-catchment analysis, where villages would be located close to good soils, so minimising daily distances to the fields and reducing the costs of transporting the crop at harvest-time.

From an archaeological perspective the interest focuses on observing contradictions to this simple expectation. Particular goods, such as rare obsidian mirrors in Mesoamerica, do not steadily decline away from source. Rather they 'peak' at places where exchange partners of similar rank or status lived. Much attention has been given to the circulation and distribution of these so-called *prestige goods* which are exchanged between élites (Renfrew and Shennan 1982; Kristiansen and Rowlands 1998). Their distribution provides information about the scale and organisation of polities and the unequal flow of goods between people within them.

The importance of trade and exchange has been stressed in the examination of change, particular in the question of how state societies and the early civilisations arose (Chapter 7).

Geographical information systems

The archaeological love affair with distribution maps has recently received a further fillip thanks to the advent of geographical information systems (GIS). This is the future of spatial archaeology. GIS has replaced the laborious business of hand-plotting artefacts on maps with computer procedures. But there is more to GIS than just saving time. The core of GIS is the database and, thanks to advances in computing hardware and software, this can incorporate more data than was possible even only 20 years ago. This allows for the management and analysis of much more complex sets of data than before. One example is provided by Richard Bradley's (1997) regional survey of the rock art found from Portugal to Scotland. Using GIS he was able to calculate for different areas the intervisibility of rock-art sites, known technically as viewshed data. The point of such an exercise is to define a hierarchy of sites in the landscape, to compare whether the most visible are also the richest in terms of the number of motifs and how close they are to one another. The GIS analysis revealed a structure and patterning to the rock-art data that had not previously been suspected.

Another great potential for GIS in archaeology is predictive modelling. We want to know more about the distribution of sites and artefacts to guide future research as well as the management of the archaeological resource. Through prediction we can test hypotheses about distributions. A recent example is provided by Robert Hosfield's (1999) study of the distribution of Lower Palaeolithic artefacts in southern England. He modelled the activities of collectors during the last century as well as the pattern of mineral extraction. This allowed predictions to be made about the likely occurrence of deeply buried sites incorporated in the river gravels of the region during the past half-million years of human occupation. Such predictions now need to be tested. An archaeological information system would add that important ingredient which is largely missing from GIS, the long-term activities of people.

The social use of space

The anthropologist Nurit Bird-David (1994, 1999; see also Strathern 1988) has made the point that there are two different ways of studying people. If we take a *relational* view of society, then what we are stressing as important in any investigation of social life is the way people relate to each other. How we all build and create society is the key. The alternative is a *modernist* view of society, where the interest is more in the formal institutions that individuals have to fit themselves into. You will see strong parallels to the top-down and bottom-up approaches to society which were discussed in Chapter 4.

At the moment it is the modernist approach that carries more weight in our accounts of how society works in all times and places. This has not always been the case. Bird-David's study of Nayaka people in southern India, who would traditionally be classed as hunters and gatherers, reveals the alternative, relational style. But not so long ago, during Europe's Middle Ages, the relational approach was also common. Individuals were not recognised as separate entities, as we see each other today, but were instead indivisible from the world (1999: 88). The Nayaka and the Normans have more in common than a neo-evolutionist interested in the difference between hunting bands and military states would ever believe possible.

An archaeological expression of this difference can be found in Matthew Johnson's (1993: 349) study of the medieval open hall (Figure 6.3). The arrangement of rooms, he argues, could be related

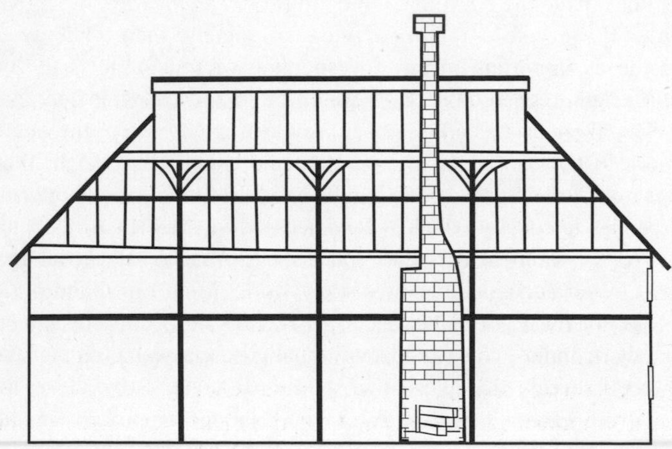

FIGURE 6.3 The changing use of space. The internal layout of a medieval open-hall (upper) and post-medieval lobby-entry house (lower). Access and privacy are very differently conceived (after Johnson 1993: figure 7.3)

to a conception of the dispersed self, an example of the way that people did not see themselves as separate individuals but rather as related. The hall is a symbolic frame with all the various roles – landlord, servant, peasant head of household, lord – all on view in face-to-face interaction. What happens with the major changes in society that led to the rise of capitalism was that this face-to-face community became partitioned. The conceptual space of the hall was physically divided, as alterations to so many buildings in England in the post-medieval period show. Everyday life now shifted to a recognition of the indivisible, the individual caught up in social relations based on class. When a peasant now visited his landlord at home he saw and experienced an alien spatial and symbolic system. Previously he was included, albeit with demarcations based on status within a single body of space. The performance and participation in lives changed fundamentally from a web of relatedness to the net of modernity.

Social space and gender

Space is about power. As such it provides a framework for the discussion of gender, the social construction of difference between men and women. Roberta Gilchrist's study (1993) of English nunneries shows how these differences can be approached by analysing the physical movements of religious men and women through the spaces they built, lived in and modified with time. She found that the architectural layout of male and female monasteries was very different. In the nunneries the most restricted and difficult areas to reach were the dormitories, while in the monasteries it was the chapter house and sacristy, which were easily accessible in the nunneries. Furthermore nunneries were located in liminal surroundings, at the threshold of changes in either the natural landscape or the townscape. This contrasted with male houses, and a further distinction lay in the fact that nunneries rarely altered the landscapes around them, unlike their male counterparts which relied on self-sufficiency in agricultural produce. As a result nunneries resembled more closely the houses of the gentry, which, Gilchrist suggests, was the social group that fostered and supported them. They were founded to interact closely with the local community. Consequently their support network lay in that direction rather than in self-sufficiency. Her archaeological study led her to conclude that:

> If nunneries looked different from monasteries, were placed in different landscape situations, and were never endowed in order to achieve self-sufficiency, this is because medieval patrons had a different purpose in mind for medieval religious women.
>
> Gilchirst (1993: 190)

Monastic architecture was therefore critical in the social construction of the gender difference between religious men and women – a good example of material culture being active in social relations rather than simply reflecting them.

Summary

Time and space are the framework for archaeological analysis and interpretation. In this chapter I have looked at the issue of temporality and how that helps us to understand the construction and use of landscapes and sites. I have returned to the issue of obtaining a representative sample. We have seen that space solves that old problem of not knowing what you are going to find before fieldwork starts. We have a research strategy that samples space for populations of artefacts, sites and landscapes, and these are built up into regions and world systems. Each level has a temporal as well as a spatial dimension, not just in terms of how long a village was inhabited or over what distances a lead ingot was traded, but rather in terms of the rhythms and repetition of human action as people went about constructing their lives.

Understanding how time and space are so intimately connected with the construction of social life opens up a huge field of exploration with archaeological data. The built environment with its constraints and possibilities can be reconstructed from plans and peopled with objects. The analysis of how space is sectored and related to the body as a source of interpretation and authority provides a most potent means of extending the archaeological imagination in new directions. It will undoubtedly impact on our next topic, the study of change.

Chapter 7

Change and stasis

At the heart of archaeological investigations lie questions about change. These are the big 'why' questions where we try to understand the move to agriculture or the factors behind the spread of people to the New World 15,000 years ago. 'Why' questions can also be much smaller in scope. They may deal with shifts in the animals hunted at a site, the transformation from mud-brick to stone architecture or from circular to rectangular houses, changes in burial customs or the appearance of new styles in art or coinage.

But change is only one side of the coin. On the reverse is stasis. When the coin is flipped it is this side that dominates the archaeological record. For long periods of time on either a prehistoric or historic timescale nothing much seems to have happened. Pottery styles remained constant. The dead were sent to meet their ancestors in much the same way. Crops were harvested and stone chipped in repetitive fashion, often for millennia on end. The question 'why no agriculture?' in a continent such as Australia becomes as interesting as investigating the origins of rice cultivation in China.

The contrast to our experience of constant technological and social change could not be more marked. Both change and stasis therefore need explaining. The notion we have that change is the only constant in our lives needs examining. Change is not an essence of the past. But of course it did happen.

Questions about change

In earlier chapters I explored issues of variability in human behaviours and the archaeological record using the dimensions of time and space. This framework is also important when asking questions about change. Change is a very scalar problem for archaeologists. We need to understand exactly how and where we are pitching our question in order to frame an appropriate explanation.

I will tackle this scalar problem by first looking at six big questions that deal with origins. Then I will move down the scale to less grand questions about why aspects of societies vary. I will examine what we mean by change and ask if we can recognise it as distinct from variation. This will involve considering complexity as a basic issue alongside scales of analysis.

Origins and the big six questions

These are questions that have focused a great deal of archaeological enquiry. Very often they run on a 20-year cycle, which is about the gestation time for large field projects to be written up. The origins cycle runs like this. An international conference is called to tackle an issue of global interest, such as the origins of agriculture (Ucko and Dimbleby 1969), urbanism (Ucko, Tringham, and Dimbleby 1972) or modern humans (Mellars and Stringer 1989). Delegates arrive with their fresh data and carefully prepared syntheses. New models and theories are put forward. The raft of information is assimilated. A large proceedings volume emerges and many spin-off volumes then follow as the issues raised are amended, tested in the field and refined by further analysis. Then, after a few years, the excitement cools. Work still continues but not with the headline-grabbing intensity of before. Interest in the question continues to quietly bubble away until the cycle hits its second decade. Another international conference is called and the pan boils over once more.

I identify five big questions that follow this cycle:

- Origins of hominids.
- Origins of modern humans.
- Origins of agriculture and domestic animals.
- Origins of urbanism and civilisation.
- Origins of modernity.

The first four questions have been there since the birth of archaeology. The fifth is evidence of archaeology's new place in the historical sciences. They are now all investigated by interdisciplinary teams. They subsume many themes, such as complexity, specialisation, power and intensification. Their implications are global. They are often referred to as revolutions, most famously by Childe (1951) with his Neolithic and Urban revolutions, the two great stages in human cultural evolution before the Industrial Revolution of the eighteenth century.

To this quintet I would add a sixth big, how and why question:

- Global colonisation by the human species.

This question has origins implications about both the earliest colonisation of habitats, continents and islands as well as their rediscovery as part of mercantile capitalism which gave us, among other things, the triangular slave trade. In other words this question covers all the other five questions under its umbrella. As we shall see below, unravelling the process of global colonisation has in fact been one of archaeology's great, but rather unsung, discoveries.

There are of course other big questions, such as origins of feudalism, or the rise and spread of world religions. Language and writing have been treated as origin questions, as have the graphic arts and key aspects of technology such as shipping, wheeled transport and metallurgy.

Much of this only recognises that we can investigate the origins of anything. But the big six are widely recognised as fundamental to archaeological endeavour. They also illustrate very well the type of explanation that archaeologists favour. I will return later to the issue of whether such questions have now served their usefulness.

Origins of hominids

This is a question about bodies and brains. We know from genetic evidence that the hominids, which include ourselves and all our fossil ancestors, split from our closest relative the chimpanzee between five and six million years ago. The reasons for this split need explaining, as does the subsequent path taken by hominid evolution. This led towards upright walking, bipedalism, and a greatly enlarged brain, known as encephalisation.

Fossil evidence from Southern and East Africa shows that by two-and-a-half million years ago some hominids had developed full bipedalism, whereas others still retained features such as long, curled fingers and toes, indicating a semi-arboreal adaptation. Moreover, hominid brain size was by this time almost double that found in chimpanzees. Such encephalisation is unique to the hominids, where brain size far exceeds what is expected in a primate of our size. This was a costly process because brains are very expensive tissues to maintain (Aiello and Wheeler 1995). Our big brains account for only about 2 per cent of our weight but use up nearly 20 per cent of all the energy we consume. They require high-quality foods.

In hominid evolution you don't get something from nothing. A balance had to be struck between the relative size of our key organs – brain, heart, kidney, liver and stomach. The evolutionary trade-off was an expanding brain at the expense of a shrinking stomach. Less gut means less food processing, which means higher-quality foods – feedback feeding on itself (Figure 7.1).

About two-and-a-half million years ago we also find the first stone tools. These simple hammers, choppers and sharp flakes would have assisted the recovery of meat and marrow from animals either brought down or scavenged. Between two and one-and-a-half million years ago we find the first hominids outside sub-Saharan Africa in the Near East and Java.

So what needs explaining are the Darwinian selection pressures (Chapter 2) for such an expensive tissue as the brain and such an odd form of primate locomotion as upright walking. Even so, the advantages can still seem obscure. Kurt Vonnegut, for example, in his novel *Galápagos*, voiced his suspicions:

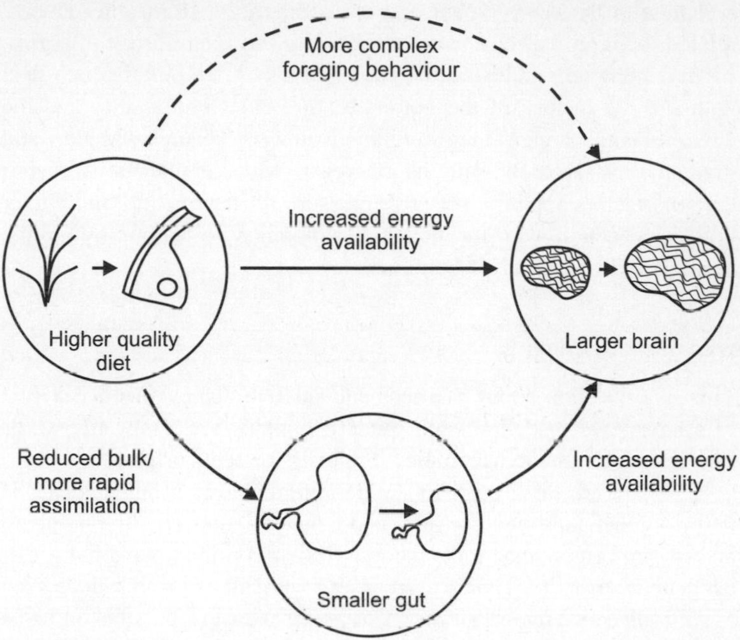

FIGURE 7.1 A causal feedback-loop between several variables to explain why we evolved larger brains (after Aiello and Wheeler 1995)

> When I was alive, I often received advice from my own big brain which, in terms of my own survival, or the survival of the human race, for that matter, can be charitably described as questionable. Example: It had me join the United States Marines and go fight in Vietnam.
>
> Thanks a lot, big brain.
>
> Vonnegut (1987: 32)

Bigger brains needed very strong selection indeed, not only because of the extra feeding costs but also because of the longer time that those bigger-brained children, born ever more helpless, needed parenting. Therefore there was unlikely to have been a single cause such as a change in the environment or even competition from other closely related hominid species who shared the savannah-forest margins. Instead, complex, multi-faceted explanations are favoured which deal with the life history of the hominids, the wider community and the environmental changes they were involved with. Change was slow and gradual, measured in millions of years. Most explanations favour external factors applying selective pressure for new bodies and bigger brains. Selection was for increased tolerance to variability in the biology and behaviour of hominids.

Origins of modern humans

This is a question about essences and relative achievement. But first of all we have to define what modern humans are. Only afterwards can we search the archaeological archives for their origins.

There are three parts to the definition. Modern humans can be defined genetically, anatomically and behaviourally. The first points to an African origin since today people in that continent have the greatest genetic diversity. This is used as an argument of origins since such genetic diversity requires time. The point of origin is believed to be between 250,000 and 300,000 years ago. The anatomical evidence also points to Africa as the continent of origin. To date the oldest modern-looking skulls come from East Africa and are some 150,000 years old. The behavioural evidence is less clear cut. It forms a checklist of traits that are found scattered across Africa from 300,000 years ago. These include changes in technology and the use of pigments, exotic stones, camp sites and marine resources. A similar scatter can be found in parts of the Old World, especially in the best researched continent, Europe.

However, around 60,000 years ago these disparate elements are combined in some places into a distinctive package that has been called the human revolution (Mellars and Stringer 1989). The pace of stylistic change accelerates and fragmentation occurs between regions. Figurative art and novel forms of northern architecture are present after 40,000 years ago, while richly appointed burials are found after 30,000 years ago. Moreover, people are now found for the first time in Australia, 60,000 years ago, and the Americas, at least by 15,000 years ago and possibly earlier.

These achievements may seem rather strung out in time. Revolution hardly seems the right word for something that takes place over 30,000 years. But that has to be put into the context of six million years of hominid evolution since we split from the chimps. On this timescale change was rapid and dramatic.

The origin of modern humans also involves the fate of other hominid species, most famously the Neanderthals. These people with their distinctive faces and bodies well suited to northern climates lived in Europe and the Middle East. Their fate has long interested archaeologists. Were they replaced by incoming modern humans, *Homo sapiens*, or did they evolve into them? The genetic and anatomical evidence is overwhelming that *Homo sapiens* replaced them. But the behavioural evidence points to at least 10,000 years of coexistence in parts of Europe. The last Neanderthals are found in southern Spain some 27,000 years ago. This was long after modern humans were widespread throughout northern Europe. The demise of the Neanderthals must now be seen as protracted and complex rather than short and simple.

Change in this question is usually tackled with evolutionary models. However, historical contingency is increasingly coming to play a part in the explanations put forward precisely because the triumvirate of genetics, anatomy and behaviour does not mesh chronologically. One hundred thousand years ago some people looked like you and me. Their genes had a modern pattern, like yours and mine, and yet they acted according to a much older script. Archaeology rather than genetics or anatomy holds the key to understanding our recent origins.

Origins of agriculture and domestic animals

This is a question about manipulation, control and progress. Famously termed by Childe (1935) the Neolithic Revolution, the package of changes in subsistence, settled villages and population numbers has been taken as a turning point in human prehistory. Traditionally the markers come as much from the widespread use of pottery, polished stone, large funerary monuments and increasingly elaborate settlements as they do from the appearance of domestic animals and cultivated crops. A contrast is often drawn with the preceding mobile hunters and gatherers. For example, early Neolithic villages in the Near East and southeastern Europe often form impressive tells or mounds, as at Karanovo in Bulgaria, and bear witness to intensive and repeated use of locations over many millennia.

In the face of these archaeological data the case for progress seemed clear cut. Neolithic peoples in the Old World manipulated the same domesticated cattle, sheep, goats, pigs and dogs, and cultivated wheat and barley, all of which formed the basis for contemporary civilisation. They lived in villages which would become towns. They had religious monuments. They represented a break with the past of the hunters and gatherers, described in the nineteenth century schemes of social progress as the stage of savagery.

The key point about the Neolithic Revolution is the control of subsistence production and the possibility of a reliable surplus that this revolution ushered in. Human affairs appeared to shift from consuming to producing. Childe's legacy has been to make many archaeologists look no further back in time for our origins than about 10,000 years ago, when the first evidence for domestic cereals and sheep are found in the Near East.

Hence those few relevant millennia were diligently searched for an explanation (see Redman 1978). Explanations have included climatic change forcing the wild ancestors of animals, cereal grasses and humans together. Differences between geographical regions have also been put forward, with people in the marginal zones intensifying production to keep up in the post-glacial world. The importance of identifying the hearth for domestication, either the fertile crescent of the Near East or the smaller Levantine corridor (Bar-Yosef 1998) has been important in evaluating such models.

The result has been to reverse the notion of progress. The farmers were in fact the failures among the hunters and gatherers. The latter can also exhibit the trappings of agriculturalists, such as cemeteries, villages and trade routes, while still hunting deer and gathering shellfish. Moreover, we need to break the Near Eastern bias and remember that the Neolithic Revolution occurred independently in China (rice and water buffalo), Sub-Saharan Africa (sorghum and cattle) and Mesoamerica (maize and turkeys). Indeed, the process of domestication has occurred in many places and at many times. Sometimes it occurred in an agricultural setting, sometimes not. Examples include dogs in Palaeolithic Europe, cats in Egypt, llamas in Peru, dingoes in Australia, elephants in India, dogs again in prehistoric North America and musk-oxen in Alaska during the 1960s.

So it is not a simple case of saying that GM foods originated in the Neolithic. Manipulation by hunters through selective breeding eventually produced 57+ varieties of dog from their wild counterparts. However, the unexpected effects of comparable selection on the productivity of key grass crops such as wheat, rice, finger millet and maize were astonishing. Thin little grasses with tiny seeds evolved into kernels of concentrated energy and power.

Change in this third question has often been put down to a prime mover where one factor is singled out as the catalyst for change. Prime movers that have been put forward over the years include population pressure, climate change and propinquity between grasses and humans. But the convergence to agriculture was global, which casts doubt on any simple prime mover. A co-evolutionary approach as explored by Rindos (1989) directly tackles the convergence. He reminds us that evolution works through undirected variation and that human innovations facilitate rather than cause evolution. Bigger ears of wheat provide the means but not the explanation for change.

Alternatively, the move to new forms of production is attributed to changes in the social requirements of production (Bender 1978). Intensification, which in this instance involved selective manipulation of the resources themselves, rather than just working harder or developing other mechanisms such as storage, has always been a response available to hunters and gatherers. Indeed, archaeological evidence for hunter-gatherer intensification is now commonplace in continents, such as Australia (Lourandos 1997), where what we know as farming was introduced by Europeans. The realisation that the Neolithic is not all that Childe cracked it up to be means that to understand the process we must look again at the historical circumstances of those societies that took up the option. It also requires that we examine those areas, such as Australia, which at the time of European contact did not have pyramids poking out of the Queensland rainforest, in order to achieve a satisfactory explanation.

Origins of urbanism and the state

This is a question about our civilised origins – not only about how technologically smart we became but how some centres of power came to dominate. This has been a popular question with colonial archaeologies (Box 1) seeking authority from the past for action in the present (Andrén 1998). Now that an agricultural surplus was possible, what could be done with it? Once again Childe's view has been very influential: turn the surplus into people and then organise them through a cadre of specialists (priests, kings, soldiers, bureaucrats).

The archaeological archives could once again be examined by means of a ten-point checklist (Box 18) to discover when society had moved from the Neolithic stage, barbarism according to the nineteenth-

Box 18: Checklist of traits for Childe's urban revolution

1. *Size*: an increase in settlement size towards urban proportions.
2. *Surplus*: the centralised accumulation of capital resulting from the imposition of tribute or taxation.
3. *Monumental public works.*
4. The invention of *writing*.
5. Elaboration of the exact and predictive *sciences*.
6. The appearance and growth of long-distance *trade in luxuries*.
7. The emergence of a *class-stratified society* based on the unequal distribution of social surplus.
8. *Composition and function of an urban centre*: freeing part of the population from subsistence tasks for full-time craft specialisation.
9. *State Organisation* based on residence rather than on kinship and involving territorial definition.
10. The appearance of *naturalistic art*.

century viewpoint, to full civilisation. Childe summed it all up very succinctly as a technological package:

> Metallurgy, the wheel, the ox-cart, the pack-ass, and the sailing ship provided the foundations for a new economic organisation.
>
> Childe (1942: 97)

More recently this has been described by Andrew Sherratt (1997) as the secondary-products revolution. Once again this applies to the Near Eastern domesticates. Secondary products include milk, animal traction and an emphasis on wool for clothing. Their appearance points to a further intensification in the agricultural process. Metals were important in the Old World but apart from copper and gold supremely unimportant in the New, where iron and bronze metallurgy were unknown.

Between 3500 and 1500 BC a combination of urbanism, writing and specialisation produced state-level societies in the Near East, Egypt, the Indus Valley and China between the Yellow and Yangtze rivers. In Mesoamerica a similar combination was in place 2000 years ago with the widespread influence of the Mayans, until their civilisation collapsed between AD 771 and 830. John Baines and Norman Yoffee have succinctly identified the common link between these geographically separate developments:

> The formation and maintenance of elites, and then of elites within elites, lie at the heart of civilisations: inequality is fundamental.
>
> Baines and Yoffee (1998: 234)

These primary states were followed by many other civilisations, for example the Inca of South America, Great Zimbabwe in southern Africa and the Minoans and Mycenaeans of Greece. The last appear to be locked into a world system relationship (Chapter 6) with the civilisations of the Near East, just as the complex societies of southwestern North America and the Mississippi Valley were with Mesoamerica.

Recasting the question as to the origins of the state, rather than of civilisation, has not been without its difficulties. Agreement over how to define the state also remains elusive (Feinman and Marcus 1998). We all know it when we see it in the form of the Mexican city of Teotihuacan, which housed 200,000 people. But what about less-obvious examples such as the complex Hawaiian chiefdoms or the pueblos in Chaco Canyon, New Mexico? Should they also qualify? Opinions differ. One feature of explaining the state is that environmental factors are accorded less importance in accounting for origins, probably because of these fuzzy definitions, and rather more when the issue of their collapse is examined.

Change in this origins question still involves a debate between a generalising approach, the comparative study of the state and historical specificity. For example, what particular features led to elite control? To what extent was the exercise of power dependent upon local circumstances, such as the availability of copper sources or trade routes to control and exploit? The role of trade, particularly the circulation of prestige goods, has been presented as crucial in setting in motion the cycles of production and social reproduction typical of these state systems (Friedman 1994). Control of production through irrigation was important in the Mesopotamian states, but elaborate and extensive water management in Papua New Guinea led only to tribes without chiefs.

The key, as Baines and Yoffee (1998) argue, is that the elites in archaic states and civilisations did not so much create the wealth that archaeologists dig up by the dumpster-load but transformed the meaning of that wealth. This was the role of those priest kings and other potentates who controlled symbolic resources. They, and only they, gave those obsidian mirrors, gold sarcophogi and elephant ivory footstools value and meaning. Elites were only interested in material redistribution in so far as it kept them in power. They were not bound by the cultural requirements of the welfare state. High culture, defined as 'the production and consumption of aesthetic items under the control, and for the benefit, of the inner elite of a civilisation, including the ruler and gods' (Baines and Yoffee 1998: 235), was the focus for the exploitation of wealth by the social order to establish the legitimacy of that order.

Origins of modernity

This is a question about attitude. The investigation of modernity, the transformation of the world under industrialisation, nationalism and capitalism, has been dominated by historians and social scientists and the expressive powers of authors and artists – modern times, modern art and a material girl (Box 19).

At its heart lies the idea of separation. Modernity implies, as Johnathan Friedman writes (1994: 143), the separation of the symbol from what it refers to. A point of origin is therefore traced to the seventeenth-century philosopher René Descartes (see Chapter 5) and his classic 'Cartesian' dualisms between mind and body, nature and culture, subject and object and the individual and society.

Box 19: What is meant by modernity
(after Friedman 1994: 214)

Modernity is a term of identity. It is used to characterise something essential in our own society and so refers to a particular historical period. The term it is usually contrasted with is *tradition*.

This separation led to immense gains in analytical and theoretical science, engineering and medicine. The approach came to dominate all aspects of human knowledge, including the study of the remote past. Unsurprisingly the literature on the origins of modernity is vast.

For our basic purposes it is permissible to cut to the chase by citing five propositions that have been applied to other, non-Western cultures, and their view of their own past (Box 20). These propositions, most closely followed in archaeology by the culture history and processual schools (Chapter 2), illustrate our traditionally close relationship to modernist approaches.

That having been said, modernity may not be unique to the European Industrial Revolution which began in the eighteenth century. Greece in the fourth and fifth centuries BC had comparable tendencies to analytical separation. However, this was not supported by industrialisation and the alienation and commodification it produced between people involved in the work process (Friedman 1994: 229).

Box 20: Five propositions about the world that a modernist view of knowledge would make
(after Friedman 1994: 137 – I have adapted them to refer to the study of the past.)

1 There is only one 'true' version of the past.

2 The past consists of an arbitrarily chosen segment of a temporal continuum which ends with the present moment.

3 The structure attributed to the past is the product of a specific kind of research carried out by those competent in the field, i.e. archaeologists.

4 The structure of the past is therefore objective, which corresponds to proposition 1. That is, there is only one, not many pasts.

5 All other structures or interpretations attributed to the past are, by implication, ideological in the sense that they are misrepresentations. This allows anthropologists to dismiss the 'natives' point of view' as only a mere folk model, a common-sense explanation. It is never of any scientific value as defined in terms of the above approaches by the competent practitioners mentioned in proposition 3. Archaeologists can be equally contemptuous of New Age interpretations of stone circles and the like.

Charles Orser (1999) has referred to our study of the industrial period as modern-world archaeology. I have previously outlined the four aspects that make it a distinct enterprise (Box 2). But why should archaeologists be studying the past 300 years at all? Wouldn't it be sensible to leave it to the historians and their mountain of written records?

A point that Sarah Tarlow (1999: 265) makes is that the transition from the medieval to the modern led to the commodification of peoples and things. Since the basics of archaeology are concerned with objects, we should be well placed to comment on the changes. However, we first have to convince historians, who seriously outnumber archaeologists working on this period, that favouring the text over the object to explain the origins of modernity may be unjustified.

Matthew Johnson, for one, makes the telling point that:

> Most agree that [modernity] has something to do with material things, how they are produced and consumed and the social and economic values people place upon them; and that the changing relationship between things, values and people has a lot to do with the origins of the modern way of life.
>
> Johnson (1993: 328–9)

We ignore objects and their transformation into commodities at our peril. Furthermore, by coming late to the game modern-world archaeology might be able to sidestep some of the origins pitfalls that have previously ensnared archaeologists. Certainly there is a good deal of debate about what to call and how to define, chronologically, the period. More importantly, modern-world archaeologists have the opportunity to assess change in a more reflexive manner than their colleagues studying the rise of Hittite civilisation. The familiar past of the past 300 years is just that and it is through objects, those broken willow-pattern plates, street plans and glass bottles, that we can begin the process of de familiarising what we think is the known past (West 1999: 1). As Susie West makes clear, this is a very different use of material culture than in prehistory, where the object of the exercise is to make the totally unknown familiar. In modern-world archaeology those objects challenge the orthodoxy. They won't do away with written records, eye-witness accounts or the works of Charles Dickens. We have to make the two work together to provide that rich interface between the 'world as lived in' and the 'world as thought' that the amalgamation of text and object can achieve.

A further advantage that modern-world archaeologists have in their study of the origins of modernity lies in their awareness of essences. The push to modernity was first accounted for in a series of important books and papers by James Deetz (1977) and Henry Glassie (1975) as a process of 'Georganization' from 1600 to 1800. The changes could be traced in the way food was prepared – individual portions rather than helpings from the common pot – and architecture, where individualism was expressed through new levels of privacy, as shown by the partitioning of rooms. Such Georgian principles help to define the trends but also encourage an essential way of thinking. Something either is or is not Georgian and hence is on the way to or has already arrived at modernity. The state of mind is stressed and curiously that 'world as lived in' quality that comes from objects is lost. The truth is we can never 'see' Georganization, just as we cannot 'see' either the Neolithic Revolution or the transition to modern humans. As Johnson remarks (1993: 345), concentrating on the rise of institutions or the desired qualities of social life can miss the point. Too much emphasis on origins takes our eye away from the changing matrices of social relations that created such institutions and qualities. Modernity and capitalism were more about constantly becoming than they were about origins with a discernible transition and a well-established start date.

Global colonisation by the human species

My final big question has received nothing like the systematic attention of the other five. Yet by asking how and why we became not only a global species, unique among mammals, but at the same time the sole extant hominid allows us to put them in perspective (Gamble 1993).

As the world was rediscovered by explorers such as Columbus and Cook, so they found that it had already been peopled. Modernity was part of the process of global rediscovery. The great discovery of prehistoric archaeology has been to show that this global peopling was a recent event in our hominid history and that outside the Old World it was entirely achieved by ourselves, *Homo sapiens*. We know that for most of our five million years there have been at any one time, and often in the same region, at least two hominid species, and in well-researched periods several more. This all ended about 25,000 years ago as the last Neanderthals in Europe and *Homo erectus* in Southeast Asia became extinct. Over only the past 60,000 years colonisation took place for the first time in Australia and the Pacific, Siberia and the Americas. It, therefore, took *Homo sapiens* roughly 1 per cent of hominid evolution to colonise 75 per cent of the

Earth – not much more time than the origins of crop agriculture or urban civilisations.

The timing strongly suggests that prime-mover explanations such as population pressure, climatic change or lucky breaks in technology such as inventing boats will not adequately account for the process. They may contribute to an understanding of how colonisation took place but not fully explain why it occurred. As Rindos pointed out for agriculture, human innovations facilitated, but did not cause, evolution.

Global colonisation is not a quest for the oldest North American or the first Australian. Rather it uses the timing and the different histories involved in the process to understand humans as colonisers. Therefore, the extent to which intensification, social as well as economic, occurred among colonising societies is very relevant. There would have been no global colonisation without domestication, the deep Pacific shows that. But neither would there have been a start to the process if mobile peoples had not intensified their own production because of revised social demands. The question then becomes one of understanding at all times and places why society changed and how the demands placed on production, distribution and consumption were met. There seems to be some similarity between the processes that put a person on Easter Island and a pyramid at Giza.

For my money, global colonisation, that great prehistoric achievement, was an unintended consequence of processes that also led, as it happened, to agriculture and the urban state. It may have involved purpose among individuals but it was never a goal. By contrast, the historical migrations that had such stated goals all occurred in the context of a full world and state power.

The problem with origins research

Origins research can be great fun. There is nothing quite like excavating the oldest goat. Similarly, the thrill of finding London's oldest banana, *c.*1560 AD dug up in 1999, also unzips a New-World view. Origins strikes a chord with the public. And remember, nobody who has found a fossil skull, the older the better, has ever damaged their career prospects. But is origins research really a worthwhile archaeological pursuit?

No – is the short answer. I have already referred to the essentialist nature of such research where definitions and checklists (e.g. Box 18) dominate the process. Origins research is like misusing an old-fashioned hearing trumpet. You place the pointed end on the thing you want to hear about – e.g. language, writing, graphic arts, agriculture – and listen for an explanation at the open end where the noise distortion is greatest. As Alexandra Alexandri (1995: 59) concludes, all this does is to trace the beginning of familiar concepts, echoes of the present in the past.

This is clearly unsatisfactory. We are confusing chronology with explanation, description with understanding. We need to attend to more voices than just that of origins research, where, at its worst, the hunt for the oldest comes to dominate the conversation. Instead, as discussed below, we need to broaden explanation to consider that lifestyles have a 'becoming' (i.e. are constantly originating) rather than an origin in time and space. Such a becoming is a continuous process of creativity, not something that is fixed in time, pinned like a butterfly in a case or lying like a banana skin on the floor.

Scale and changes to the system

While origins research needs to carry a health warning – 'The Chief Archaeologist advises: Too many "firsts" can lead to dialogues with the deaf' – there is no escaping the narrative focus it continues to provide, equivalent in other disciplines to the search for cold fusion, Fermat's last theorem or a cure for the common cold.

I have briefly sketched our current approaches to origins questions because if we lift the lid on such research we find that underneath the more familiar scales of change are addressed. These scales involve all the entities and the temporal and spatial scales discussed in Chapters 3 and 6. Now this was one of the appeals of the systems approach whereby change was traced in the component subsystems of an entire socio-cultural adaptation (Figure 2.2). Hence at the levels of intra-site, site and region a trajectory of change can be plotted for the subsistence, trade, settlement, population, craft specialisation, and symbolic and religious subsystems. The extent to which these interlocked is then examined. It is understanding how change arose in these subsystems that has led to the many archaeologies briefly mentioned in Chapters 1 and 2, for example settlement, economic, cognitive, demographic and environmental archaeology.

In the same way, artefact types and their attributes can be examined as they change through time and across space. Explanation is then often sought in terms of new functions or changes in ideology. Hodder's (1982: 73) study of calabashes in East Africa concludes that these important daily objects are integral to the social relations between young men and women and older men. As the economic and social fortunes of the former have fluctuated, this is expressed through changes in design. Material symbols are used to disrupt the dominant social order.

Be local, think global

Representations of time are important in the process of explanation. Archaeology has a vertical vision, thanks to stratigraphy, as well as a linear notion of time. The sections we dig through a cave, a Bronze Age tell or a medieval town demand an explanation, even if nothing seems to change. The vertical strongly emphasises the narrative structure of the way we describe and explain the past. The temporal segments we observe are also of variable length, and obtaining a continuous sequence is rather like building up a tree-ring chronology from many different trees. If change occurs in our trench, then we build explanations for the change in relation to changes in other trenches nearby and further afield.

All of this is part of the professional use of our archaeological imagination. The basic point to grasp is that explaining the structure of archaeological archives in time and space will always be a contest between the local and global. For example, you excavate the floorplan of a seventeenth-century tenement in Southampton. What you are interested in are data that shed light on the rise of mercantile capitalism. The link may seem tenuous while you empty the contents of a rubbish pit.

As a result it is always tempting to explain the local by the local, but this must be resisted, or at least tested (Wobst 1978). Explaining change in the components of a system or in the segment available in a survey or excavation may seem tempting in terms of immediate conditions. The explanation would sound like this: 'they selected those stone tools because they needed to cut up that rhino whose bones they lie beside', or, 'the shift in the later part of the tell sequence to fully threshed, clean grain rather than the earlier mixed grain and weed assemblage points to local changes in consumption, storage and field management and may correlate with a few larger structures, i.e. elites taking charge, which appear elsewhere on site'.

No doubt in many cases such explanations are basically correct. But archaeology, because it is about objects, simultaneously samples different spatial and temporal scales. Time and again we see how variation is caused by regional as much as a local factors.

When change is not change but variation

Therefore the really big question is when is it possible to talk of change rather than just document variation? That is another appeal of the big five questions. They deal with qualitative and quantitative differences in organisation, lifestyle, environmental impact, human biology, geographical expansion and inter-connectedness that just can't be ignored.

But there are many smaller changes – a new pot style, a shift from a dispersed to a nucleated settlement pattern, the repositioning of chimneys from the centre to one or both ends of rural cottages – that are of a lesser scale but also need explaining. Most of these are in effect dealing with variation.

For change to occur we need to identify two factors. Obviously there is a chronological element. Secondly, since all individuals and indeed cultures exhibit variation (see Figure 3.3, polythetic sets) we need to have a view on the limits to variation. Change happens when those limits are exceeded, as I show below for evolutionary landscapes. But change is neither a property nor an essence of the entities we study. Variation and stasis, on the other hand, most certainly are.

I define change as organisation *based on novel* social premises. By contrast variation is the accommodation of novel conditions *within* existing social premises. If the Neolithic Revolution has validity as one of the hinges in human history, then it is because society moved to new forms of appropriation and not because humans evolved a taste for mutton. Variation always exists. Change requires a new structure.

Now this may seem like splitting hairs. But change and variation are important, owing to the types of explanation involved. Variation, as we have seen, is well catered for by evolutionary approaches – culture history, contextual investigations and processual studies. Those moving chimneys in the cottages of rural England would, respectively, be put down to cultural transmission, cultural norms, structuring principles of identity and gender or functional requirements following a change in temperature or wind direction. The explanation of variation is based, as we have seen (Chapter 2), on differing views of culture, the nature of variation itself, human agency and the role of scientific method in a causal process. As a result there will always be few real changes to explain in archaeology but a very great deal of variation to account for.

Neo-evolutionary accounts of variety and change

Sometimes it is simplest to decide on what we don't want in order to find out what we need. Neo-evolutionary schemes are a prime example. They should not be confused with neo-Darwinian approaches.

Neo-evolution was 'new' because it revisited the nineteenth century schemes of social progress with an anthropological awareness. The ladder of savagery, barbarism and civilisation that Morgan proposed in 1877, and which Childe was still using in 1951, was then replaced by the scheme of band, tribe chief and state (Service 1962; Sahlins 1963; Fried 1967). This influential framework, shown in Box 21, has provided archaeologists with ethnographic descriptions to work towards in their studies of function and change. The framework proved very useful as a systems approach to social change.

But the categories are disputed. Chiefdoms, for example, are classed as redistributive societies, although redistribution is found in many other societies on the scale of band to state societies. Ethnographically, chiefdoms encompass a great range, so much so that the difference between the ranking and stratification of social roles and positions is not always clear. Neither have neo-evolutionists ever

Box 21: A typology of societies favoured by neo-evolutionists (after Earle 1994)

<table>
<tr><th>Childe</th><th>Service</th><th>Sahlins</th><th>Fried</th></tr>
<tr><td>Civilisation</td><td>State</td><td>State</td><td>State</td></tr>
<tr><td rowspan="2">Civilisation</td><td rowspan="2">Chiefdom</td><td>Complex</td><td>Stratified society</td></tr>
<tr><td>Simple</td><td rowspan="2">Ranked society</td></tr>
<tr><td>Farmers (barbarism)</td><td>Tribe</td><td>Big man</td></tr>
<tr><td>Hunter/gatherers (savagery)</td><td>Band</td><td>Head man</td><td>Egalitarian</td></tr>
</table>

been very clear about the division between 'simple' chiefdoms and tribal societies led by charismatic 'big men', a status commonly observed in Papua New Guinea, where established political rulers are very rare. The fuzziness is also apparent at the band level where many hunter-gatherer societies exist that are certainly not egalitarian. Hence the further division by some into simple and complex hunters.

Neo-evolution provides an excellent example of a top-down approach (Chapter 4) to the classification and study of society. Band society is an institution created by anthropologists so that they can go about their business of revealing society (Gamble 1999). The individual quickly vanishes, like a government statistic.

Complexity

While archaeologists no longer talk of progress, either to describe or to explain the changes in society they study, we often view change as a complexification.

Something becomes complex when it is made up of ever more parts. It is literally folded together in more dense and intricate ways. Complexity is another of those terms that attracts a trait list in order to compare simple and complex hunters or tribes with chiefdoms. However, what are needed are measures of complexity rather than a presence/absence list. Moreover, rather than pick complexity to pieces we need to recognise, as James McGlade and Sander van der Leeuw (1997: 14) point out, that the basic feature of any complex system is that it is more than the sum of its parts. Complexity is irreducible.

The investigation of complexity once seemed well suited to a systems approach where structural differences are dependent upon the organisation and flow of information as the diverse and disparate units, or subsystems, are integrated. Hence for Kent Flannery (1972) complexity is measured via *segregation*, or differentiation, and *centralisation*, the degree of connectedness in the system. Randall McGuire (1983) has examined the components of complexity as variables in cultural evolution. He points out that the concept often includes so much that it becomes a catch-all and explains nothing. His solution is to simplify the concept. He does this by emphasising the vertical and horizontal axes in social structure. In this way measures of complexity can be made for comparative purposes. These involve *inequality*, measured in terms of access to resources, and *heterogeneity*, which refers to the number of social persona in the system. Most importantly, we should not expect these two variables to correlate positively but instead consider them independently in the process of social change.

It is only in the very long term that we can see that change tends towards more complex systems of organisation. That of course is archaeology's unique time perspective. But once again change and complexity do not represent the old-fashioned drive to progress – savagery, barbarism and civilisation. Elsewhere, Shirley Strum and Bruno Latour (1987) reserve *complex* to describe primate societies and *complicated* to characterise the simple, repeated actions that structure much of human social life. These habitual actions organise life by making it more routine and hence both more predictable and more variable. The implication is that for social evolution to occur we first had to become more simple, not more complex.

Mechanisms and models

I can identify the big questions, although remember the health warning, and I can propose what represents change rather than variation. But I still have to discuss the mechanisms and models that account for the overwhelming evidence for stability, the rare moments of change and long-term developments in complexity among the many scales of our archaeological entities.

We fight shy of terms such as 'progress' because that is a legacy, quite rightly, that archaeologists are trying to shed. Instead, biology provides a better set of metaphors to clarify our basic principles simply because biology deals with growth in complexity in organisms, where the egg and sperm race becomes the marathon of multicellular life. Biology also deals with long-term change in the form of speciation. Biology does not explain culture, but it does, as in the case of cultural transmission (Chapter 2), provide a co-evolutionary way of thinking about the problem.

Language and development

Terry Deacon (1997) has argued that language, a trait that in anyone's book would ratchet up complexity and signify change, is best explained with such a co-evolutionary perspective. The origins of language were not just a brain thing. Neither were they just down to other biological processes such as the evolution of a suitable voice-box. They did not take place either inside or outside the brain but rather at that critical interface where biology and culture interact.

In Deacon's view how we became a symbolic species using language without even thinking about it is best explained as a developmental process. Changes in growth affected components of the biology of hominids, particularly their brains. But these took place in response to selection from the lives they led and the sort of people they were.

The result is a non-linear model of change for what we regard as a fundamental capacity of being human. There was no simple straight line from grunting to singing *Nessun dorma* at the World Cup. There was no single cause or selective pressure for change. Why should spoken language confer advantages in either scoring goals or finding a mate? While chat-up lines have no doubt improved in five million years, thanks to language, so too has our ability to head the ball into the back of the net, because at the same time we acquired a forehead.

The Neolithic Revolution and the end of biology?

My point is that much change is an unintended consequence of the complex interaction of biology and culture with which we are all involved. This produces exaptations, fit by reason of form, rather than adaptations, fit by reason of design (Gould and Vrba 1982; Gould 1991). Animal domestication was not an adaptation, the product of selection to forge a new economic niche. Animals had been part of human economies for hundreds of thousands of years. They were therefore always available for use, either in the same way as hunted resources or in new ways tethered to the homestead. They were exapted as required, rather than adapted to produce the requirement of more, predictable food.

All too often the Neolithic Revolution is presented as the slackening of biology's grip on the process of cultural change. With the first wheat the biological fetters dropped from our potential for cultural growth and diversity.

To believe this would be to return to the progressive evolution of the nineteenth century. Instead Deacon's co evolutionary interface still operates. Variation is being adapted and exapted into novel patterns. Individuals and populations are very much constrained by hereditary biology – just think of disease resistance. Change continues to occur neither inside nor outside our biology, neither inside nor outside culture, but as part of that complex interaction between the two.

The evolutionary landscape

Many of the issues concerning complexity, stasis and change were illustrated by the biologist C. H. Waddington in his brilliant book *Tools for Thought* (1977). He supplied the metaphor of the evolutionary landscape to describe biological growth as well as the constraints that account for stasis.

His landscape is a surface with valleys and hills. It exists in multi-dimensional space, since it is an attractor surface conditioned by natural selection. It therefore bends and flexes, so its topography is not constant but rather responsive to the selective pushes and pulls. Where once there was a single valley now a fork occurs. Where hills once stood we now find a flat plain.

The entity under investigation, and Waddington was very interested in the behaviour of complex systems such as the world's economy, is integral to this evolutionary landscape. Waddington conceived of it as a ball bearing rolling down the valleys and, with enough momentum, up the sides of the hills. On occasion the momentum would take it over into another valley. Moreover, which path it rolled down when it came to a fork also contributed to change. It is important to stress how integral the landscape and the entity are to each other. The one does not exist without the other and the familiar distinction between external and internal forces (see below) is not being made.

Regulating the system and organising the flow

One of Waddington's central ideas was *canalisation*. In evolutionary biology canalisation predicts that natural selection will tend to replace flexible adaptive responses to continuing environmental constraints with genetic predispositions. This is how behaviour becomes fixed. Canalisation is what makes systems stable and predictable. As Waddington put it:

> In many systems we come across, some type of stability has been an important property. A natural living system has usually acquired some degree of stability by natural selection (it would have fallen apart and died out if it wasn't stable enough); in artificial systems man commonly designs a series of checks and counter-checks to ensure stability.
>
> Waddington (1977: 104)

He then identified two of these checks: *homeostasis*, which preserves a value at a given state, and *homeorhesis*, which preserves a flow.

Archaeologists spent a great deal of time talking about the former when the systems model was popular. Hence a homeostatic feature would be an environmental hazard, periodically reducing population to a sustainable level, or a granary presided over by an elite who redistributed the surplus and so avoided civil unrest. Feedback in terms of information flows was considered important for regulation, and stability, to occur. Disruptions to the feedback mechanisms were potential explanations for change.

Homeorhesis has been considered less, although, notably, in the application of catastrophe theory to the analysis of how small variations can lead to unexpectedly dramatic change (Renfrew and Cooke 1979). Potentially homeorhesis is much more interesting, as it leads us back to the complexities of those attractor surfaces.

This is the landscape where non-linear modelling of dynamic, i.e. changing, systems comes to the fore. As put by James McGlade and Sander van der Leeuw (1997: 14), a non-linear approach rejects explanation as a linear, progressive unfolding of events. For them a non-linear approach requires a different vision of history and the causes of change. They see the process as a series of unexpected consequences, known as contingency. These arise from the interplay of processes that can be both deterministic and stochastic, randomly generated. Their bottom line is to encourage the discovery of more and more dimensions of variability in our data rather than to trim them into convenient packages to make plausible narratives.

What makes a good explanation in archaeology

Explanation is never easy. It depends upon the paradigm you follow (Chapter 2). For example, Randall McGuire (1992) discusses the advantages that would accrue from aligning archaeological explanation to Marxist theory and in particular the power of the Hegelian dialectic that this would bring. Neo-Darwinists, on the other hand, prefer the explanatory power of natural selection, while processual and interpretive approaches favour, respectively, science and social theory. The preferred option for many, and for culture historians in particular, is to arrange the entities in chronological order and simply describe what happened – to let the explanation emerge by putting their ducks in a row. If there is an explanation it is that change is somehow inherent in the system. Things will get better, or worse, with enough time.

Explanation needs to be taken seriously because simple descriptions of this nature are an insult to the richness of the archaeological record. It is only when we attempt explanation that we begin to understand how the objects of the past actually can assist us in that process of self-knowledge. Description is part of the job, but it remains half finished without an attempt at why and how.

My guidelines for a good explanation in archaeology are as follows:

- Does it abolish the inside/outside, nature/culture dualisms that I have examined in earlier chapters?
- Does it avoid circularity, as in culture explaining culture?
- Does it suggest ways to collect new data to try another draft of the same explanation?
- Does it account for more of the archaeological data than previous explanations?
- Does the narrative avoid turning the past into what we are simply familiar with in the present?
- Does it strike you as plausible and if so is the plausibility sufficient for the question being asked?
- Does the explanation spin a stronger cable, as advocated in Chapter 4?

Tacking as the explanatory exercise

The last point structures the discussion. In Chapter 4 I compared the exercise of spinning an explanatory cable (Figure 4.3) with tacking a sailboat against the wind. This is how we build explanation in archaeology, by tacking between scales of analysis, time, space and entities, and the different resolutions, for example: fine and coarse grained (Chapter 6), in our data. This is how we build up the argument: not as a house of cards but, as Alison Wylie (1993) described it, by adding another strand to the cable.

Tacking helps to reunite archaeology by making a virtue of flexibility (Figure 7.2). These are familiar tacks between opposites. What

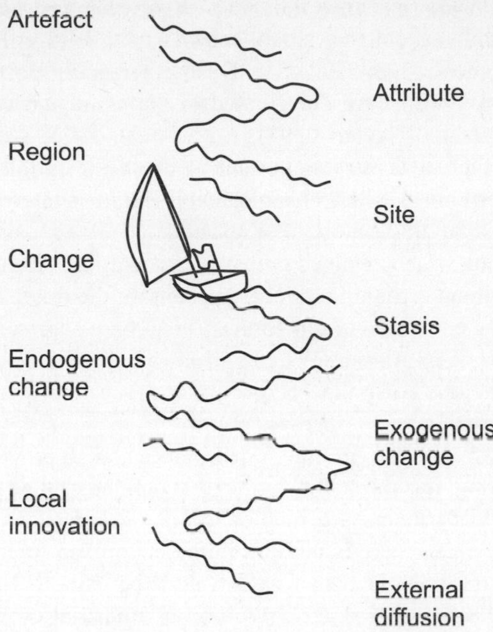

FIGURE 7.2 The archaeological strategy of tacking between different levels of data, spatial and temporal scales, and concepts

we have learnt is that rarely is it so simple. The alternative is to keep those oppositions, or dualisms, separate like port from starboard. Then explanation is a matter of coming down firmly on one side or the other, 'Steady as she goes!', 'Defend your position!', 'Prepare to repel all boarders!', even though you know you are already on the explanatory rocks.

Endogenous and exogenous change

Many archaeological explanations revolve around the importance of internal (endogenous) or external (exogenous) factors in change. The classic external factors are environmental changes. These can include long-term climatic cycles as well as short-lived events such as the eruption of Santorini, once thought to have destroyed Minoan Crete. The thousand-year cold, dry snap, known as the Younger Dryas, which marks the move from Clovis to Folsom projectile points in North America, may well have contributed to the extinction of that continent's megafauna (Haynes 1993).

However, it is very important to avoid the pitfall of environmental determinism. The archaeological literature is littered with failed explanations of this nature. For example, Childe's oasis theory of domestication which involved climatic deterioration, or Carneiro's geographical circumscription model to account for the origins of the state. Certainly the environment sets limits. Cereal-based agriculture is never going to work in Alaska. Water will always be a limiting factor in Egypt and central Australia irrespective of the scale of society, ranging from hunter-gatherer to pharonic empire.

But while the environment determines and so provides a degree of canalisation, it is the social system that dominates the process. Most of the world's habitats are neither icy nor hot deserts. Rather they present a choice. There is nothing in the oak-mixed forest and grassland habitats of England that says it *must* be exploited by a mobile foraging lifestyle, settled agriculture or an industrial economy. Social and economic change has proceeded according to the demands set on the environment by the social relations that dominate production and consumption.

Internal, endogenous change can be equally blinkered. For example, the role accorded to elites in social change has been much investigated, particularly in relation to models of how chiefdoms and early states developed. Elites manipulate exchange networks and bring benefits by organising the redistribution of agricultural surplus. The system, not to mention the people, needs them. Apparently the only fee they charge is that large palace on the hill. Contextual explanations generally prefer internal factors. Styles of monuments and artefacts change to reflect new power relationships structured by age and gender. The tests of plausibility and circularity need to be applied in both examples.

The solution is to reaffirm the mutual relationship between internal and external, dissolve the difference, as discussed in Chapter 5. The separation of organism and environment is unhelpful because it distracts explanation from considering the whole. Therefore one way to recognise a good explanation is to test it for that mutual recognition.

Diffusion and migration: innovation and autonomy

These mechanisms have, since the beginning, been the stock explanations for change and variation. The diffusion of ideas and the migration of peoples has accounted for the appearance of new pottery types, metal objects, tombs and settlements as well as major changes such as the spread of agriculture into Europe. The concepts take us back to the roots of the subject with the people–culture hypothesis (Chapter 3) and the cultural norms that express ethnicity and identity (Chapter 8).

There is no escaping the fact that both occurred. Some Saxons did migrate to England. The Romans did invade and conquer, and aspects of being Roman diffused ahead of their arrival. What is at issue is the easy option that *any* change is explained as the movement of people or of those people's ideas. Firstly, this reduces the world to producers and consumers. An active centre, as in the *ex oriente lux* models that favours the Near East (Chapter 1), always has all the best ideas and exports them to a grateful periphery. Some years ago Colin Renfrew (1973a) turned this on its head and showed, thanks to calibrated radiocarbon dating, how Bronze Age Wessex developed independently of Mycenaean Greece. Independent invention and autonomous development is as valid a starting position as diffusion and replacement.

Secondly, the issue of ethnicity has its own problems, as I will examine in the next chapter. Who exactly did the Saxons really think they were? What was involved in Romanization? New data continues to muddy such explanations. For example, the expansion of agriculture into Europe has been presented as a wave of advance from the Near East into southeastern Europe and then northwards through the fertile basins of central Europe. This process, dated by radiocarbon, took some 4000 years – equivalent to an annual advance of 1 km. While the cereals and some of the animals, cattle, sheep and goats, had to disperse from the source area, it is only recently with genetic studies that doubt has been cast on the notion that the covered wagons of the first farmers inched their way into a Europe of hunters and gatherers, brushing them aside like the British colonists did the Australian Aborigines. Genetic information on today's Europeans shows instead that they have comparatively few genes from the Near East. Proportionately, the largest set of European genes can be dated to the recolonisation, by small hunting groups, of parts of the continent following the retreat of the ice sheets 14,000 years ago – some 6000 years before the Neolithic package arrives.

Stasis and rates of change

Some of these examples raise the issue of rates of change, a return to the scalar problem mentioned at the beginning of this chapter.

In the Lower Palaeolithic, stasis ruled. The biface technology of the Acheulean appears in East Africa one-and-a-half million years ago. It remained basically unchanged for more than a million years. During this time it is found in India, western Asia and Europe. Not only was stone technology very similar over this long time frame, but other evidence about lifestyles exhibits a comparable conservative character. Geography makes little difference. The uppermost levels at Olduvai Gorge, on the equator in Tanzania, are a similar age, 600,000–400,000 years old, to well-preserved Acheulean locales in southern England: Boxgrove, Swanscombe and Hoxne. But these locales, almost 7000 km apart, have the same low-density scatter of bones and stones as well as the same types of artefact. Against such an ecological gradient today we would expect the ethnography of mobile hunters and gatherers to reveal very different campsites and technology, not to mention variation in art and ritual. During the Late Stone Age/Upper Palaeolithic, 15,000 years ago, a similar north–south comparison reveals a similar picture (Gamble and Soffer 1990; Soffer and Gamble 1990).

The Acheulean is a particularly extreme form of stasis. During its span there was significant hominid evolution involving several fossil species and a marked encephalisation. In later periods the rate of change not surprisingly speeds up. But nonetheless it is common to find cultures persisting for a thousand years in very recognisable forms. In the period 20,000 to 5,000 Robert Foley, using a worldwide sample of archaeological cultures, found that their lifespans were on average between 2000 and 5000 years. At a finer scale of analysis many of the phases within the major traditions of North American prehistory lasted for some 200 to 400 years (Fagan 1991a) or some ten to twenty generations.

These lifespans can be compared with the period divisions in the Mayan lowlands (Figure 7.3). The four broad divisions that are used to discuss the rise, and repeated collapse, of the Mayan state range between 300 and 600 years. Joyce Marcus (1998) has calculated the cyclical changes in the geographical size of the polities within this region. As you can see, there were dramatic shifts in scale within the classic divisions. The constant increase in polity size during the Early Classic can be compared with the stasis of the Postclassic until the late burst in the fifteenth century. What this figure shows is that archaeological terminology, especially that of periods, can lull you into a feeling that nothing is happening. But once you drill into the database you will find those evolutionary landscapes bending and flexing. Stasis and change are therefore relative terms that need measuring if they are to have any meaning.

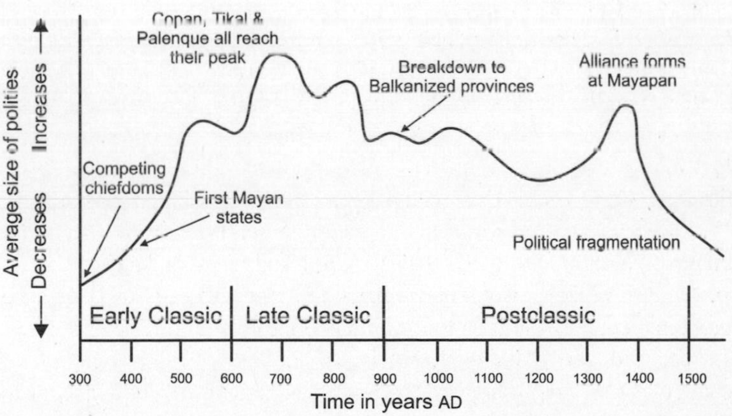

FIGURE 7.3 Political change through time. The cycles of growth and collapse of the Maya State (after Marcus 1998)

Summary

I have now examined some of the big questions that archaeologists tackle. It is currently through these that we make our major contribution to the wider world of human knowledge. There is great curiosity about our past and our origins. New fossil skulls frequently hit the headlines and the newscasts. However, on the inside pages change and stasis are what archaeologists grapple with in their explanations. The lifespan estimates I have just given above for archaeological entities serve to show that on a variety of timescales stasis dominates the picture. Canalisation, as described by Waddington, of both the organisation (homeostasis) and the flow (homeorhesis) helps us to conceptualise how this might occur. Selection for change and selection for stasis are equally powerful mechanisms. However, what these simple lifespan figures mask is the everyday role of individuals in the creation of society within the parameters set by canalisation and selection. Stasis should never be interpreted in the negative sense of stagnation or cultural passivity. Within these periods of 200 or 2 million years there were vibrant societies based on human creativity. Our task is now to explore such canalisation, where identity emerges as the last basic issue to tackle.

Chapter 8

Identity and power

What is the identity of the person who was buried in the ship at Sutton Hoo 1400 years ago? We have a name, Raedwald, but as we saw in Chapter 4 that is rather like calling the family pet Frodo. Giving a dog a name does not necessarily establish its identity. The rich grave goods are much more help, especially if you take the view that the power of that identity rests in the trappings of status, in this case kingship. The relative amounts of that power are also expressed by such measures as the craftsmanship of the objects, the distance from which they came, the content of gold and silver, their quantity and the fact that such wealth was ritually disposed of, taken out of circulation, thrown away. The body was not preserved at Sutton Hoo. But the fact that the corpse was dressed in full parade kit – sword, helmet and Sam Browne belt – has led to the automatic assumption that this was a male.

Of course this is an essentialist view of the social categories of kingship and gender identity. We expect kings to have richer burials. Otherwise they wouldn't obviously be kings. We expect fancy swords and big

gold buckles to represent powerful males. In circular fashion we expect their identities to have the properties of power and to be accompanied by objects that also have those characteristics. They attract those fine items because they are a king and because they are male. We expect them to be both magnates and magnets.

The alternative that I will explore here is that power is more subtle than that. It is more varied and resides not so much in categories as in overlapping relationships. Power is a network rather than a set of institutions. We all construct our own networks on a daily and lifetime basis. We use objects to do this and, as we saw in Chapter 4, they construct us. Therefore we, people and objects, all have power by virtue of being in these networks and not because of some inherent property in the social structure into which we are born. Such network power varies, but it is through that process of construction that our identities emerge.

Two identities

Identity and power therefore have two archaeological aspects. We can investigate them *within* archaeological data, as at Sutton Hoo. The major categories are ethnicity, class, gender, sexuality, age and the body. We must also consider the identities that are derived *from* such studies and which often lead to claims of contemporary nationalism and ethnicity based upon the authority of the past. Martin Carver puts this well when he summarises the wider debate over the Sutton Hoo finds. The Sutton Hoo cemetery lasted for less than a hundred years until continental Christianity swept over this part of eastern England and its pagan identity disappeared:

> This episode is seen as the first round in an ideological argument between the benefits of independent enterprise and those of a European union, which has exercised the British ever since.
>
> Carver (1996: 706)

The basic point about identity, power, ethnicity and nationalism is that the archaeological facts that we use to explore these concepts are some of the most theory-laden in the whole subject. The reason for this is quite simple. The past is not a neutral subject. It is not something, like trainspotting, that is only of interest to hobbyists in anoraks on station platforms. It cannot be ignored because, as the history of Europe alone has shown over the past 70 years, it will come and drive you from your home, your land and your country.

What we mean by power

I have used the term power throughout this book. It is now time to examine the concept more closely. Power is very often seen as an entity, something that some people have and others do not. Power and position are seen as going together, hand in glove. This view usually stresses the negative aspects of power as force, coercion, imposition. As a result power becomes a property and an implicit explanation of change, as in 'a shift in power'. One of its properties is asymmetry, for example in a world system (Chapter 6), where centres and peripheries have very different effects upon each other.

Power in these circumstances is often presented as a one-way relationship. Perhaps the most famous expression of this view was set down by the classical historian Thucydides. It takes the form of a lengthy debate between the mainland power of Athens and the small Cycladic island of Melos which, in 416 BC, had refused to join Athens' empire. The Athenians were very upfront about the situation:

> *Athenians*: 'For you know as well as we do, that, when we are talking about relations between human beings, the standard of justice is based on the equality of power to compel and that the strong do what they have the power to do, while the weak accept what they must.'
>
> And the reply:
>
> *Melians*: 'You should not destroy the principle of the common good, that is, that all who fall into danger should be treated with fairness and justice . . . And this is the principle which affects you too, since in your own fall you would incur the most terrible vengeance and be an example to the rest of mankind.'
>
> Sparkes (1982: 319)

The dialogue changed no one's position. After a long siege the Melians surrendered and all the men of military age were massacred.

The alternative to such a negative representation is not to deny that massacres happen but instead to see power as a process that flows and changes. It is inherent neither in artefacts nor actions but emerges from the relationships that revolve around the human and material worlds. It is therefore an epiphenomenon, the result of interaction, rather than somehow basic or natural to the system, as implied by the Athenians.

Our old friend scale is once again important. Much of social theory is concerned with tying together the micro- and macro-levels of interaction and power. To what extent do individuals have power? How do they produce and use it and how far are they constrained by wider social structures?

Gender and power within archaeology

Scale, power and gender studies are closely linked. As we saw in Chapter 2 the rise of an archaeology of gender needed an assault on the power structures among archaeologists themselves. Moreover, the demonstration that gender can be studied in the past by archaeologists has begun at the micro-scale. It involves the analysis of individual artefacts, houses and sequences of manufacture rather than the big origins questions I examined in the last chapter. The strategy has been to find gender in the details rather to claim its universal properties (Nelson 1997: 95).

One consequence of these studies of the past is that the route to understanding how we construct our own identities in the present, and the power that goes with it, is now much clearer. Daniel Miller and Christopher Tilley (1984) talk of power *to* and power *over*. In the former a person or network has power to act and influence. This is a consequence of any social relationship or action. We all have power to act. We also invest the institutions of power – the state, the family, the law, the city – with similar power to transform. When power *to* also involves power *over*, then a relationship of domination exists.

Therefore a feminist archaeology pursuing an archaeology of gender potentially has power to transform the discipline. This is done through the overlapping and very variable actions, interests, commitments and output of those subscribing to that ideology. Some inroads have already been made into that power *over*, which undoubtedly exists in the various archaeologies described in Chapter 2. Among these an archaeology of gender may feel that currently it has more chance of receiving a sympathetic hearing from the community of interpretive archaeologists. At the moment the scale remains small, though in some practitioners' minds (e.g. Nelson 1997) a future goal is to achieve power over an androcentric archaeology.

When essence is OK

Let me be clear on one important point here. If power resides in a relationship, then it might be regarded as another essentialist argument, like those I have criticised a good deal in this book. But it is not for a simple reason. If there is good causal reason, as in the statement 'engine-oil reduces friction', then there is no problem in stating that an essential property of engine oil is its ability to stop friction. The problem is that it does not tell us very much beyond the obvious. In evolutionary studies that would be known as the adaptive fallacy, as in 'human feet are adapted for upright walking'. Well they would be wouldn't they? Otherwise they wouldn't be human feet and you would fall over. The difference in saying that power resides in relationships but avoiding the 'so-what?' response is that this is the starting point for understanding, not the end point for explanation.

Bodies and sexuality

If gender is a socially constructed category, a vehicle for identity, then so too are our bodies and sexuality. For example, homosexuality was invented as a social category in the late nineteenth century, emphasising that the construction of sexuality is a modern project. Lynn Meskell (1999: 97) points out that the ancient Egyptians had no word comparable to our notion of sexuality. We should therefore be wary of imposing our particular interests onto their lifestyles. But 3500 years ago there certainly existed culturally created contexts for the experience and expression of sexual life. These were not a series of neat categories but rather, as Meskell argues, the assumption of roles and permutations in different contexts. They are revealed to us through tomb paintings and domestic architecture.

In the same way the body needs to be rethought. Should we regard it as another artefact? Or rather should we view artefacts in the same way as bodies? The emphasis on the treatment and movement of bodies and objects around the tombs of Neolithic Britain indicates that we might. In Julian Thomas' economy of substances (1996: 164) we see the recombination and redeposition of items such as skulls, pots and stone axes, which allowed the renegotiation of meaning in Neolithic society. The body was also an artefact among other artefacts in the Neolithic ritual landscapes of southern England. These include burial chambers and monuments such as Stonehenge and Avebury, with their processional avenues, ditches and specially constructed sightlines. Here the body experienced the landscape and it is our route to understanding those landscapes (Barrett 1999: 258–60).

The body can also be a source of display, as in sculpture, frescoes and other media. Classically, the house is a metaphor for the body and over time a container of successive bodies (West 1999: 105). Houses, like motor cars, are representations of the person and the self. Because they are containers they are if you like mini-landscapes; society in microcosm.

But in approaching the body as an artefact or display, Meskell (1999: 42–4) argues that we have overemphasised its power to represent something and largely ignored another dimension of power, namely the experience of our own bodies, which we live in and live through. Applied to archaeology this 'body as lived' approach requires the wealth of iconography and texts and the cornucopia of artefacts that come with an ancient civilisation such as Egypt. Her point is well taken. We need to guard against separating our bodies as lived from the construction of our individual identities. But to do this we also need to carry the mute body of prehistory with us rather than step over its corpse on the road to civilisation and the lure of texts.

Power, practice and discourse

The temporal approach to power can also be formalised in terms of scale. Christopher Gosden (1994: 137) links power to the performances that take place in public time. Here the individual comes face to face with what seems most natural in his or her world. This includes those rituals and monuments that exist only because they are part of long-term time. Power and knowledge are therefore very closely linked. If we take the view of the philosopher Michel Foucault, then power resides in discourse. He used this term to refer to all the conditions that are needed for the production of knowledge. Discourse refers to data as well as to concepts, their history and the social conditions that produce and use knowledge. This book is part of a discourse about the past and what archaeologists do. So too is a museum exhibit, an archaeological excavation and a visit to ancient ruins. The approach to understanding power that a discourse approach gives us is very top-down. Power precedes. Hence one of Foucault's best-known books is entitled *The Archaeology of Knowledge*. Power is a structure, because the many discourses we engage in by dint of being social are also structures. To push the metaphor a bit further to make the point more clearly, we are 'imprisoned' or 'captured' by these structures. It comes as no surprise that Foucault wrote a great deal about discipline, prison, mental asylums and sexuality as his examples of changing discourses.

Of course there is an alternative and one that I have already outlined in Chapter 4 when discussing society. Gosden contrasts the top-down approach to power with the bottom-up approach. Rather than power and knowledge residing in discourse, they are created through practice, as in Pierre Bourdieu's concept of *habitus* (see below) and Gosden's landscape of habit (Chapter 6). I prefer to define practice as routine actions rather than the more commonly encountered 'meaningful actions of knowledgeable agents', which sounds tautologous to me. Power stems from action – I think we could all agree on that. Therefore the structures and institutions of society that we encounter are all products of daily practice, rituals of renewal and creation (see the papers in Dobres and Robb 2000). Practice therefore gives much greater weight to the actions of individuals at the micro-scale and less

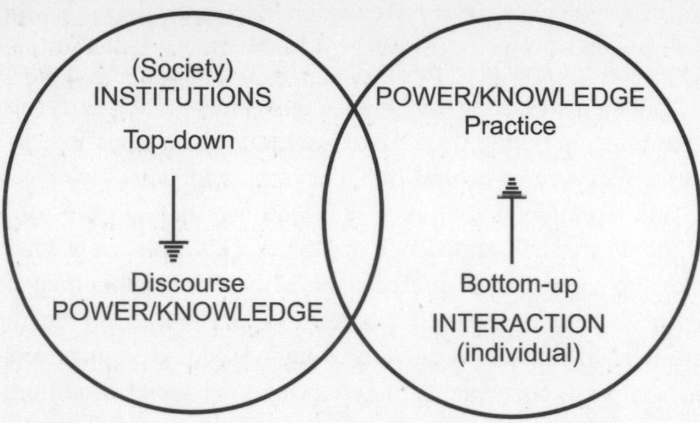

FIGURE 8.1 The overlapping networks of knowledge about society and the individual that archaeologists have used

to the overarching macro-scale structures. But practice also breaks down the dichotomy between individual and society by treating them as one (Figure 8.1). Thus we can escape from the Cartesian theatre, with its many and much-loved oppositions (Chapter 5).

The identity within

At one level we are all concerned with constructing our personal identity, that sense of self. At another we belong to much larger communities that influence what that self will be and against which it will be tested. Understanding power and using concepts such as *habitus* and landscape of habit can help to clarify the issue of how we become socialised.

As Siân Jones puts it:

> the *habitus* is made up of durable dispositions towards certain perceptions and practices (such as those relating to the sexual division of labour, morality, tastes and so on), which become part of an individual's sense of self at an early age, and can be transposed from one context to another.
>
> (Jones 1997: 88)

I would only add that for me those durable dispositions she speaks of stem from those routine, oft-repeated actions. As Gilchrist puts it, *habitus* is your 'common-sense knowledge which is socially constructed with reference to the material world' (1993: 16). The *habitus* is a 'collective unconscious' built up from experience rather than consciously mastered. You are what you make yourself to be. Obviously there are constraints. Action and interaction are limited by the senses, the physical structure of the body, and the differences between people's bodies based on age, sex and activity. The networks that result from interaction are, as I have shown (Chapter 4), not only limited by the resources – emotional, material and symbolic – that define them, but also made possible by them.

It is the twin aspects of power to simultaneously offer opportunities as well as impose constraints that leads us to an understanding of how canalisation works. In those evolutionary landscapes described by Waddington (Chapter 7), or the landscapes of habit outlined by Gosden (Chapter 6), we routinely dig the canals down which the flow of social life proceeds. They are not dug for us. To be 'stuck in a rut' only suggests that you are capable of digging a new rut. Flex those durable dispositions in your landscape of habit, push the envelope a little, change your routine actions and so nudge Waddington's ball bearing into a new rut. But remember that everyone else is digging their own self-defining rut and so collectively the canal gets deeper. The landscape changes through other forces than yours alone.

Back to style

How does all this help the archaeologist? Basically it takes us back to our understanding of similarity and gets us to think again about its significance as that attribute of objects called style. I discussed similarity and the principle of popularity in Chapter 3 and showed how archaeologists have generally assumed that the more similar artefacts and cultures are, the more interaction took place between individuals and groups. This was refined by Wobst with his much tighter definition of style as information exchange. Wiessner then provided, as we have also seen (Chapter 5), a definition of style as 'a means of non-verbal communication to negotiate identity' (1990:

108). Her underpinning idea is that psychologically we derive our identities through comparison. She puts this into an evolutionary context by pointing out that those who create a positive self-image in this manner are also putting themselves at a selective advantage. This comes about because the style adopted encourages others to engage in desirable social activity.

Wiessner's main point, as we saw earlier, was to distinguish between an *assertive* and an *emblemic* style (1983: 257–8; 1990). She contrasted the stylistic variation in material culture that is personally based (assertive) with that that is group based (emblemic). Two types of identity were therefore created. Style manages this without words. At the group level, style works by referring to conscious affiliation, what might be called ethnicity in some contexts. At the personal level, the stylistic references may be more down to habit. As Stephen Shennan has pointed out (1989a: 22), because assertive style is neither unique to individuals nor universally prescribed there will be a good deal of variation among individuals within a culture. It is this variation that provides the seedbed for emblemic uses of style, of which ethnicity (see below) is a particular example.

But, before we get too carried away, I also examined in Chapter 5 the notion that the social component of our data resides in style. This depends on a particular way of looking at the world. In particular, it comes from the division of subject and object, material culture and person, style and function (Boast 1997). *Habitus* and the landscape of habit makes such a division unnecessary. And with it goes the analytical power of style. Identity is less a feature coded into designs on pots, or the shape of houses, than an ongoing process firmly embedded in the practices of daily life. In other words it is less the product of thought, 'I will colour my hair orange because I think people with orange hair are cool', than the result of action, 'My hair is orange because that's me. Her hair is brown because that's her. What's your problem?'

Spotting the habitus

Style may not be the great ally we once thought it was to get at social life or identity from archaeological data. But how do we conceptualise the *habitus* and these landscapes of habit? Lets face it, the *habitus* is a great idea but it is distinctly fuzzy round the edges for a 'soaked in the data' subject like archaeology. Archaeologists know there is a reality out there which is the past. We trip over it when out fieldwalking to pick up survey data. We can pat a pot appreciatively and tell you its cultural heritage. We can point on our timelines to a style zone. We can map distributions based on similarity in form, shape, attributes and that thing called style. *Habitus*, by comparison, is out there like the truth in the *X-files*.

This criticism returns us to our archaeological imagination and the different archaeologies I outlined in Chapter 2. All of those approaches share common ground in recognising ways in which the past can be studied. Then they part company. Culture historians generally prefer description. Processualists like the rigour of the scientific method. Neo-Darwinists appeal to a higher authority – Darwin – and the power of natural selection. Finally, interpretive archaeologists settle for a self-reflexive, multi-aspectual approach. The development of a professional archaeological imagination which these approaches encapsulate has been to move away from the common-sense. However, not all of them are ready to question what is handed down to a study of the past from the contemporary concerns of society about peoples, nations and things. Marxist and feminist approaches are well aware of how an interest in the past is often framed for us.

Ignoring these last developments leads to an impoverished imagination. Many archaeologists still believe, despite the processualists' demonstration to the contrary 30 years ago, that the subject is terminally limited either by the nature of the data that survives or by the ability of science to produce fresh analytical insights. This is the crunch at the core of Hawkes' onion, which I discussed in Chapter 4. Landscapes of habit will not fit neatly onto distributions of house types or vessel decoration. But how could they, since the visual output of one is not based on the premises of the other? Just as the demonstration of an archaeology of gender had to return to the detail rather than tackle the universals, so the study of identity needs to reformulate and reconceptualise the problem.

The existence, archaeologically, of practice and the *habitus* is, however, apparent in the sheer diversity of material culture that archaeologists have discovered. Michelle Hegmon (1998) in rejecting style as the way to understand this diversity, nonetheless focuses on seven regularities that still merit further investigation (Box 22). Some of them are familiar. Number 7, for example, was Wobst's point about target populations and stylistic messaging. Numbers 3 and 4 could be a translation of Wiessner's assertive style.

Box 22: What the patterns in the data seem to tell us but which we don't yet fully understand

(based on Hegmon 1998: 277, with additions)

1 Complex technologies (for example metallurgy) seem to be heavily loaded symbolically.

2 Decorations that cross-cut a number of media (pots, textiles, metals) are likely to be symbolically meaningful.

3 Very simple decoration may not be particularly significant at a conscious level. It may tell us more about everyday interaction between individuals and the contexts in which objects are made.

4 The objects used in everyday life have an important role in defining who people are socially and are relevant to the concept of *habitus*.

5 Aspects of production that are taught in a relatively formal manner may be useful indicators of learning contexts.

6 Elaboration of non-visible objects (such as medallions or tattoos worn under clothing) are more likely to communicate with yourself and your intimate and effective networks, including your ancestors, rather than with your extended network partners.

7 Highly visible elaboration is likely to involve communication with your extended network but does not always involve group distinctions but rather your ability to negotiate such far-flung networks in time and space.

Overlapping patterns and many networks

What I have added to Hegmon's patterns (Box 22) is the notion that these regularities can be understood in terms of the networks that we all construct (Chapter 4). Moreover, the elements in these networks, other people and objects, are treated in a similar way, because both exist as the result of relationships. Without such relationships there would be no social world, and no distinctively human social world. Our material world of garden gnomes, plates, computers, houses and jumbo jets is therefore replete with cross-cutting distributions of social relationships, linked into a coherent whole by people in motion. The image I have of the landscape of habit with all its many practices being enacted at all sorts of different scales is of overlapping networks (see Figure 6.1). This is my way of sharpening the fuzzy picture.

Julian Thomas (1996: 178) provides a fully worked-out example. He has argued, in the case of Neolithic southern Britain, that what existed were spatially segregated practices distributed across the landscape. These we recognise as tombs, henges, enclosures, fields, flint mines, pits with animal bones and distinctive pottery. Any identity or social grouping was therefore defined by a series of cross-cutting criteria that worked like this:

> Some activities may have been restricted on the basis of age sets, some according to gender . . . , some by membership of kin groups, some by agnation [relations by marriage], and some by other sodalities such as hunting societies, sorcerer's lodges and so on. In all probability, many of these groupings crossed over the boundaries of any formal social units such as tribes, clans or lineages.
>
> Thomas (1996: 178–9)

Elsewhere he refers to Neolithic Britain as comprising 'multiple overlapping communities' (Thomas 1996: 180). It was neither a single society nor a mosaic of tribal groupings. Now such a model does have an empirical reality in the cross-cutting distributions of styles and decorations on Neolithic objects. We are also propelled towards that bottom-up view of how these intricate, overlapping webs of relationships were constructed. The vocabulary of networks I explored in Chapter 4 helps us to grasp the idea using familiar terms and so broaden our archaeological imaginations to encompass the unfamiliar *habitus* and landscape of habit. It is in their construction, rather than in the properties of style, that identity emerges.

Boundaries: natural

The change in emphasis to a vocabulary of *habitus* also helps the archaeologist in considering the key concept of boundaries. We like bounded entities. That is why islands like Orkney, Malta, Iceland and Papua New Guinea are very popular laboratories for the study of social and political systems and their long-term properties of stasis and change. Islands are particularly suitable for measuring inputs and outputs. Goods and peoples flow in and out as archipelagos are fought over and exploited by mainland states. By focusing on islands we can trace the cultural shifts of groups as historically diverse as the Vikings and Anglo-Saxons in northwestern Europe and Britain, Mycenaeans and Minoans in the Aegean, and the competitive spread of Muslim and Buddhist religions through the islands of Indonesia.

Islands can also be centres of innovation. As a result they have been used to model in microcosm the processes of change that are more difficult to grasp on the continents, where defining a particular region is never easy. For example, the archipelagos of the Pacific have been important for the study of social evolution. The independent rise of chiefdoms in Hawaii, Fiji and New Zealand have provided impetus precisely because they are seen as bounded units to the study of autonomous development.

Islands are an extreme case and in many instances their isolation has been overstated. The vast Pacific Ocean and the cold North Sea acted as highways, *not* as barriers to contact. The significance of islands lies in their making the job of defining regions that much easier (Chapter 6). But in many cases they are very small regions and hence atypical.

Boundaries on the continents are just as permeable but the job of drawing up regions is much more difficult. Cyril Fox contrasted the highland and lowland zones of Britain and evocatively entitled his essay *The Personality of Britain* (1932). His form of environmental determinism proposed that identity is shaped by climate and landscape as much as by history and culture. Regional building styles in wood or stone reflect a culture of the possible, which only serves to confirm a view that until empires arrived life was local and that innovation came from elsewhere.

Instead the lesson that science-based archaeology has repeatedly reinforced is that the local view misrepresents the scale of human action in the past. Radiocarbon dating freed Europe from *ex oriente lux* diffusion, where the answer to the question 'What's new?' always came, before the arrival of American know-how, from the Near East (Chapter 1). Instead the possibility was opened up of autonomous economic and social development, as in Colin Renfrew's snappy title *Wessex Without Mycenae* (1968), which heralded a new prehistoric world order. Characterisation studies of ceramics, metals and stones such as obsidian revealed that even mundane items such as cooking pots were often transported, wherever they are known, over many kilometres from the source of the raw material. These findings relate to the prehistoric, classical and historic worlds. And now genetic studies are reversing the patterns of simple diffusion linked to the supposed economic superiority of the first farmers (Chapter 7). Natural boundaries have never looked more unnatural.

Boundaries: cultural

Boundaries must also be considered at the scales of human interaction, from the macro to the micro.

At the grand scale, boundary markers such as the Limes that the Romans built to fence-off barbarian Germany are very popular objects for archaeologists to study. Hadrian's Wall in England, which did the same job against the Scots, is probably the most studied archaeological monument in the country and a World Heritage Site to boot. Boundaries are also chronological, as in the Norman invasion of 1066 and in 1492, which marks the end of pre-Colombian America.

When it comes to boundaries around social groups we find ourselves back among those text and non-text arguments (Andrén 1998) that I explored in Chapter 1. Often the aim seems to be to produce a tribal ethnography linking style zones to named geographical groupings. This applies to prehistoric Australia as well as to Iron Age societies in Africa and Europe and the states of the ancient Near East and Mesoamerica. The basic point is that a boundary sees an interruption in similarity. This could be a cessation of interaction or a change in the type of interaction from, say, exchange to warfare.

Boundaries can be gendered. They exist because they have been culturally constructed. Martin Hall (1997: 227) has shown how, in the layout of Cape Town, South Africa, gender structured not only the colonial city but also the surrounding countryside. The gridded streets and symmetrical manor houses imply the stamp of a gendered social order. Contemporary accounts reveal the freedom of males in public display as they moved through the streets while their women were kept indoors. Much remains to be done, as Hall readily admits, to go beyond these implications and uncover through the study of household contents how gender relations were articulated in everyday life. The probate record of one early settler in 1827 is a masculine document recording the owners possessions, including his African servants. By contrast the items excavated from the well in his backyard provide not only an individual portrait of the owner – gout-suffering, short-sighted and military-minded – but also evidence for the European women in the household – shoes, dolls, jewellery, thimbles.

Male : female boundaries may seem clear cut in this example. However, our interest must reside less in the dichotomy and more in the process of domination and its resistance, much of which would have been worked out in the material realm. It is through the fine detail that the micro-scales of gender relations will be resolved with the macro-framework of power.

At the micro-scale, boundaries exist around settlements, houses, graves and persons. Ditches, walls, pits and clothing are all examples of the cultural divisions that divide the indivisible. Hence categories emerge. These may be easy to identify archaeologically but difficult to interpret. For example, the precision with which a new city such as Canberra, the capital of Australia, is laid out contains to a Western perception many boundaries and an ordered appreciation of space. However, when viewed by an Australian Aborigine, Frank Gurrmanamana, the geometry of Canberra appears as primordial chaos instead of an orderly arrangement (Jones 1985). The straight roads, property boundaries, mowed lawns and zoned activity that we see when driving around Canberra's artificial Lake Burley-Griffin is to Gurrmanamana an unnamed, 'natural', landscape with no significance, since the people who inhabit it have forgotten the rights that the land demands. By contrast the savannahs of northern Australia where Gurrmanamana lives, a 'wilderness' to our perception, have also been transformed in both the physical and metaphorical sense as a result of continuous human action.

But all is not doom and gloom for those periods of archaeology that do not have eye-witness accounts. Within houses boundaries exist. Matthew Johnson (1993: 341) shows how space came to be demarcated in different ways (Figure 6.3) between the late-medieval and post-medieval periods. Class interests were eventually served as segregation between people within the same space turned into the occupation of separate rooms which now contained their status and their private lives within a capitalistic structure of social relations. Just as the ancient Egyptians had no word for sexuality (see above), so the late-medieval texts are largely mute on the identities being expressed by the architecture of the time. As Johnson argues:

> Identities were negotiated through movement through space, placement of actions, and visual and iconic images such as heraldry; not in the first instance through writing things down.
>
> Johnson (1999b: 77)

This eloquently summarises the power of material culture to access areas of the human past once thought to be the sole prerogative of the text. There will always be disagreement over identifying boundaries and attributing significance to them. Consequently it is better to investigate the process of boundary maintenance, which leads us directly to the size of networks.

Consuming identity and cutting the network

Identity is not something that is given. Even though your status might be ascribed by the fact of your birth, as in hereditary kingship, you will still create your identity within that role. Identity, like power, is both enabling and constraining.

Identity, as we have seen, is best conceptualised as a set of overlapping fields: different practices which add up to a *habitus* or, as I prefer, an archaeological landscape of habit. This view stresses the individual and the web of networks we all create. The temporal and spatial scales of these networks varies and the resources we use to negotiate them are likewise varied (Chapter 4). Creating identity is therefore dependent on a wide range of different selective pressures. We are canalised, though often this is habitual rather than consciously deliberate. The important point to grasp, as emphasised by anthropologist Johnathan Friedman, is that what people do is not merely representative of who or what they are but basically constitutive (1994: 107). He uses the example of Western fashion in urban Zaire. Designer labels do not just declare your allegiance to a group. Their consumption is the means by which you possess any identity at all by relating to others. In his study of consumption in contemporary society Daniel Miller reaches a similar conclusion:

> The consumer society exists when, as in industrial societies today, most people have a minimal relationship to production and distribution such that consumption provides the only arena left to us through which we might potentially forge a relationship with the world.
>
> Miller (1995: 17)

Archaeologists can investigate the same relatedness through their myriad material cultures and extend it to their general model of culture as repetitious patterning in time and space. The difference is that besides the activity of consumption, people in the past were more directly involved in forging links with the world through production and distribution. This difference lies at the heart of two rather different theories of exchange.

When objects are commodities, as in our own society, relationships, as Miller states, are created through collective ownership, distribution and consumption. Importantly objects are regarded as having symbolic and material significance, just as they have been seen by archaeologists to have passive and active styles (Chapter 5).

The alternative is where social relations rather than commodities shape the significance of objects and hence how we deal with one another. Here, as Marilyn Strathern points out (1988: 172), social relations can only be turned into other social relations. So, when objects are exchanged they become other social relationships. The material and the symbolic are therefore fused rather than analytically separate. Moreover, the objects have identities. When a transaction involving feathers, shells or salt takes place you also give a bit of yourself. Those pots and rare stones are integral to the system of relatedness.

But networks and relatedness cannot go on forever. I outlined in Chapter 4 how three networks – intimate, effective and extended – have expected sizes that depend on the resources – emotional, material and symbolic – that are used to create them. These, however, form rather weak boundaries. The resources cross-cut. For example, symbolic resources such as a statue of the Virgin Mary on the mantelpiece can be part of your intimate network. It is also possible to get emotional with strangers.

The basic point for archaeologists is how networks are cut. An individual maintaining those three ideal networks is at the same time engaged in the practice of boundary maintenance. From what I said in Chapter 6 about the difference between relational and modernist approaches to society, we should expect this because of the modernist view of identity. From this perspective networks are cut when the resources can no longer be negotiated into a relationship through transactions. 'Not fade away' may be the desire, but in practice there are only so many network partners an individual can maintain. The refrain is much more often 'Get off of my cloud!'.

If you prefer to stress the importance of relatedness in studying how people interact (Bird-David 1999) then the loss of immediacy can sever the principle. But once again it is the break in social transactions that leads to a boundary. The importance for archaeology is that we should not be looking for hard and fast boundaries. Rather the interruptions in the social world are the result of complex, interleaved practices. Many of these boundaries are permeable in terms of items, resources and individuals which flow through time and space.

Neither should we be misled by style, in the shape and distribution of artefacts, which at first glance might seem to help. I could show you many maps with crisp changes in space, as well as time, of objects that stylistically are chalk and cheese. These encourage us in our belief that we are studying something real, and yes of course there is a pattern there. However, I hope I have now said enough to make it clear why understanding that pattern is not just a simple matter of equating distribution with identity, as many archaeologists still maintain. Trying to be precise about boundaries will always be hazardous and is well illustrated by the next major topic: ethnicity.

The identity from

Ethnicity forms a boundary concept between the investigation of identity *within* the past and the uses of the past to create an identity *from*. I have intentionally left this key concept in archaeology until now because so much of what we know about the past comes from its application rather than from what is so often assumed to be the inherent nature of cultural data.

Who are you?

Let me illustrate just how theory laden the archaeological facts are with concepts of ethnicity by asking: Who do you think you are? How do you classify yourself? By your bodily phenotype, how you see yourself – skin colour, hair type, stature, sex – or your inner genotype – the history of your genes? Would you instead stress the importance of the culture you live in with all its weird and wonderful ways of greeting people, behaving at table, and body language in different social gatherings, not to mention what you wear, how you cook ('you are what you eat'), and so on? Are your various identities attributable to your body, class, sexuality, age and gender sufficient to draw a boundary around your ethnic status?

Answering such questions in any multicultural society would produce a very complex array of traits. Be reflexive about it. Ask yourself why you use some categories and not others to classify yourself and other people. Do those categories and the significance you attach to them differ between your effective and extended network and the company of complete strangers whom you see every day? I think you will find very quickly that most of your categories are very polythetic (Chapter 3). Do we see groupings because, like one of those archaeological detectives (Chapter 4), we are great classifiers? Categories work well when the traits are kept minimal. As you expand the number of traits to reflect the complexity of the situation, you will find the boundaries dissolving.

Yes, you might counter, but living in Southampton, Denver or La Plata is very different to living in a rural community in Africa, India or China, where the opportunity for cultural and biological diversity is much smaller. There the boundaries are less permeable simply because the range of variation is much less. That argument does not stand up for long. Just because we expect rural communities to be conservative does not mean that people are not actively creating their roles. Richard Lee discovered that the !Kung San bushmen at their waterhole in the Kalahari desert of southern Africa were quick to change their affiliations as the economic climate of the region shifted. Traditional hunters and gatherers could soon become wage labourers in the region's cattle industry, thus exchanging a key trait of their ethnicity foraging for ranching.

Ian Hodder (1982: 18–21) also found that individuals moved between ethnic groups in East Africa. His study of material culture indicated sharp boundaries because individuals change their dress at the 'frontier'. The boundaries might indicate a form of ethnicity but have little to say about the pattern of mobility, which contradicts the view that ethnicity is historically fixed to a place. Ethnicity is therefore malleable and contingent. There is no reason to suppose that it was not the same in the past. These examples make it difficult to sort out some of the claims archaeologists make.

Ethnicity

Perhaps a definition will help:

> Ethnicity must be distinguished from mere spatial variation and should refer to self-conscious identification with a particular social group at least partly based on a specific locality or origin.
>
> Shennan (1989a: 14)

Self-conscious identification is the basic point. For example, there are many white Australian Aborigines who totally confound the racial and ethnic stereotype. But they self-consciously identify for reasons of descent, history, residence and oppression with the general ethnic category Australian Aborigine.

How can archaeologists cope with self-conscious identification? The recent child burial from Laghar Velho in Portugal poses the problem (Darte *et al*. 1999). Dated to 24,500 years ago it appears to its discoverers, after careful measurement and study, to be a hybrid between Neanderthals (*Homo neanderthalensis*) and modern humans (*Homo sapiens*). Since these categories are regarded as separate species, we could also reasonably claim an ethnic distinction. The mixture of anatomical features does not help us in determining what this child thought about his/her identity. However, the one pierced shell found with the body could point to a self-conscious affiliation with *Homo sapiens*, with whom such objects are common, rather than with Neanderthals, with whom they are very rare. Alternatively he/she could have slipped the simple necklace on-and-off anytime he/she passed across the 'frontier'.

But what assumptions, what theory-laden facts, are really on display in this extreme example? Judgements about affiliation could bring us very close to the disreputable history of archaeology and anthropology that judged people, morally and practically, by how they looked. At its worst this led to the programme of eugenics, where deliberate intervention was proposed to change the human blueprint. Ethnic cleansing and holocausts attest to the practical application of such obnoxious beliefs.

In hindsight such statements can seem innocuous. For example, Samuel Laing in his hugely popular *Human Origins* published in 1895 conveys the racism of the times based on an effortless sense of European superiority:

> The form of the chin seems to be wonderfully correlated with the general character and energy of the race. It is hard to say why, but as a matter of fact a weak chin generally denotes a weak, and a strong chin a strong, race or individual.
>
> Laing (1895: 395)

But spotting such 'chinless wonders' is a deadly serious and very dangerous matter, especially when science underpins social policy (Gould 1984). Neither does it diminish when applied to ancient skulls, precisely because archaeology was once used to authorise the uncritical application of such bogus approaches to the living. 'Styles' of heads and bodies were, and continue for some observers, to be indicative of intelligence, industriousness and the capacity for progress.

Neither does a hundred years seem to make much difference in the application of prejudice based on a reading of anatomy. Nelson Mandela, when practising law in Johannesburg in the 1950s, came across an instance where the classification of people under apartheid legislation led to similar judgements:

> I once handled the case of a Coloured man who was inadvertently classified as an African . . . The magistrate seemed uninterested in both my evidence and the prosecutor's demural. He stared at my client and gruffly asked him to turn round so that his back faced the bench. After scrutinising my client's shoulders, which sloped down sharply, he nodded to the other officials and upheld the appeal. In the view of the white authorities in those days, sloping shoulders were one stereotype of the Coloured physique. And so it came that the course of this man's life was decided purely on a magistrate's opinion about the structure of his shoulders.
>
> Mandela (1995: 175)

Definitions are not always helpful.

The ethnic imperatives

The basis of ethnicity, and the significant role archaeology has played in its current form, has been dissected by Sîan Jones (1997). She traces the idea of a people represented by, but not constitutive of, their material culture into the nineteenth century. Subsequently we have merely elaborated on two central ideas. The first she refers to as the *primordial imperative* where ethnicity is best summed up as being 'in the blood'. According to this imperative, ethnicity is a form of sociobiology. We inherit it as part of the biological makeup that conditions our social life. I am English not just because I carry an umbrella on the sunniest of summer days but because I was born English. This is a convenient doctrine to many who use ethnicity as a political slogan, since we cannot apparently do anything about it. To renounce ethnicity would be like cutting off your right arm.

The second key idea identifies the *essentialist imperative*. Here culture, whether defined by anthropologists or archaeologists, is directly equated with ethnicity. Johnathan Friedman (1994) argues that culture, and by implication ethnicity, is a typical outcome of modernist thinking in western countries that turns cultural difference into ideal types. It is a very simple equation, and one followed by archaeologists. The different cultural practices in the world therefore become the essence of ethnic identities. End of analysis. Let your society do your thinking for you.

The ethnic trinity

The essence of ethnicity, that a bowler hat and a beret really do distinguish the English from the French, merges with the primordial inheritance flowing in our veins. These imperatives are founded on three expectations that stem from the idea of culture that I have examined, and criticised, time and again throughout this book. These are boundedness, similarity and continuity (Jones 1997: 136). These properties which underpin so much archaeological methodology are the reasons we can recognise patterns in our data. By reference to the two imperatives, archaeologists have supplied their patterns with meaning by interpreting their significance as ethnic markers.

But what does it matter? Archaeology, you might say, only deals with dead things and has no influence on the present. Nothing could be further from the truth. Remember the past is not a neutral subject. It is a source of authority for action in the present. It shapes political ideologies. Let me give you two examples from politicians who have led the fight for independence and freedom in their countries.

In 1961, just before his long imprisonment for leading the struggle against apartheid, Nelson Mandela visited Egypt:

> I spent the whole morning of my first day in Cairo at the museum, looking at art, examining artefacts, making notes, learning about the type of men who founded the ancient civilisation of the Nile valley. This was not amateur archaeological interest; it is important for African nationalists to be armed with evidence to refute the fictitious claims of whites that Africans are without a civilised past that compares with that of the West. In a single morning, I discovered that Egyptians were creating great works of art and architecture when whites were still living in caves.
>
> Mandela (1995: 353)

India's first prime Minister, Pandit Nehru, wrote *The Discovery of India* from his prison cell in 1944. He also looked to the monuments and relics of the past to chart the future road to independence:

> These journeys and visits of mine, with the background of my reading, gave me an insight into the past. To a somewhat bare intellectual understanding was added an emotional appreciation, and gradually a sense of reality began to creep into my mental picture of India, and the land of my forefathers became peopled with living beings, who laughed and wept, loved and suffered; and among them were men who seemed to know life and understand it, and out of their wisdom they had built a structure which gave India a cultural stability which lasted for thousands of years.
>
> Nehru (1946: 51–2)

Faced with imperial power and state oppression the readings of the past by these two leaders provided alternatives.

Nationalism and the Nazis

However, not all claims on the past have been made in such just causes. While patriotism has been described as the last refuge of the scoundrel, so too might nationalism be termed the first haven of the archaeologist. As Marguerita Díaz-Andreu and Timothy Champion discuss (1996: 3–8), the wave of nationalism that swept Europe at the end of the eighteenth century converted the production of history into a patriotic duty. The existence of nations had to be demonstrated. A past was required which needed to be described. Archaeology was both created by nationalism and helped create the nation states we now take for granted.

In 1849 as the independent Danish state was being forged, the archaeologist J. J. A. Worsaae called his countrymen to arms:

> The remains of antiquity thus bind us more firmly to our native land; hills and vales, fields and meadows, become connected with us, in a more intimate degree; for by the barrows [prehistoric burial mounds], which rise on their surface, and the antiquities, which they have preserved for centuries in their bosom, they constantly recall to our recollection, that our forefathers lived in this country, from time immemorial, a free and independent people, and so call on us to defend our territories with energy, that no foreigner may ever rule over that soil, which contains the bones of our ancestors, and with which our most sacred and reverential recollections are associated.
>
> Worsaae (1849: 149–50)

Antiquities, as we saw in Chapter 1 with the work of C. J. Thomsen, were very important in Denmark. They were tangible products, unearthed as the country industrialised and as the middle classes rose to political ascendancy, not only here but across the western world. Institutions such as national museums which expressed this new order sprang up in all the countries of Europe.

Denmark's struggle was to regain the independence it had once apparently enjoyed in Viking and prehistoric times. By contrast, and using the same notions of culture and peoples, the German archaeological tradition began to support reasons to expand. One major difference lay in the different histories of these states. Denmark had historical claims to being a nation state. Germany did not. It was only unified in 1871, a year after Italy. Before that there had not been *a* Germany and only *an* Italy in the Roman period. These very unhistorical nations used the past to underpin their nationalist agendas. Germany stressed prehistory, Italy looked back to the glories of the Roman imperial past.

The ultra-nationalist German archaeologist Gustav Kossina extended the nineteenth-century agenda. Already in 1911 he had delivered a lecture on *German Prehistory, An Eminently National Discipline*. In 1926, a few years before Childe's famous formulation of an archaeological culture, he set down his core principle which linked people to archaeological provinces (see page 57).

But as Heinrich Härke points out (1992: 204–5) in his discussion of this archaeological bogeyman, such innocent-sounding statements rested on ethnocentric notions of racial supremacy. There was an underlying belief in a Nordic, Aryan race that was superior to other races in both physical and intellectual qualities.

Kossina was very much against *ex oriente lux* that Gordon Childe would later champion using similar concepts of culture but combined with a very different political philosophy (Chapter 3). Instead, Kossina's heartland lay to the north, not the east. The repeated movements south of the Nordic races was for him the dynamic in both European and world history (Härke 1992: 205).

Kossina died in 1931, two years before the founding of the Third Reich. His interpretations and methods were influential on Nazi ideology, which sought reasons to invade and annex neighbouring countries which they saw as formerly part of the Aryan homeland. The SS commander Heinrich Himmler founded the *Deutsches Ahnenerbe*, an organisation whose task was to create a scientific theory of German dominance. Archaeology was a leading discipline in this enterprise. Research was politicised and had to be ideologically useful to the Third Reich. Combined with the worst sort of physical anthropology the categorisation of peoples and cultures and the development of an ultimate solution in the name of ethnic purity were visited upon Europe. Among many atrocities underpinned by a bogus theory of the past was the invasion of Denmark and the suppression of Worsaae's free and independent people.

Alternative power: who owns the past?

I have dealt with identities from archaeology on the large scale: ethnicity and nationalism. The final question to ask is if there are alternatives to the equation of culture with people? Jones for one thinks there is, so long as we change the very notion of how ethnic identity is constructed (1997: 140). The mindset to get out of is the one that sees the past as fixed, with the only changes coming from new discoveries. This approach states that artefacts and monuments, ancient cities and landscapes are static because they belong to the past; the older they are, the more rooted to the spot they become. It is therefore a short step within this mindset to plucking the objects out of the past to use them in the present. It is easy to insist on boundedness, similarity and continuity in the patterns we draw up on our plans and distribution maps. The past, and all the identities it contains and can support, is like a freeze-frame on the video. The flow of creativity is stopped and the past is owned just like any other commodity.

A good example of this is provided by legislation about monuments. Most countries have laws that protect and bring into the safekeeping of the state either all or a selected range of antiquities. The World Heritage Convention sponsored through UNESCO does something similar with its list of World Heritage Sites, which have to be nominated. Once approved it is the responsibility of that country to manage them and hold them in trust for all the peoples of the world.

But such legislation, while clarifying rights and obligations to the material remains of the past, raises issues of who owns it? Local concerns can differ significantly from national interests. First Nations such as the Australian Aborigines or Native North Americans have a very different view of relics to which they claim affinity. Moreover, the keeping of many objects in the museums of the world rather than where they were originally deposited raises issues of ownership.

A most famous case such as the return of the Parthenon [Elgin] Marbles as requested by the Greek Government from the British Museum highlights the issues that elsewhere may involve returning simple stone tools. The respective artistic merits or even the historic importance of an object or set of objects is conflated with the issues of universality, the control of the centre and its relationship with the identities of the periphery.

Conclusion: archaeology, the future

What more can happen to archaeology? The past will always be contentious. Archaeologists will increasingly find themselves in ethical stands over the rights of their profession and the interests of others with claims on the past. The identity of the archaeologist, that professional use of the archaeological imagination, will also undergo changes and be interpreted very differently than it was even 30 years ago. To face this challenge we need to go back to basics and rethink the static view of the past. We need to accept it as an overlapping set of contexts and interests from which many identities, including ours as archaeologists, are forged. How we construct our own identities through our involvement with the past is just one interpretation among many of the business of being involved with the past.

But there will be little left to contest and build with if the archaeological resource is not managed. The pace of destruction has been very rapid in the past 50 years. The mechanisation of agriculture and forestry and the growth of cities and infrastructure projects, for example dams, highways and airports, has removed much archaeology and placed what remains at a premium. In the United Kingdom the pace of destruction of sites and landscapes that do enjoy some legal protection is still disheartening, as the recent Monuments at Risk Survey (MARS) discovered (Darvill and Fulton 1998). A finite resource, the archaeological record, is disappearing bit by bit, year by year rather like the Amazonian rainforest.

Imagine a world where the remote past is excluded and only the present, and maybe the future, is celebrated. But this time it is not a ghastly marketing mistake, as happened with London's Millennium Dome, but instead a gruesome reality. The past, prior to the modern world, no longer physically exists because it has been ploughed, bulldozed, tarmacked and eroded away. I wonder, could we have archaeology without material remains? Well certainly not the archaeology that I have described in this book. The stimulus for our professional archaeological imagination and the public enjoyment of the past comes from those objects and landscapes that, for the past 300 years, archaeologists have been trying to protect and record. This is the stuff of archaeology: those monuments and artefacts of stone, bronze, iron and, if we are lucky, precious metal. More of it awaits investigation and interpretation. These data will also need to be incorporated into the story we tell. In order to protect this resource and with it the future of our archaeological imagination, archaeologists must become managers (Cooper *et al.* 1995) as well as interpreters, excavators, promoters and analysts of the past. This vital area needs another book, *Archaeological Management, the Basics*, rather than this briefest of postscipts. It will be through the training that archaeologists receive and the professionalism they attain that the future of the past will be secured. I therefore end almost as I began. Archaeology is basically about three things: objects, landscapes and what we make of them, now and for the future. Archaeology is quite simply the study of the past through material remains and with that activity come responsibilities.

References

Aiello, L. and P. Wheeler (1995) 'The expensive-tissue hypothesis: the brain and the digestive system in human and primate evolution'. *Current Anthropology* 36: 199–221.

Alexandri, A. (1995) 'The origins of meaning'. In I. Hodder, M. Shanks, A. Alexandri, V. Buchli, J. Carman, J. Last and G. Lucas (eds) *Interpreting Archaeology; Finding Meaning in the Past*, pp. 57–67. London: Routledge.

Andrén, A. (1998) *Between Artifacts and Texts: Historical archaeology in global perspective*. New York: Plenum.

Andrews, G. and R. Thomas (1995) 'The management of archaeological projects: theory and practice in the UK'. In M. A. Cooper, A. Firth, J. Carman and D. Wheatley (eds) *Managing Archaeology*, pp. 189–207. London: Routledge.

Arnold, D. E. (1985) *Ceramic Theory and Cultural Process*. Cambridge: Cambridge University Press.

Ascher, R. (1961) 'Analogy in archaeological interpretation'. *Southwestern Journal of Anthropology* 17: 317–25.

Bailey, G. N. (1983) 'Concepts of time in quaternary prehistory'. *Annual Review of Anthropology* 12: 165–92.

Baillie, M. G. L. (1995) *A Slice Through Time: Dendrochronology and precision dating*. London: Batsford.

Baines, J. and N. Yoffee (1998) 'Order, legitimacy and wealth in Ancient Egypt and Mesopotamia'. In G. M. Feinman and J. Marcus (eds) *Archaic States*, pp. 199–260. Santa Fe: School of American Research.

Bar-Yosef, O. (1998) 'On the nature of transitions: the Middle to Upper Palaeolithic and the Neolithic revolution'. *Cambridge Archaeological Journal* 8: 141–63.

Barker, P. (1982) *Techniques of Archaeological Excavation*, (second edition). London: Batsford.

Barrett, J. (1999) 'The mythical landscapes of the British Iron Age'. In W. Ashmore and B. Knapp (eds) *Archaeologies of Landscape*, pp. 253–65. Oxford: Blackwell Publishers.

Bellwood, P. (1978) *Man's Conquest of the Pacific*. Auckland: Collins.

Bender, B. (1978) 'Gatherer-hunter to farmer: a social perspective'. *World Archaeology* 10: 204–22.

Bettinger, R. (1991) *Hunter-Gatherers: Archaeological and evolutionary theory*. New York: Plenum.

Binford, L. R. (1962) 'Archaeology as anthropology'. *American Antiquity* 28: 217–25.

Binford, L. R. (1964) 'A consideration of archaeological research design'. *American Antiquity* 29: 425–41.

Binford, L. R. (1972a) *An Archaeological Perspective*. New York: Academic Press.

Binford, L. R. (1972b) 'The new archaeology – an American archaeologist gives his own opinion'. *The Listener* 87: 174–6.

Binford, L. R. (1973) 'Interassemblage variability – the Mousterian and the "functional" argument'. In C. Renfrew (ed.) *The Explanation of Culture Change*, pp. 227–54. London: Duckworth.

Binford, L. R. (1978a) *Nunamiut Ethnoarchaeology*. New York: Academic Press.

Binford, L. R. (1978b) 'Dimensional analysis of behaviour and site structure: learning from an Eskimo hunting stand'. *American Antiquity* 43: 330–61.

Binford, L. R. (1980) 'Willow smoke and dogs tails: hunter-gatherer settlement systems and archaeological site formation'. *American Antiquity* 45: 4–20.

Binford, L. R. (1981a) *Bones: Ancient men and modern myths*. New York: Academic Press.

Binford, L. R. (1981b) 'Behavioral archaeology and the Pompeii premise'. *Journal of Anthropological Research* 37: 195–208.

Binford, L. R. (1983) *In Pursuit of the Past*. London: Thames and Hudson.

Binford, L. R. and S. R. Binford (1966) 'A preliminary analysis of functional variability in the Mousterian of Levallois facies'. *American Anthropologist* 68: 238–95.

Binford, S. R. and L. R. Binford (eds) (1968) *New Perspectives in Archaeology*. Chicago: Aldine.

Binford, S. R. and L. R. Binford (1969) 'Stone tools and human behaviour'. *Scientific American* 220: 70–84.

Bird-David, N. (1994) 'Sociality and immediacy: or, past and present conversations on bands'. *Man* 29: 583–603.

Bird-David, N. (1999) '"Animism" revisited: personhood, environment, and relational epistemology'. *Current Anthropology* 40: 67–91.

Boast, R. (1997) 'A small company of actors: a critique of style'. *Journal of Material Culture* 2: 173–98.

Bordes, F. (1950) 'L'évolution buissonnante des industries en Europe occidentale. Considerations théoretiques sur le paléolithique ancien et moyen'. *L'Anthropologie* 54: 393–420.

Bordes, F. (1972) *A Tale of Two Caves*. New York: Harper and Row.

Bordes. (1973) 'On the chronology and contemporaneity of different Palaeolithic cultures in France'. In C. Renfrew (ed.) *The Explanation of Cultural Change: Models in Prehistory*, pp. 217–26. London: Duckworth.

Bordes, F. and D. de Sonneville-Bordes (1970) 'The significance of variability in palaeolithic assemblages'. *World Archaeology* 2: 61–73.

Bowden, M. (1991) *Pitt Rivers: The life and archaeological work of Lieutenant-General Augustus Henry Lane Fox Pitt Rivers, DCL, FRS, FSA*. Cambridge: Cambridge University Press.

Bradley, R. (1997) *Rock Art and the Prehistory of Atlantic Europe*. London: Routledge.

Brain, C. K. (1981) *The Hunters or the Hunted?* Chicago: Chicago University Press.

Brooks, A. and B. Wood (1990) 'The Chinese side of the story'. *Nature* 344: 288–9.

Brumann, C. (1999) 'Writing for culture: why a successful concept should not be discarded'. *Current Anthropology* 40: 1–27.

Bryson, B. (1995) *Notes from a Small Island*. London: Black Swan.

Carrithers, M. (1990) 'Why humans have cultures'. *Man* 25: 189–206.

Carver, M. (1996) 'Sutton Hoo'. In B. Fagan (ed.) *The Oxford Companion to Archaeology*, pp. 705–6. Oxford: Oxford University Press.

Carver, M. (1998) *Sutton Hoo: Burial ground of kings?* London: British Museum Press.

Champion, T. C. (ed.) (1989) *Centre and Periphery: Comparative studies in archaeology*. London: Unwin Hyman.

Childe, V. G. (1925) *The Dawn of European Civilisation*. London: Cape.

Childe, V. G. (1929) *The Danube in Prehistory*. Oxford: Oxford University Press.

Childe, V. G. (1935) 'Changing methods and aims in prehistory'. *Proceedings of the Prehistoric Society* 1: 1–15.

Childe, V. G. (1936) *Man Makes Hiself*. London: Watts.

Childe, V. G. (1942) *What Happened in History*. Harmondsworth: Penguin.

Childe, V. G. (1947) *Archaeology as a Social Science*, University of London, Institute of Archaeology, Third Annual Report, pp. 49–60.

Childe, V. G. (1951) *Social Evolution*. London: Watts.

Childe, V. G. (1956a) *Society and Knowledge*. New York: Harper.

Childe, V. G. (1956b) *Piecing Together the Past: The interpretation of archaeological data*. Harmondsworth: Penguin.

Chorley, R. J. and P. Haggett. (eds) (1967) *Models in Geography*. London: Methuen.

Clark, J. D. and J. Walton (1962) 'A late stone age site in the Erongo mountains, South West Africa'. *Proceedings of the Prehistoric Society* 28: 1–16.

Clark, J. G. D. (1952) *Prehistoric Europe: The economic basis*. London: Methuen.

Clark, J. G. D. (1957) *Archaeology and Society* (third edition). London: Methuen.

Clark, J. G. D. (1968) 'Australian stone age'. In K. Jazdzewski (ed.) *Liber Iosopho Kostrzewski octogenaria a veneratoribus dicatus*, pp. 17–28. Warsaw: Ossolineum, Polish Academy of Sciences.

Clarke, D. L. (1968) *Analytical Archaeology*. London: Methuen.

Clarke, D. L. (ed.) (1972a) *Models in Archaeology*. London: Methuen.

Clarke, D. L. (1972b) 'A provisional model of an Iron Age society and its settlement system'. In D. L. Clarke (ed.) *Models in Archaeology*, pp. 801–69. London: Methuen.

Clarke, D. L. (1977) 'Spatial information in archaeology'. In D. L. Clarke (ed.) *Spatial Archaeology*, pp. 1–32. London: Academic Press.

Clarke, D. L. (1979) *Analytical Archaeologist*. London: Academic Press.

Conkey, M. and J. Spector (1984) 'Archaeology and the study of gender'. *Advances in Archaeological Method and Theory* 7: 1–38.

Cooper, M. A., A. Firth, J. Carman and D. Wheatley (eds) (1995) *Managing Archaeology*. London: Routledge.

Courbin, P. (1988) *What is Archaeology?* Chicago: University of Chicago Press.

Darte, C., J. Mauricio, P. Pettitt, P. Souto, E. Trinkaus, H. van der Plicht and J. Zilhao (1999) 'The early Upper Palaeolithic human skeleton from the Abrigo do Lagar Velho. (Portugal) and modern human emergence in Iberia'. *Proceedings of the Natonal Academy of Science* [USA] 96: 7604–9.

Darvill, T. and A. K. Fulton (1998) *MARS: the Monuments at Risk Survey of England*. Poole: School of Conservation Sciences, Bournemouth University.

Dawkins, R. (1976) *The Selfish Gene*. Oxford: Oxford University Press.

de Laet, S. (ed.) (1994) *History of Humanity. Volume 1, Prehistory*. London: UNESCO and Routledge.

de Lumley, H. (ed.) (1976) *La Préhistoire Française*. Paris: CNRS.

Deacon, T. (1997) *The Symbolic Species: The co-evolution of language and the human brain*. Harmondsworth: Penguin.

Deetz, J. (1977) *In Small Things Forgotten: The archaeology of early American life*. New York: Anchor Books.

Dennett, D. (1991) *Consciousness Explained*. Harmondsworth: Penguin.

Díaz-Andreu, M. and T. Champion (1996) 'Nationalism and archaeology in Europe: an introduction'. In M. Díaz-Andreu and T. Champion (eds) *Nationalism and Archaeology in Europe*, pp. 1–23. London: UCL Press.

Dietler, M. and I. Herbich (1998) 'Habitus, techniques, style: an integrated approach to the social understanding of material culture and boundaries'. In M. T. Stark (ed.) *The Archaeology of Social Boundaries*, pp. 232–63. Washington, DC: Smithsonian Institution Press.

Dobres, M.-A. (2000) *Technology and Social Agency*. Oxford: Blackwell Publishers.

Dobres, M.-A. and J. Robb (eds) (2000) *Agency in Archaeology*. London: Routledge.

Doran, J. and R. Hodson (1975) *Mathematics and Computers in Archaeology*. Edinburgh: Edinburgh University Press.

Douglas, M. and B. Isherwood (1978) *The World of Goods: Towards an anthropology of consumption*. London: Allen Lane.

Dunnell, R. C. (1978) 'Style and function: a fundamental dichtomy'. *American Antiquity* 43: 192–202.

Earle, T. (1994) 'Political domination and social evolution'. In T. Ingold (ed.) *Companion Encyclopedia of Anthropology*, pp. 940–61. London: Routledge.

Fagan, B. M. (1991a) *Ancient North America: The archaeology of a continent*. London: Thames and Hudson.

Fagan, B. M. (1991b) *Archaeology: a brief introduction* (fourth edition). New York: Harper Collins.

Fagan, B. M. (1992) *People of the Earth: An introduction to world prehistory*. New York: Harper Collins.

Feinman, G. M. and J. Marcus (eds) (1998) *Archaic States*. Santa Fe: School of American Research.

Flannery, K. V. (1967) 'Culture history versus cultural process: a debate in American archaeology'. *Scientific American* 217: 119–22.

Flannery, K. V. (1972) 'The cultural evolution of civilizations'. *Annual Review of Ecology and Systematics* 3: 399–426.

Flannery, K. V. (1973) 'Archaeology with a capital S'. In C. Redman (ed.) *Research and Theory in Current Archaeology*, pp. 47–53. New York: Wiley.

Flannery, K. V. (ed.) (1976) *The Early Mesoamerican Village*. New York: Academic Press.

Fox, C. (1932) *The Personality of Britain*. Cardiff: Cardiff National Museum and University of Wales.

Frank, A. G. (1993) 'Bronze Age world system cycles'. *Current Anthropology* 34: 383–429.

Fried, M. H. (1967) *The Evolution of Political Society: An essay in political anthropology*. New York: Random House.

Friedman, J. (1994) *Cultural Identity and Global Process*. London: Sage.

Gamble, C. S. (1986) *The Palaeolithic Settlement of Europe*. Cambridge: Cambridge University Press.

Gamble, C. S. (1987) 'Archaeology, geography and time'. *Progress in Human Geography* 11: 227–46.

Gamble, C. S. (1993) *Timewalkers: The prehistory of global colonization*. Stroud: Alan Sutton.

Gamble, C. S. (1998) 'Palaeolithic society and the release from proximity: a network approach to intimate relations'. *World Archaeology* 29: 426–49.

Gamble, C. S. (1999) *The Palaeolithic Societies of Europe*. Cambridge: Cambridge University Press.

Gamble, C. S. and O. Soffer (eds) (1990) *The World at 18 000 BP. Volume 2, Low latitudes*. London: Unwin Hyman.

Geertz, C. (1975) *The Interpretation of Cultures*. London: Hutchinson.

Gell, A. (1992) *The Anthropology of Time*. Oxford: Berg.

Geneste, J.-M. (1988) 'Systemes d'approvisionnement en matières premières au paléolithique moyen et au paléolithique supérieur en Aquitaine'. *L'Homme de Néandertal* 8: 61–70.

Gero, G. and M. Conkey (eds) (1991) *Engendering Archaeology: Women and prehistory*. Oxford: Blackwell Publishers.

Giddens, A. (1984) *The Constitution of Society*. Berkeley: University of California Press.

Gifford, D. P. (1981) 'Taphonomy and paleoecology: a critical review of archaeology's sister disciplines'. *Advances in Archaeological Method and Theory* 4: 365–438.

Gifford-Gonzalez, D. (1993) 'You can hide, but you can't run: representation of women's work in illustrations of Palaeolithic life'. *Visual Anthropology Review* 9: 23–41.

Gilchrist, R. (1993) *Gender and Material Culture: The archaeology of religious women*. London: Routledge.

Glassie, H. (1975) *Folk Housing in Middle Virginia*. Knoxville: University of Tennessee Press.

Goodall, J. (1986) *The Chimpanzees of Gombe. Patterns of behaviour*. Cambridge, Mass.: Belknap Press.

Gosden, C. (1994) *Social Being and Time*. Oxford: Blackwell Publishers.

Gosden, C. (1999) *Anthropology and Archaeology: A changing relationship*. London: Routledge.

Gould, R. A. (1980) *Living Archaeology*. Cambridge: Cambridge University Press.

Gould, S. J. (1984) *The Mismeasure of Man*. Harmondsworth: Penguin.

Gould, S. J. (1991) 'Exaptation: a crucial tool for an evolutionary psychology'. *Journal of Social Issues* 47: 43–65.

Gould, S. J. and E. S. Vrba (1982) 'Exaptation – a missing term in the science of form'. *Palaeobiology* 8: 4–15.

Greene, K. (1995) *Archaeology: An introducton. The history, principles and methods of modern archaeology*. London: Routledge.

Haggett P. (1965) *Locational Analysis in Human Geography*. London: Edward Arnold.

Hall, M. (1997) 'Patriarchal façades: the ambivalence of gender in the archaeology of colonialism'. In L. Wadley (ed.) *Our Gendered Past: Archaeological studies of gender in southern Africa*, pp. 221–36. Johannesburg: Witwatersrand University Press.

Härke, H. (1992) 'All quiet on the western front? Paradigms, methods and approaches in West German archaeology'. In I. Hodder (ed.) *Archaeological Theory in Europe: The last three decades*, pp. 187–222. London: Routledge.

Harris, E. C. (1989) *Principles of Archaeological Stratigraphy* (second edition). New York: Academic Press.

Hawkes, C. (1954) 'Archaeological theory and method: some suggestions from the old world'. *American Anthropologist* 56: 155–68.

Haynes, C. V. (1993) 'Clovis-Folsom geochronology and climatic change'. In O. Soffer and N. D. Praslov (eds) *From Kostenki to Clovis: Upper Palaolithic-Paleo-Indian adaptations*, pp. 219–36. New York: Plenum.

Hearne, C. M. and M. J. Heaton (1994) 'Excavations at a Late Bronze Age settlement in the Upper Thames Valley at Shorncote Quarry near Cirencester, 1992'. *Transactions of the Bristol and Gloucestershire Archaeological Society* CXII: 17–57.

Hegmon, M. (1998) 'Technology, style and social practices: archaeological approaches'. In M. T. Stark (ed.) *The Archaeology of Social Boundaries*, pp. 264–79. Washington, DC: Smithsonian Institution Press.

Hodder, I. (1982) *Symbols in Action*. Cambridge: Cambridge University Press.

Hodder, I. (1990) 'Style as historical quality'. In M. W. Conkey and C. A. Hastorf (eds) *The Uses of Style in Archaeology*, pp. 44–51. Cambridge: Cambridge University Press.

Hodder, I. (1991) *Reading the Past*, (second edition). Cambridge: Cambridge University Press.

Hodder, I. (1999) *The Archaeological Process: An introduction*. Oxford: Blackwell Publishers.

Hodder, I. and C. Orton (1976) *Spatial Analysis in Archaeology*. Cambridge: Cambridge University Press.

Hosfield, R. (1999) *The Palaeolithic of the Hampshire Basin: A regional model of hominid behaviour during the Middle Pleistocene*. Oxford: British Archaeological Reports, British Series 286.

Ingold, T. (1993) 'The temporality of the landscape'. *World Archaeology* 25: 152–73.

Ingold, T. (1994) 'Introduction to culture'. In T. Ingold (ed.) *Companion Encyclopedia of Anthropology*, pp. 329–49. London: Routledge.

Isaac, G. (1978) 'The food sharing behaviour of proto-human hominids'. *Scientific American* 238: 90–108.

Johnson, A. W. and T. Earle (1987) *The Evolution of Human Societies*. Stanford: Stanford University Press.

Johnson, M. (1993) 'Notes towards an archaeology of capitalism'. In C. Tilley (ed.) *Interpretative Archaeology*, pp. 327–56. London: Berg.

Johnson, M. (1999a) *Archaeological Theory: An introduction*. Oxford: Blackwell Publishers.

Johnson, M. (1999b) 'Reconstructing castles and refashioning identities in Renaissance England'. In S. Tarlow and S. West (eds) *The Familiar Past?*, pp. 69–86. London: Routledge.

Jones, R. (1985) 'Ordering the landscape'. In I. Donaldson and T. Donaldson (eds) *Seeing the First Australians*, pp. 181–209. Sydney: George Allen and Unwin.

Jones, S. (1997) *The Archaeology of Ethnicity: Constructing identities in the past and present*. London: Routledge.

Keeley, L. H. (1988) 'Hunter-gatherer economic complexity and "population pressure": a cross-cultural analysis'. *Journal of Anthropological Archaeology* 7: 373–411.

Kelly, R. (1995) *The Foraging Spectrum: Diversity in hunter-gatherer lifeways*. Washington, D.C. and London: Smithsonian Institution Press.

Kessing, R. M. (1981) *Cultural Anthropology: A contemporary perspective*. Fort Worth: Holt, Rinehart and Winston.

Kidder, A. V. (1924) *An Introduction to the Study of Southwestern Archaeology*. New Haven: Papers of the Southwestern Expedition, Phillips Academy, no. 1.

Kirch, P. V. (1984) *The Evolution of the Polynesian Chiefdoms*. Cambridge: Cambridge University Press.

Kristiansen, K. (1998) *Europe Before History: The European world system in the second millennium BC*. Cambridge: Cambridge University Press.

Kristiansen, K. and M. Rowlands (1998) *Social Transformations in Archaeology: Global and local perspectives*. London: Routledge.

Kuper, A. (1999) *Culture: The anthropologist's account*. Cambridge, Mass.: Harvard University Press.

Laing, S. (1895) *Human Origins*. London: Chapman and Hall.

Leech, R. (1999) 'The processional city: some issues for historical archaeology'. In S. Tarlow and S. West (eds) *The Familiar Past?*, pp. 19–34. London: Routledge.

Leone, M. P. (ed.) *Contemporary Archaeology: A guide to theory and contributions*. Carbondale: Southern Illinois University Press.

Leroi-Gourhan, A. (1993) *Gesture and Speech*. Cambridge: MIT Press.

Lourandos, H. (1997) *Continent of Hunter-gatherers: New perspectives in Australian prehistory*. Cambridge: Cambridge University Press.

Lubbock, J. (1865) *Pre-Historic Times, as Illustrated by Ancient Remains and the Manners and Customs of Modern Savages*. London: Williams and Norgate.

Lyman, R. L. (1994) *Vertebrate Taphonomy*. Cambridge: Cambridge University Press.

Lyman, R. L., M. J. O'Brien and R. C. Dunnell (1997) *The Rise and Fall of Culture History*. New York: Plenum.

Mandela, N. (1995) *Long Walk to Freedom*. London: Abacus.

Marcus, J. (1998) 'The peaks and valleys of ancient states: an extension of the dynamic model'. In G. M. Feinman and J. Marcus (eds) *Archaic States*, pp. 59–94. Santa Fe: School of American Research.

McGlade, J. and S. van der Leeuw (1997) 'Introduction: archaeology and non-linear dynamics – new approaches to long-term change'. In S. van der Leeuw and J. McGlade (eds) *Time, Process and Structured Transformation in Archaeology*, pp. 1–31. London: Routledge.

McGuire, R. (1983) 'Breaking down cultural complexity: inequality and heterogeneity'. In M. B. Schiffer (ed.) *Advances in Archaeological Method and Theory*, vol. 6, pp. 91–142. New York: Academic Press.

McGuire, R. H. (1992) *A Marxist Archaeology*. San Diego: Academic Press.

McIntosh, J. (1999) *The Practical Archaeologist*. London: Thames and Hudson.

McNairn, B. (1980) *Method and Theory of V. Gordon Childe*. Edinburgh: Edinburgh University Press.

Mellars, P. A. (1970) 'Some comments on the notion of "functional variability" in stone tool assemblages'. *World Archaeology* 2: 74–89.

Mellars, P. A. and C. Stringer (eds) (1989) *The Human Revolution: Behavioural and biological perspectives on the origins of modern humans*. Edinburgh: Edinburgh University Press.

Meskell, L. (1999) *Archaeologies of Social Life*. Oxford: Blackwell Publishers.

Miller, D. (1994) 'Artefacts and the meaning of things'. In T. Ingold (ed.) *Companion Encyclopedia of Anthropology: Humanity, culture and social life*, pp. 396–419. London: Routledge.

Miller, D. (1995) 'Consumption as the vanguard of history: a polemic by way of an introduction'. In D. Miller (ed.) *Acknowledging Consumption: A review of new studies*, pp. 1–57. London: Routledge.

Miller, D. and C. Tilley (eds) (1984) *Ideology, Power and Prehistory*. Cambridge: Cambridge University Press.

Miller, D., M. Rowlands and C. Tilley (eds) (1989) *Domination and Resistance*. London: Unwin Hyman.

Mintz, S. W. (1985) *Sweetness and Power: The place of sugar in modern history*. New York: Viking.

Mithen, S. (1993) 'Individuals, groups and the Palaeolithic record: a reply to Clark'. *Proceedings of the Prehistoric Society* 59: 393–8.

Morgan, L. H. (1877) *Ancient Society*. New York: World Publishing.

Moser, S. (1998) *Ancestral Images: The iconography of human origins*. Stroud: Alan Sutton.

Nehru, J. (1946) *The Discovery of India*. New Dehli: Jawaharlal Nehru Memorial Fund.

Nelson, S. M. (1997) *Gender in Archaeology: Analyzing power and prestige*. Walnut Creek: Altamira Press.

O'Brien, M. (ed.) (1996) *Evolutionary Archaeology: Theory and application*. Salt Lake City: University of Utah Press.

Orser, C. (1999) 'Negotiating our "familiar" pasts'. In S. Tarlow and S. West (eds) *The Familiar Past?*, pp. 273–85. London: Routledge.

Paddayya, K. (1995) 'Theoretical perspectives in Indian archaeology: an historical review'. In P. J. Ucko (ed.) *Theory in Archaeology: A world perspective*, pp. 110–49. London: Routledge.

Patrik, L. E. (1985) 'Is there an archaeological record?'. In M. B. Schiffer (ed.) *Advances in Archaeological Method and Theory*, vol. 8, pp. 27–62. New York: Academic Press.

Peacock, D. P. S. (1968) 'A petrological study of certain iron Age pottery from Western England'. *Proceedings of the Prehistoric Society* 34: 414–27.

Piggott, S. (1965) *Ancient Europe*. Edinburgh: Edinburgh University Press.

Pitt-Rivers, A. H. L. (1887) *Excavations in Cranborne Chase*, vol 1. Privately published.

Preucel, R. and I. Hodder (eds) (1996) *Contemporary Archaeology in Theory: A reader*. Oxford: Blackwell Publishers.

Prown, J. D. (1993) 'The truth of material culture: history or fiction?'. In S. Lubar and W. D. Kingery (eds) *History from Things: Essays on material culture*, pp. 1–19. Washington, D.C.: Smithsonian Institution Press.

Redman, C. L. (1978) *The Rise of Civilization: From early farmers to urban society in the Ancient Near East*. San Francisco: W. H. Freeman.

Renfrew, C. (1968) 'Wessex without Mycenae'. *Annual of the British School of Archaeology at Athens* 63: 277–85.

Renfrew, C. (1972) *The Emergence of Civilisation: The Cyclades and the Aegaen in the third millennium BC*. London: Methuen.

Renfrew, C. (1973a) *Before Civilization*. London: Jonathan Cape.

Renfrew, C. (1973b) *Social Archaeology*. Southampton: University of Southampton.

Renfrew, C. (1977) 'Space, time and polity'. In J.Friedman and M.Rowlands (eds) *The Evolution of Social Systems*, pp. 89–112. London: Duckworth.

Renfrew, C. (1982) 'Explanation revisited'. In C. Renfrew, M. J. Rowlands and B. A. Segraves (eds) *Theory and Explanation in Archaeology: The Southampton conference*, pp. 5–23. New York: Academic Press.

Renfrew, C. and P. Bahn (1991) *Archaeology*. London: Thames and Hudson.

Renfrew, C. and K. L. Cooke (eds) (1979) *Transformations: Mathematical approaches to culture change*. New York: Academic Press.

Renfrew, C. and S. J. Shennan (eds) (1982) *Ranking, Resource and Exchange*. Cambridge: Cambridge University Press.

Renfrew, C. and J. M. Wagstaff (eds) (1982) *An Island Polity: The archaeology of exploitation in Melos*. Cambridge: Cambridge University Press.

Rindos, D. (1985) *The Origins of Agriculture: An evolutionary perspective*. New York: Academic Press.

Rindos, D. (1989) 'Darwinism and its role in the explanation of domestication'. In D. R. Harris and G. C. Hillman (eds) *Foraging and Farming: The evolution of plant exploitation*, pp. 27–41. London: Unwin Hyman.

Sackett, J. R. (1990) 'Style and ethnicity in archaeology: the case for isochrestism'. In M. W. Conkey and C. A. Hastorf (eds) *The Uses of Style in Archaeology*, pp. 32–43. Cambridge: Cambridge University Press.

Sackett, J. R. (1982) 'Approaches to style in lithic archaeology'. *Journal of Anthropological Archaeology* 1: 59–112.

Sahlins, M. (1963) 'Poor man, rich man, big man, chief: political types in Melanesia and Polynesia'. *Comparative Studies in Society and History* 5: 285–303.

Schiffer, M. B. (1976) *Behavioral Archaeology*. New York: Academic Press.

Service, E. R. (1962) *Primitive Social Organization: An evolutionary perspective* (second edition). New York: Random House.

Service, E. R. (1966) *The Hunters*. Englewood Cliffs, NJ: Prentice-Hall.

Shanks, M. and C. Tilley (1987a) *Reconstructing Archaeology: Theory and practice*. Cambridge: Cambridge University Press.

Shanks, M. and C. Tilley (1987b) *Social Theory and Archaelogy*. London: Polity.

Shennan, S. (1989a) 'Introduction: archaeological approaches to cultural identity'. In S. J. Shennan (ed.) *Archaeological Approaches to Cultural Identity*, pp. 1–32. London: Unwin Hyman.

Shennan, S. J. (1989b) 'Cultural transmission and culture change'. In S. E. van der Leuuw and R. Torrence (eds) *What's New? A closer look at the process of innovation*, pp. 330–46. London: Unwin Hyman.

Shennan, S. J. (1993) 'After social evolution: a new archaeological agenda?'. In N. Yoffee and A. Sherratt (eds) *Archaeological Theory: Who sets the agenda?*, pp. 53–9. Cambridge: Cambridge University Press.

Sherratt, A. (1997) *Economy and Society in Prehistoric Europe: Changing perspectives*. Edinburgh: Edinburgh University Press.

Skibo, J. M., W. H. Walker and A. E. Nielsen (eds) (1995) *Expanding Archaeology*. Salt Lake City: University of Utah Press.

Soffer, O. and C. S. Gamble (eds) (1990) *The World at 18 000BP, Volume 1: High latitudes*. London: Unwin Hyman.

Sollas, W. J. (1911) *Ancient Hunters and Their Modern Representatives*. London: Macmillan.

Sparkes, B. A. (1982) 'The melian dialogue of Thucydides *Historiae* V. 84–116'. In C. Renfrew and J. M. Wagstaff (eds) *An Island Polity: The archaeology of exploitation in Melos*, pp. 319–22. Cambridge: Cambridge University Press.

Spector, J. (1993) *What This Awl Means: Feminist archaeology at a Wahpeton Dakota Village*. St Paul: Minnesota Historical Society Press.

Spencer, H. (1876–96) *The Principles of Sociology*. London: Williams and Norgate.

Sperber, D. (1996) *Explaining Culture: A naturalistic approach*. Oxford: Blackwell Publishers.

Spriggs, M. (ed.) (1984) *Marxist Perspectives in Archaeology*. Cambridge: Cambridge University Press.

Sterner, J. (1989) 'Who is signalling whom? Ceramic style, ethnicity and taphonomy among the Sirak Bulahay'. *Antiquity* 63: 451–9.

Stiner, M. C. (1994) *Honor Among Thieves: A zooarchaeological study of Neandertal ecology*. Princeton, NJ: Princeton University Press.

Strathern, M. (1988) *The Gender of the Gift: Problems with women and problems with society in Melanesia*. Berkeley: University of California Press.

Strathern, M. (1996) 'Cutting the network'. *Journal of the Royal Anthropological Institute* 2: 517–35.

Stringer, C. and C. Gamble (1993) *In Search of the Neanderthals: Solving the puzzle of human origins*. London: Thames and Hudson.

Strum, S. S. and B. Latour (1987) 'Redefining the social link: from baboons to humans'. *Social Science Information* 26: 783–802.

Tarlow, S. (1999) 'Strangely familiar'. In S. Tarlow and S. West (eds) *The Familiar Past?*, pp. 263–72. London: Routledge.

Taylor, W. W. (1948) *A Study of Archaeology*. Menasha: Memoirs of the American Anthropological Association 69.

Thomas, D. H. (1998) *Archaeology* (third edition). Fort Worth: Harcourt Brace.

Thomas, J. (1995) 'Where are we now?: archaeological theory in the 1990s'. In P. J. Ucko (ed.) *Theory in Archaeology: A world perspective*, pp. 343–62. London: Routledge.

Thomas, J. (1996) *Time, Culture and Identity: An interpretive archaeology*. London: Routledge.

Tilley, C. (1993) 'Introduction: Interpretation and a poetics of the past'. In C. Tilley (ed.) *Interpretative Archaeology*, pp. 1–27. London: Berg.

Tilley, C. (1996) *An Ethnography of the Neolithic*. Cambridge: Cambridge University Press.

Trigger, B. G. (1989) *A History of Archaeological Thought*. Cambridge: Cambridge University Press.

Tylor, E. B. (1865) *Researches into the Early History of Mankind and the Development of Civilization*. London: John Murray.

Tylor, E. B. (1871) *Primitive Culture*. London: John Murray.

Ucko, P. J. and G. Dimbleby (eds) (1969) *The Domestication and Exploitation of Plants and Animals*. London: Duckworth.

Ucko, P. J., R. Tringham and G. W. Dimbleby (eds) (1972) *Man, Settlement and Urbanism*. London: Duckworth.

Veit, U. (1989) 'Ethnic concepts in German prehistory: a case study on the relationship between cultural identity and archaeological objectivity'. In S. J. Shennan (ed.) *Archaeological Approaches to Cultural Identity*, pp. 35–56. London: Unwin Hyman.

Vita-Finzi, C. and E. S. Higgs (1970) 'Prehistoric economy in the Mount Carmel area of Palestine, site catchment analysis'. *Proceedings of the Prehistoric Society* 36: 1–37.

Vonnegut, K. (1987) *Galápagos*. London: Grafton Books.

Waal, F. D. (1982) *Chimpanzee Politics*. London: Jonathan Cape.

Waddington, C. H. (1977) *Tools for Thought*. London: Paladin.

Wadley, L. (ed.) (1997) *Our Gendered Past: Archaeological studies of gender in southern Africa*. Johannesburg: Witwatersrand University Press.

Wainwright, G. J. (1989) 'Saving the Rose'. *Antiquity*: 430–5.

Wallerstein, I. (1974) *The Modern World System: Capitalist agriculture and the origins of the European world economy in the nineteenth century*, vol. 1. New York: Academic Press.

Wallerstein, I. (1980) *The Modern World System*, vol. 2. London: Academic Press.

Wenke, R. J. (1990) *Patterns in Prehistory: Humankind's first three million years*. New York: Oxford University Press.

West, S. (1999) 'Social space and the English country house'. In S. Tarlow and S. West (eds) *The Familiar Past?*, pp. 103–22. London: Routledge.

Wheeler, R. E. M. (1954) *Archaeology from the Earth*. Harmondsworth: Penguin.

White, L. A. (1959) *The Evolution of Culture: The development of civilization to the fall of Rome*. New York: McGraw-Hill.

Whittle, A. (1996) *Europe in the Neolithic: The creation of new worlds*. Cambridge: Cambridge University Press.

Wiessner, P. (1983) 'Style and social information in Kalahari San projectile points'. *American Antiquity* 48: 253–76.

Wiessner, P. (1990) 'Is there a unity to style?'. In M. W. Conkey and C. A. Hastorf (eds) *The Uses of Style in Archaeology*, pp. 105–12. Cambridge: Cambridge University Press.

Willey, G. R. (1966) *An Introduction to American Archaeology, Volume 1: North and Middle America*. Englewood Cliffs, NJ: Prentice-Hall.

Wilson, D. (1862) *Prehistoric Man*. London: Macmillan.

Wilson, E. O. (1975) *Sociobiology: The new synthesis*. Cambridge, Mass.: Bellknap.

Wobst, H. M. (1977) 'Stylistic behaviour and information exchange'. In C. E. Cleland (ed.) *Papers for the Director: Research essays in honor of James B. Griffin*, vol. 61, *Anthropological papers*, pp. 317–42: Museum of Anthropology, University of Michigan.

Wobst, H. M. (1978) 'The archaeo-ethnology of hunter gatherers or the tyranny of the ethnographic record in archaeology'. *American Antiquity* 43: 303–9.

Woodburn, J. (1991) 'African hunter-gatherer social organization: is it best understood as a product of encapsulation?'. In T. Ingold, D. Riches and J. Woodburn (eds) *Hunters and Gatherers 1: History, evolution and social change*, pp. 31–64. New York: Berg.

Worsaae, J. J. A. (1849) *The Primeval Antiquities of Denmark*. London: Parker.

Wylie, A. (1985) 'The reaction against analogy'. *Advances in Archaeological Method and Theory* 8: 63–111.

Wylie, A. (1991) 'Gender theory and the archaeological record: Why is there no archaeology of gender?'. In J. M. Gero and M. W. Conkey (eds) *Engendering Archaeology: Women and prehistory*, pp. 31–54. Oxford: Blackwell Publishers.

Wylie, A. (1993) 'A proliferation of new archaeologies: "beyond objectivism and relativism"'. In N. Yoffee and A. Sherratt (eds) *Archaeological Theory: Who sets the agenda?*, pp. 20–6. Cambridge: Cambridge University Press.

Wylie, A. (1995) 'An expanded behavioral archaeology: transformation and redefinition'. In J. M. Skibo, W. H. Walker and A. E. Nielsen (eds) *Expanding Archaeology*, pp. 198–209. Salt Lake City: University of Utah Press.

Index